# Great British Journeys

# Great British Journeys

## Nicholas Crane

WEIDENFELD & NICOLSON

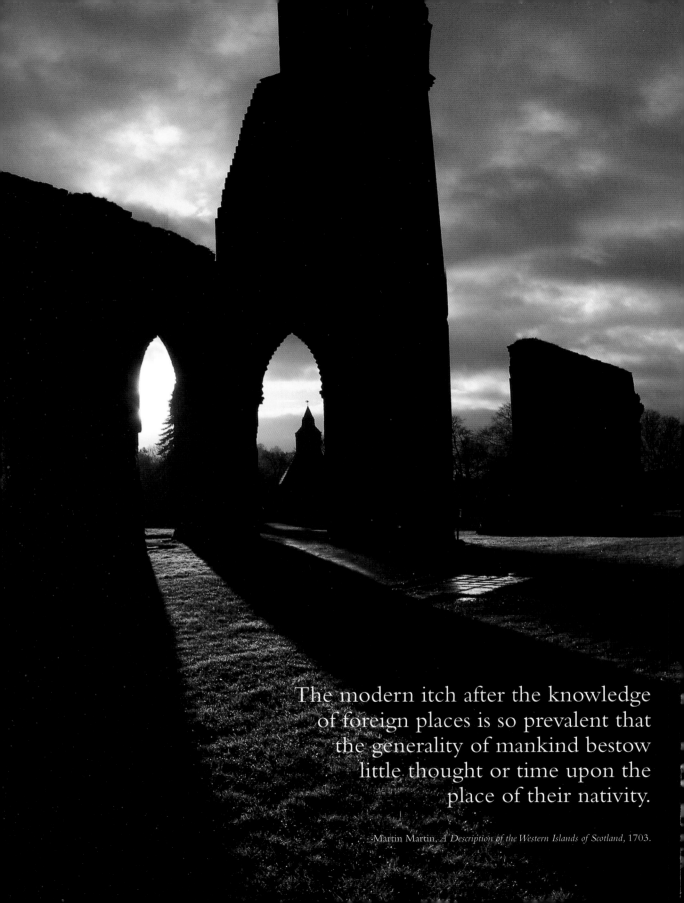

The modern itch after the knowledge
of foreign places is so prevalent that
the generality of mankind bestow
little thought or time upon the
place of their nativity.

Martin Martin, *A Description of the Western Islands of Scotland*, 1703.

# Contents

Introduction *Page 6*

Gerald
of Wales 1188
\* \* \*
*A crusader
in Wales*
*Page 12*

John
Leland 1536–45
\* \* \*
*The madness
of maps*
*Page 42*

Celia
Fiennes 1698
\* \* \*
*On horseback
through England*
*Page 72*

Daniel
Defoe 1724–6
\* \* \*
*The secret
tourist*
*Page 102*

William
Gilpin 1770
\* \* \*
*One man
in a boat*
*Page 132*

Thomas
Pennant 1772
\* \* \*
*Highlands
and islands*
*Page 162*

William
Cobbett 1822–6
\* \* \*
*Champion of the
countryside*
*Page 192*

H.V.
Morton 1929–33
\* \* \*
*By bull-nose
to Skye*
*Page 222*

Further Reading
*Page 254*

Acknowledgments
*Page 255*

*Previous pages:* Bwlch yr Eifl, Lleyn Peninsula, North Wales.
*Left:* Glastonbury Abbey, Somerset.

# Introduction

W<small>HO</small> discovered Britain? We're familiar with the image of adventurers departing these shores to explore the blanks on the world map. But who explored these islands? What did they find? And how do the narratives they left behind help us to understand modern Britain?

\* \* \*

A few years ago, I walked the length of England in a straight line. Actually, it wasn't quite a straight line. I did allow myself the luxury of straying one thousand metres each side of the line. I walked, slept, and procured my provisions within an imaginary, 2,000-metre wide, glass-walled corridor which ran up and down dale from the Northumbrian coast to the English Channel. Naturally, there were obstacles to overcome. I had to wade the Tyne, hitch a lift in a sailing dinghy across a reservoir, and ask the Army if they would mind escorting me through the live firing ranges on Salisbury Plain. By the time I caught sight of Poole Harbour (the Royal Marines helped out with that one), I'd walked across landscapes which ranged from Pennine moors to the industrial West Midlands and the undulating corn country of Wessex. My accommodation had ranged from a five-star shepherd's barn to a one-star puddle in the Pennines, and I'd enjoyed unexpected encounters with gamekeepers, war-veterans, poachers, retired hippies and farmers. The people I met, and the places I saw, were a wonderful cross-section of life and landscapes. I felt as if I was seeing my own country for the first time. It took me nearly two months to walk the length of England. The problem wasn't the distance, but the sheer density of interest. On some days I barely managed five miles. On one day, I actually walked back up the line to visit something I'd missed. It was while I was walking along two degrees west that I began to wonder who discovered Britain.

Britain is a much bigger than it looks on the map. Wrapped up in 11,000 miles of coastline is an extraordinarily diverse collection of landscapes. We have it all, from teetering peaks and gentle downs, to saltmarshes and beech woods. In Britain, you are never more than a mile from new scenery. So much variety lends itself to narrative exploration. It's not difficult to imagine Mesolithic hunters sharing tales of sights seen on foraging trips to the tidal swamps of the Severn estuary, or of Saxon explorers pushing into Dumnonia and returning home with stories of frightful capes and of tin beyond their wildest dreams. Unfortunately, they left no written records of their travels. It is not until the Middle Ages that we start to find complete records of British journeys. In the accounts of men such as William of Malmesbury, Gerald of Wales and William Worcestre, a picture emerges of a class of professional travellers criss-crossing the country on journeys that took several weeks at a time.

Beinn an Ôir, Jura.

Government agents, emissaries, messengers, kings and archbishops all had pressing reasons to take to the road.

The mode of transport and the state of the roads meant that long-distance travel in Britain frequently became expeditionary. On foot, you could cover around twenty-five miles a day, and on horse, around thirty miles. But once wheels were involved, journey times stretched. Queen Elizabeth's baggage train of over two hundred, two- and four-wheeled carts, crawled along at ten miles a day. These rates of travel barely changed until the turnpike revolution of the eighteenth century, when roads were straightened, widened and levelled.

By modern standards, pre-turnpike roads were absolutely appalling. On the road from Cardiff to Swansea, Gerald of Wales nearly lost his horse in quicksand – not the kind of misfortune likely to happen on the M4 today. Celia Fiennes had to ride through deep floods in Suffolk and Cambridgeshire and was thrown from her horse in Hampshire. In Cheshire, she was accosted by highwaymen. As late as the eighteenth

Glencoe, Scotland.

century, Daniel Defoe rode his horse along the beaches of north Norfolk, because that *was* the coast road. Signposts and road atlases were barely seen before the eighteenth century, and it was standard practice to hire local guides before tackling obstacles such as moors and estuaries.

Travel was an adventurous activity. Celia Fiennes found herself sharing a bedroom with frogs and snails on one occasion. Sailing the coast of western Scotland (because in those days there were virtually no roads north of Skye), Thomas Pennant came within a puff of being shipwrecked after straying into an uncharted loch. And that was in 1772, the year that Captain Cook set off to explore the shores of Antarctica. It was the eighteenth century that saw a huge surge in British travel narratives. Pennant helped to fill in the last blanks on the travellers' map of Scotland, and down south, the age of tourism had already kicked off.

Far from quenching the spirit of British exploration, improved roads and accurate maps triggered an era of rediscovery. In taking his voyage down the River Wye,

William Gilpin wasn't pioneering a route through uncharted territory. At the time, the Wye was the riparian equivalent of a rural trunk road, busy with freight barges and local industry. Gilpin's aim was to educate a generation in the art of looking. Cobbett did the same, directing our eyes to poverty and corruption.

The Hampshire Downs.

So who were the discoverers? I don't mean the passers-by like Pytheas the Greek, or war junkies like Tacitus, but the real explorers, who devised a journey and recorded what they had seen and learned. The list turned out to be very long, but it was a fairly straightforward task to prune it down into eight of the greatest. In each case, they had to reveal Britain as it had not been seen before, and to have left behind a narrative of some kind. As a group, they had to span as much history as possible, and as much of Britain as possible.

The finalists are an eclectic bunch who travelled between the 1180s and the 1930s. Meet them in a lift, and you'd be rubbing shoulders with a naturalist and a spy, a couple of Churchmen, a minor aristocrat, a journalist, a political activist and a librarian. A couple of them had seen the inside of prison, one would go mad and the motorist privately believed that Britain might be better governed from Berlin. Their motives for travelling ranged from royal commission to newspaper commission, and from spiritual enlightenment to political conviction. Variously, they recorded their journeys as field notes, as travel journals and as published narratives. But all eight shared a common interest in British landscapes. As topographical audits, their journeys are invaluable records of lost landscapes, and as explorers, they inspire us to view this remarkable archipelago with a renewed sense of wonder.

Traeth Maelgwyn, Dovey Estuary.

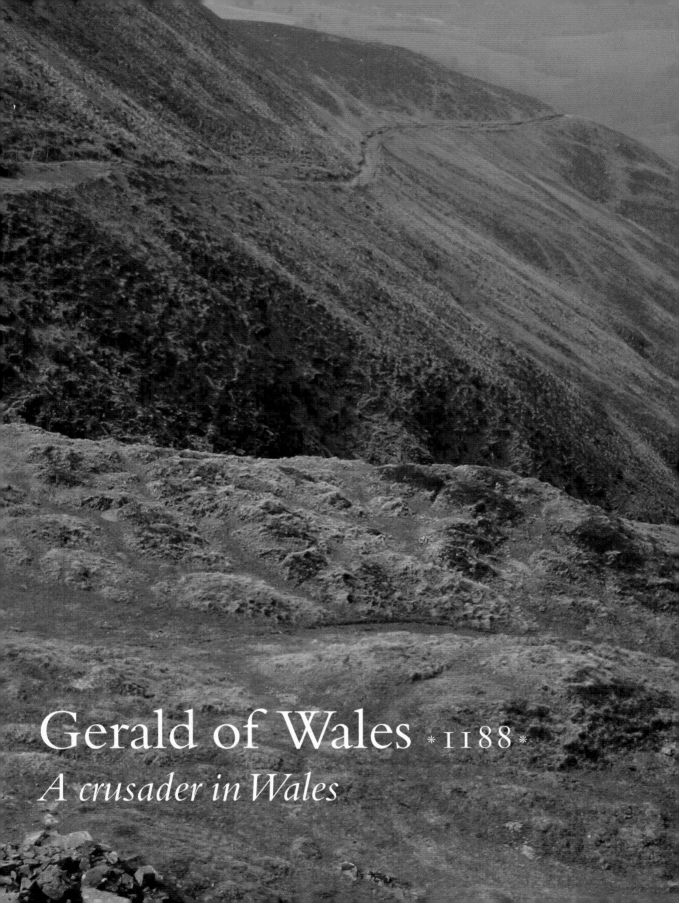

# Gerald of Wales *1188*

*A crusader in Wales*

# Route Taken by Gerald of Wales During his Journey of 1188

**Legend:**
- ‑ ‑ ‑ Route by land
- —— Route by water
- Castle
- Abbey or Cathedral
- Town or City

0 10 20 30 Miles

N W E S

Rhuddlan
Chester
Anglesey
Bangor
Whitchurch
Caernarfon
Snowdonia
Yr Eifl
Nefyn
Oswestry
Lleyn
Traeth Bach
Shrewsbury
Cardigan Bay
Cadair Idris
Towyn
Dovey Estuary
Aberystwyth
Ludlow
Radnor
Leominster
Strata Florida
River Teifi
St Dogmael's Abbey
Cardigan
Lampeter
Hay-on-Wye
Hereford
Cenarth
Nevern Castle
Black Mountains
St David's
Whitland
Brecon
Newgale Beach
Carmarthen
Haverfordwest
Abergavenny
Kidwelly
Usk
Manorbier Castle
Swansea
Margam Abbey
Newport
Gold Cliff
Briton Ferry
Cardiff

THE hunter-gatherers who explored Britain as the ice sheets melted left no record of their extraordinary treks, and so the earliest complete account of a genuinely great British journey was not written until the twelfth century, when the garrulous son of a Norman knight undertook an epic circuit of Wales to raise crusaders for a misguided adventure in the Middle East. Riding through a land before the age of maps. Giraldus Cambrensis – Gerald the Welshman – has been hailed as the first serious natural historian of Wales and one of the founders of British geography. Three manuscript copies of the first version of *The Journey through Wales* have survived, although it is the third version (Gerald's final revision) which was translated by Lewis Thorpe in the 1970s, and endures today as the standard edition.

* * *

About a year ago, I tried to follow a section of Gerald's route through the hills of Powys. Rain had been falling for days and the track had turned into a flooded cesspit of mud and dung. My boots were filled with water and I was soaked to the skin. The wind was so strong that the rain smacking the hood of my jacket sounded like gravel hitting glass. Beyond a field-gate, the track divided. As I extracted the map from an inside pocket, a gust of wind caught the sodden folds and ripped it in half. Crouching in the slime, I took a compass bearing on each of the diverging tracks then transferred the bearings to the pieces of the map. There was no doubt about it. I was lost. How on earth, I wondered, had an Archbishop found his way through these hills eight hundred years ago?

The earliest great British journey to be fully recorded began at the city gates of Hereford one spring day in 1188. Heading west for a little-known land was the Archbishop of Canterbury, the King's Chief Justiciar, a Bishop, the Court Chaplain, and a retinue of episcopal attendants, servants and soldiers. The month of March was a few days old. Above the meandering Wye, vineyards slept behind sunny walls. In the fields, ploughman turned the stiff, winter soil while women and children tugged at weeds. Wagons loaded with manure creaked through the ruts, and flocks of sheep could be seen gathering for the trek to upland grazing. On the steep valley sides, the forests were taking colour.

Hindsight recognises that these were good days for England. The seasons were predictable. Planting began in April, and the months of June, July and August were reliably warm and settled. Average summer temperatures were 0.7–1.0 degree Celsius warmer than they are today. Harvests were dependable and winters mild. A century

*Previous pages:* **Bwlch yr Eifl, Lleyn Peninsula, North Wales.**

after the Normans stormed ashore at Pevensey to annihilate Harold's Anglo-Saxon army, England had become the stable, northern colony of Europe's most powerful 'empire' – a vast federation of Angevin dominions which stretched all the way from the Pyrenees to the Grampians. For the man in the field, life could have been a lot worse. The English economy was growing faster than at any time in the medieval period and a new breed of merchant was adjusting pleasurably to the ethos of profit. To the tinkle of silver, shiploads of wool and corn were being exported to the cities of

Flanders. England's population of around three million was reproducing as never before, and would double between 1086 and 1300. Ports were growing in the east, and towns were being created in the west. Markets were appearing. Land itself was breaking free of its feudal yoke and beginning to change hands for money. In England's richest, most populous region, East Anglia, Bishop Herbert de Losinga built a titanic cathedral. After thirty years of energetic rule under Henry II, England was secure and prosperous.

Gerald knew Hereford as one of the foremost centres of learning in the kingdom. William de Vere, the bishop here from 1186 to 1199, was one of many scholars adopting new scientific knowledge from the Arabic world.

It was against this backdrop of domestic well-being that England's ruling classes decided to join the forces of the 'Holy Empire' in a crazed adventure in the Middle East. Their demon had been born in Tikrit, close to Baghdad, and he had risen to launch an Islamic jihad against the Christian presence in Palestine. When Saladin took Jerusalem in October, 1187, Henry II responded to the call for an immediate crusade. A swingeing 'Saladin tithe' was ordained, and the Archbishop of Canterbury was despatched to Wales to recruit crusaders.

As he rode westward along the Wye, Archbishop Baldwin knew that he was embarking upon a journey of some risk. His own king regarded the Welsh as 'a wild people who cannot be tamed', while an earlier Archbishop of Canterbury had

The storming of Jerusalem by Saladin on October 3, 1187 (*right*), and Henry II (*left*), who sent the Archbishop of Canterbury into Wales to recruit crusaders.

complained that the Welsh were 'Christians in name only … barbarians'. Baldwin was out of his depth. A humble monk from Devon, he had become Abbot of the Cistercian house of Forde in the tranquil Axe valley before being appointed Bishop of Worcester and then – in 1184 – Archbishop of Canterbury. A gentle, sincere man, softened by the southern shires of England, he did not speak Welsh, and was not familiar with the wilder parts of Britain. He would be the first Archbishop of Canterbury ever to set foot in Wales.

Riding with Baldwin – in a role which ranged from diplomat to local 'fixer' and recruitment officer – was the Court Chaplain to Henry II. Gerald de Barri was uniquely suited to easing the Archbishop's passage through Wales. An Anglo-Norman-Welsh hybrid, his father was a Norman knight, William de Barri, and his mother was the daughter of the Welsh princess, Nest, who'd been a mistress of Henry I. Gerald had been educated in Latin and the classics at the Benedictine Abbey of St Peter in Gloucester, and after visits to Paris, he had been awarded benefices in both Wales and England, where he'd been instrumental in purging the diocese of St David's of corrupt churchmen. After being appointed Archdeacon of Brecon, he moved closer to the Angevin orbit in 1184, when he was made Court Chaplain to Henry II, who used him as a go-between when dealing with Welsh princes. But Gerald had another, more discreet, role on the Archbishop's mission. Three years earlier, he had accompanied Prince John to Ireland, from where he had drawn material for two books, *The Topography of Ireland*, and *The Conquest of Ireland*. Now he had ambitions to write about Wales.

The 1,400-foot heights of Hergest Ridge loom over the route taken by the Archbishop's mission as it threaded through the troubled border zone.

Towards the end of that first day on the road, the Archbishop's entourage emerged from the shadow of Hergest Ridge onto a level, triangular vale framed by rounded mountains. At the western apex of this triangle rose the great earth mound and timber battlements of Radnor, the frontier outpost built and held by the Braiose family. Climb the mound today and it's hard not to think of Radnor as a Norman Alamo. From the grassy crown, you can look down on the roofs of the village, and the rectangular grid of Norman streets. It seems impregnable, but only eight years after Henry II's crusaders called by, the castle was destroyed by the Welsh. Radnor lay at the limit of Anglo-Norman control; the mountains which lifted the western horizon were part of the interior of 'Welsh Wales' – a vast no-go region for the likes of English Archbishops.

New Radnor, from the mound of the Norman castle which controlled the valley.

Some of the most powerful men in the British Isles were gathered at Radnor that evening. Waiting at the castle for the travellers was the Prince of South Wales, Rhys ap Gruffydd ap Rhys – first-cousin-once-removed of Gerald. For over thirty years 'The Lord Rhys' had played a game of defiance and submission with Henry II. He had won and lost land, but by 1188 he controlled the old kingdom of Deheubarth, a vast territory which stretched north to the Dovey and west to the coast of Pembrokeshire. To keep the peace, Henry had appointed Rhys his deputy in Wales. Having ridden with the Archbishop from Hereford, Chief Justiciar Ranulf de Glanville, was there too. An East Anglian baron, de Glanville was Henry II's right-hand man in England. Others from Wales included the Bishop of St David's, Peter de Leia, and the son of the Prince of Elfael.

To this motley group of mixed interests, the Archbishop delivered the mission's inaugural sermon and call for recruits to the cause. For the benefit of Welsh speakers, an interpreter stood beside Baldwin. No sooner had Baldwin finished, than the first man sprang forward. It was the Court Chaplain, Gerald de Barri. 'I myself,' he writes, 'was the first to stand up … I threw myself at the holy man's feet and devoutly took the sign of the Cross.'

This seems to have been a prepared double-act, concocted in advance by Gerald and the Archbishop: 'It was the urgent admonition given some time before by the King,' admitted Gerald later, 'which inspired me to give this example to the others, and the persuasion and oft-repeated promises of the Archbishop and the Chief Justiciar, who never tired of repeating the King's words.' Lest readers doubt his sincerity, Gerald added: 'I acted of my own free will, after anxiously talking the matter over time and time again, in view of the insult and injury being done at this moment to the Cross of Christ.'

The Court Chaplain's theatrics worked, and as soon as Gerald had taken his vow, the Bishop of St David's, Peter de Leia, followed his example. Then Einion ab Einion Clud, the son of the Prince of Elfael, stepped forward to take the Cross, 'and many others too'. Conspicuously failing to take the Cross, was the Lord Rhys, although Gerald diplomatically allows that the prince 'went home quite determined to make the holy journey'. This less-than-unanimous endorsement of a counter-jihad should have warned the Archbishop that his mission would be challenging.

* * *

Ahead of the mission lay a daunting circumnavigation of Wales. Gerald himself had estimated that Wales was about eight days travel in length and four days in its breadth. A complete circuit should therefore take twenty-four days. In fact, the mission would spend thirty-four days on the road and a further seventeen days resting and preaching. The total distance they would ride through the mud and stones of Wales would be around a thousand miles – equivalent to riding from London to Milan. Anyone attempting a feat like this today would find the day-to-day logistics a formidable adventure. Route-finding, difficult terrain, weather and procuring food for horse and rider, would be a constant preoccupation. But Gerald seldom mentions the trials of the road. To the medieval long-haul traveller, the discomforts were no more remarkable (and just as tedious) as the trials of modern air travel. Gerald is far more concerned with the nature of the land he is passing through. He refers to himself as 'a careful investigator of natural history', a universal discipline which allowed him to explore everything created by God, from archaeology, hydrology and zoology, to anthropology, geography and history. Gerald's was a young, dynamic world, rich with wonder. Wherever he looked, he saw evidence of God's ingenuity and wisdom. His catch-all curiosity lit upon anything from killer-toads and the occult, to Welsh history, sea-level change and divine retribution. Travelling was an opportunity to harvest the fruits of Creation.

The edgy border garrison of Hay-on-Wye, where men came running to join the Holy War. Twenty-eight years later, both town and castle were burned during a local rebellion.

From Radnor, the mission rode over the hills towards the valley of the River Wye, which they forded – probably in the shallows near Clyro – to reach Hay-on-Wye. The castle stood on a strategically-sited mound above the river-cliff of the Wye, with a ravine cut by a tributary running along one side of the mound. The mound is still there, with the tarmac road on one side, and the old cattle market on the other. Today, Hay is is a bibliophiles paradise, its narrow streets lined with so many second-hand bookshops that it's impossible not to tread its pavements without falling into a reflective trance. The sudden appearance on Hay's streets of the Archbishop of Canterbury eight hundred years ago did not have quite the same effect: 'After the sermon' reports Gerald, 'we saw a great number of men who wanted to take the Cross come running towards the castle … leaving their cloaks behind in the hands of the wives and friends who had tried to hold them back.'

Few of Hay's recruits had any idea of the perils involved in making a three thousand mile journey by land and sea, or knew what it was like to face a blizzard of arrows from Turkish horsemen, although they may well have been familiar with the fate of forebears who had taken the Cross. The Brut recorded that, forty years earlier, some pilgrims from Wales 'were drowned on the sea of Greece, in going with the Cross to Jerusalem'. At around the same time, the Brut of Gwent noted that so many Welsh pilgrims left for the Holy Land, that 'their absence was severely felt'. Once the Cross and the vow were taken, the pilgrimage was enforced by a penalty of excommunication. Only in exceptional circumstances could absolution be granted. In the flailing limbs and the screams and the shouts of loved-ones, a distant Holy War erupted in communities who knew little of the world beyond their own valley walls. Every husband who vowed to free the Holy Land – or to die in the attempt – was breaking his marriage vow. Families splintered as men fell for the spell of the Cross ... or took advantage of a marital exit strategy. Under canon law, wives could prevent their husbands participating in the crusade on the grounds that a prolonged absence abrogated their marriage vows. All knew that there was little chance of returning from the Holy Land.

From Hay, the mission probed deeper into the Welsh heartland, following the Wye upstream. While the river curled to Baldwin's right, the dark face of the Black Mountains reared up on his left. There were streams to ford, and beyond the castle at Bronllys, gentle, wooded hills which opened presently to reveal Llanddew: Gerald's archdeaconery.

Today, Llanddew is little more than a hamlet. The remains of Gerald's home stand in the garden of the old vicarage, The corner of his hall can be seen, and his doorway, and the well. Over the waving trees, one can glimpse the distant tilt of the Brecon

Llandew, deep in the mountains of south Wales. 'This is convenient enough for my studies and my work,' wrote Gerald, 'and here I pass my time in a sort of happy-go-lucky mediocrity.'

Beacons. It is a quiet place, and still feels remote. The Ordnance Survey map carries a hint of Llanddew's former eminence, labelling its south-facing slope 'Bishop's Meadow'. When Henry VIII's topographer, John Leland, rode by in the 1530s, Gerald's archdeaconery had 'fallen douen for the more part', while the Bishop's Palace had become 'no thing but an onsemeli ruine'. Two hundred years earlier, this had been Gerald's home; the place where he pared his quill, meditated and prayed. 'I occupy a tiny dwelling-place,' he writes of Llanddew, 'convenient enough for my studies and my work.' To a modern suburbanite, Gerald's home wouldn't seem so 'tiny'. The ruined gable suggests that he had room to swing more than a few cats. Gerald gives the impression that he is content with his modest seclusion at Llanddew: 'The house gives me pleasure and it is conducive to thoughts of the next world,' he muses. 'I would not change it for all the riches of Croesus.'

Not riches, maybe, but Gerald would have traded Llanddew for St David's. For over a decade, he had been manoeuvring to free Wales from domination by the Archbishopric of Canterbury, and key to this aim was the raising of St David's to an archbishopric. But first Gerald had to become the Bishop of St David's, and in this, he had been thwarted by his travelling companion, Peter de Leia, who had beaten Gerald in the election twelve years earlier. Gerald now found himself shackled by this journey to the two men – the Archbishop of Canterbury and the Bishop of St David's – who stood between him and ecclesiastical freedom for Wales.

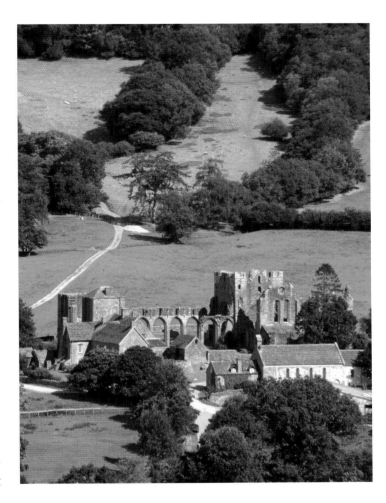

The Black Mountain sanctuary of Llanthony, whose secluded Augustinian abbey was held by Gerald to be 'most suited to the practice of religion'.

Gerald was a dreamer, and at Llandew, he drifts off on one of his periodic digressions to a nearby mountain valley so that he can share his favourite religious house. Established in the early 1100s, the abbey of Llanddewi Nant Honddu ('The English have corrupted the name to Llanthony') had been in the spiritual vanguard of religious reform in Britain. Gerald knew Llantony intimately, possibly even trained there. Snuggled into a valley 'no more than three arrow-shots in width', it is, sighs Gerald, better located than 'any of the other monasteries in the whole Island of Britain.' Its church, he writes, is built with squared stones and roofed with sheets of lead, which the architect in Gerald praises for being 'admirably suited to the nature of the place'. And that nature was one of contemplation. Setting up the abbey's daughter house in Gloucester as an emblem of the modern, vice-ridden, acquisitive world, he asks that the sanctuary on the Honddu be reserved for those whose minds are tuned to spirituality. Let those, he asks, who prefer books and prayers, and helping the needy, come to the Honddu, with its promise of eternal bliss and 'the concourse of angels'. Those who strive for earthly possessions, for entertainment and the company of mortal men, can go to Gloucester and 'clamour about the affairs and the pretences of the world'. It is Gloucester's chase for ever greater wealth, Gerald reminds us, which causes vice 'and all of the cares which follow in its train'. Here, in Llanthony, 'let the golden mean continue to flourish'. And then he is away, strewing the page with elegant phrases plucked from Ovid and Horace, Lucan and Petronius. 'Mortal appetite for success is insatiable!' 'Why can we not learn to temper our desires and be satisfied with what we have?' Last time I visited Llanthony the snow was slanting hard against the old red sandstone of its ruined walls.

\* \* \*

Separating the wilder reaches of inner Wales from the fertile, colonised, Anglo-Norman valleys of the south, were the Black Mountains. Gerald is unclear whether the mission cut through the heart of the mountains to reach the Usk valley, or skirted their western flank. 'From Llanddew,' he writes, 'we made our way along the rugged pass of Coed Grwyne or Grwyne Wood, by a narrow trackway overgrown with trees.'

The view north-westwards towards the valley of the Wye, from the crest of the Black Mountains above Grwyne Fawr. With horses and baggage, it would have been a difficult ascent.

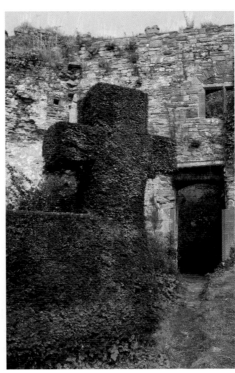

The border castle at Usk, which the Archbishop was in such a hurry to reach. Here, they were just a one-day ride from the coast, and the relative safety of Newport.

At least two authorities have identified the pass of 'Coed Grwyne' as the saddle at the head of the valley of Grwyne Fawr, in the Black Mountains, but it would have made far more sense to have avoided the 1,800 foot climb and simply followed the old Roman road down the Usk from Brecon to Abergavenny. Perhaps the 'Coed' Gerald refers to was a lost place-name at Blwch (Welsh for 'pass'), where the modern A40 still climbs to a tight notch in an outlying ridge of the Black Mountains. Shutting out the grunting coaches and streams of cars, it isn't difficult to imagine this as a rugged, overgrown mountain track.

Baldwin was no mountaineer, and Gerald writes that the archbishop was 'in a hurry to reach Usk Castle'. Down here, as they closed on the coast, the Archbishop could expect a more positive response to his sermons. And the Usk valley proved fruitful. After the sermon at Abergavenny, 'many took the Cross'. By the stone keep at Usk Castle, 'a large group of men was signed with the Cross'. At Newport, where the Usk runs into the sea, 'many people were persuaded to take the Cross'. Gerald's references to 'many' taking the cross are made at the expense of actually providing a figure. If we are to assume that Gerald's final figure of three thousand recruits for the entire mission is a modest exaggeration, and that they actually recruited around 2,500, then the mission was conscripting an average of around fifty a day. At the same time in Mainz, it is said that no less than thirteen thousand took the cross in a single day. Admittedly, the gathering at Mainz was a grander affair (among others, the German Emperor was there) than one of Baldwin's back-country sermons, but it would be unsurprising if the Archbishop was not impatient to increase his tally.

The promontory of Gold Cliff, an ancient landmark on the low-lying, northern shore of the Severn.

\* \* \*

The mouth of the Usk was a turning point marked by a natural signpost Gerald calls the 'Golden Rock'. It is still there, jutting into the Bristol Channel like a stranded hulk: 'High above the water,' writes Gerald, 'not far from Caerleon, there stands a rocky eminence which dominates the River Severn. When the sun's rays strike it, the stone shines very bright and takes on a golden sheen.'

Up on the brow of the cliff where the grass has been eroded around the modern navigation beacon, you can see stratified layers of bronze-coloured alluvium – Gerald's golden rock. In medieval times this was the most important landmark on this stretch of coast, both for shipping and land travellers; it has survived on the Ordnance Survey as 'Gold Cliff'. Here, the Archbishop's mission joined the well-travelled coast road to St David's, still ten days or so to the west. But in leaving behind the less-trodden tracks and ominous forests of inner Wales, the mission was now confronted by dangerous river crossings.

The problem was not just the width of the rivers at their outlets. The tides of the Severn Estuary have the largest range in the British Isles, and the estuaries which the coast road crossed were notorious for their quicksands, shifting sand-bars, strong currents and sudden floods. Gerald sets the scene for this litany of aquatic trials by telling a story about a notorious ford just beyond Newport. Almost facing Gold Cliff was a 'small stream known as the Nant Pencarn', which 'winds through the district called Wentloog'. The river can probably be identified as

Gerald's map of Europe, leading the viewer's eye from the British Isles at the bottom, to Rome at the top. The long inlet of the Severn is clearly marked 'Sabrina', and separates Wales from England.

the Ebbw, on Wentlooge Level (a farmhouse close to the river is still called Pen-carn). Today, the Ebbw – or 'wild horse river' – has been strangled by suburbs, factories and a motorway, but in the days before the Level was drained for farmland, the river was 'passable only at certain places and by certain fords, more because of the way in which it has hollowed out its bed and of the muddiness of the marshland which surrounds it than through the depth of its waters'. Gerald goes on to say that in earlier times the public road had crossed the river at a place named Rhyd Pencarn – which he translates as 'the ford beneath the overhanging rock'. Fords, like forests and passes, had many associations with calamity, and here Gerald repeats one that he got from the Scottish seer, Merlin Silvester, who prophesied that, should 'a strong man with a freckled face cross over Rhyd Pencarn on his way to lead an invasion of South Wales', the Welsh could expect to get beaten. Gerald had cause to believe this, since his own, strong, freckled King Henry II, had indeed galloped through this ford en route to defeat The Lord Rhys in 1163. Eight hundred years on, the river can be found beyond some scrubland. Canalised between concrete, and speckled with refuse, the 'Nant Pencarn' has lost a little of its romance.

'Of all the houses belonging to the Cistercian order in Wales,' wrote Gerald of Margam Abbey, 'this was by far the most renowned for arms and charity.'

Of the various river-mouths the mission was forced to ford on its journey west, the worst by far lay just beyond the Cistercian monastery of Margam. Little survived Henry VIII's monastic purge, but walls, arches and the shell of the chapter house still stand beside Junction 38 of the M4, mute on mown lawns. In 1188, the monastery was thriving in its secluded cleft below the tumulii-dotted heights of Mynydd Margam. Here, the travellers received 'the most open-handed hospitality', and must have ridden from the gates in good spirits. Immediately, they were faced by an alarming change of scenery. Outside Margam, the broad coastal plain they'd followed from the mouth of the Usk, was pinched out of existence by a forested wall which reached to the tide line.

Anticipating difficulties, the misssion was to be guided that day by the local prince, Morgan ap Caradog ap Iestyn. Following the road along the sands below the hills, first they had to cross the Afan. In a premonition of what was to follow, the riders were 'delayed for some time' as the ebbing tide combined with the flow of the river to make the Afan

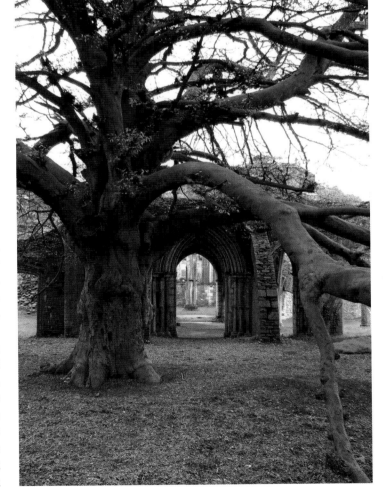

unfordable. Today, the river is shuttered between suburban terraces and concrete highway walls. Try to wade it (I did, and it was fast and surprisingly deep) and you realise how, and why, the crusaders ran into trouble. The Afan's unnerving turbulence is due to it falling 1,600 feet during its thirteen-mile course.

Far worse was to follow. Anxious not to be caught by the tide, the mission hurried along the coast road towards the next obstacle: the River Neath, notorious, writes Gerald, for being 'the most dangerous and difficult of access of all the rivers of South Wales, on account of its quicksands'.

Set off in Gerald's hoof-prints today, and you find the six miles of sands from Margam to Neath buried beneath the derelict site of the Margam steelworks, a housing estate, (appropriately-named Sandfields), and a decomposing wasteland of metal tubing, pylons and tanks which used to be one of the largest petrochemical works in Europe. Where Gerald and his companions splashed across tidal sands, two thousand workers mass-produced Styrene, Ethanol, Vinyl Acetate and Isoproponal, a colourless solvent used for automotive windscreen wash.

As the riders approached the mouth of the Neath, they split into two groups. Several of the packhorses took a lower route, and – for fear of quicksand – appear to have been trotting. Gerald's packhorse was caught and began sinking. Nervous servants ran across the quicksand to the stricken animal and hauled at the harnesses and ropes. Gerald records that the animal was 'almost sucked down into the abyss' and

Fast flowing mountain rivers like the Afan forced medieval travellers to use the narrow coastal strip, where they had to face the dangers of wide, tidal estuaries.

that tragedy was averted, though 'not without some damage done to my books and baggage'.

The danger was far from over. Their guide, Morgan, entreated them all to move slowly and carefully but, writes Gerald, 'against the advice of our leader, our fear of the unusual surface made us hurry across the quicksands'. They had not reached the river, and this was no place to be caught by an incoming tide. Quoting Virgil, Gerald noted that 'Terror gave us wings'. The travellers appear to have suffered further problems with the sands, for Gerald adds that they endured 'considerable danger and quite a few upsets' before the river came in sight. It was only as they realise that they have 'won through' that they heed Morgan's advice and accept that 'it is better to advance more slowly and with great circumspection over such dangerous terrain'.

The Neath itself proved far too difficult to ford, 'for the passages through the river change with every monthly tide and they cannot be located at all after a heavy fall of rain, when the waters are swollen with floods and inundations'. They crossed by boat, probably at the

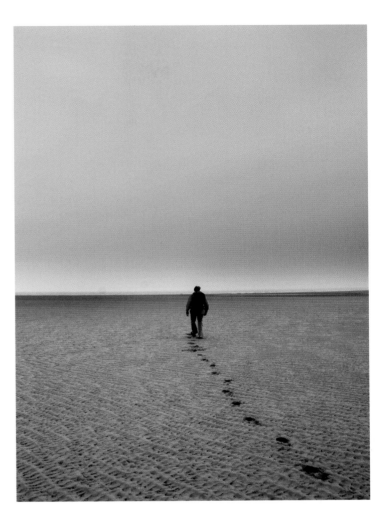

Quicksands here at the mouth of the River Neath, trapped Gerald's packhorse.

spot now known as Briton Ferry, where the river squeezes between a pair of low foothills. The Neath pilot who ferried me across the river here, told me that local boatmen still speak of the days when poorer travellers had to wade across a submerged, wooden causeway. In sight of the old ford, the giddy stalks of the M4 lean skyward bearing a modern road which can whisk motorists all the way to London in less time than it took Gerald to ride ten miles of seashore.

Exhausted, the mission spent the night in the castle at Swansea, where Gerald overheard two monks talking about the episode in the quicksand. 'It's hard country, this,' said one. 'Not at all,' quipped the other. 'Yesterday we found it far too soft.'

\* \* \*

For Gerald, the Neath was a personal deliverance; this river marked the boundary between the diocese of Llandaff and that of St David's. Ahead of him lay his own birthplace and the city of his dreams. Once again, he was on home turf, and as the mission made its way towards St David's, he prepared to spring back onto his pages bathed in a virtuous aura. His first chance came at Haverfordwest.

Beyond the Neath, the mountains backed away from the shoreline and the travellers were able to follow a safer route through the populous countryside of Dyfed. This should have been perfect recruiting country, and yet Gerald suggests that the mission was struggling. Apparently, plotters in Cardigan and St David's were attempting to disrupt Baldwin's tour, and – by failing to record large-scale responses to the Archbishop's sermons since Swansea – Gerald implies that the recruitment drive was flagging. Then, at Haverfordwest, Gerald reappears for another of his dramatic turns. Taking over from Baldwin, he addresses the crowd, first in Latin and then in French. Admitting that few among his audience understood a word, he claims that many of them were 'moved to tears ... rushing forward in equal numbers to receive the sign of the Cross'. Modesty was not one of Gerald's handicaps.

Having set the mission on its feet again, Gerald launches into a promotional digression on the kingdom of Dyfed. A patchwork of woods and fields surrounded on three sides by a ragged coast, Dyfed was blessed with the riches of land and sea. 'Of all the different parts of Wales,' enthuses Gerald, 'Dyved, with its seven cantrefs, is at once the most beautiful and the most productive.'

In that warm, stable twelfth-century climate, there is food in abundance: 'This is a region rich in wheat,' he continues, 'with fish from the sea and plenty of wine for sale.' Gerald had been born here over forty years earlier, and his narrative takes a sentimental ramble through his childhood home at Manorbier, down by the sea. Then, as now, the turrets and crenellations of his father's seat rise above a sandy beach and rocky headland. Gerald refers to his home as a 'fortified mansion', but later accretions have turned the de Barri 'mansion' into an enormous castle. Among the more recent walls and turrets lurk places which Gerald knew as a boy. The most impressive is the hall-block built by Gerald's father at around the time of Gerald's birth. William de Barri broke with Norman convention and integrated his keep with the curtain wall, creating an extended domestic complex which fed an enormous hall. To the sides were the buttery, pantry and kitchen. Above the buttery are the ruins of William's withdrawing room. Some have speculated that Gerald was born up here, in one of the first rooms to catch the morning sun.

Outside the walls is Gerald's boyhood playground. The little valley between the castle and church still carries its stream between ponds where Gerald used to fish. The ruins of the mill that he mentions can also be seen, although his 'attractive orchard' has now disappeared beneath the carpark and public lavatories. And the storms of intervening centuries have piled sand against Manorbier's walls, separating Gerald's home from the open sea. He writes of the view from the rocky headland to the south of the bay, and if you take the footpath there today, you can choose the spot where Gerald sat and gazed: 'Boats on their way to Ireland from almost any part of Britain scud by before the east wind, and from this vantage point you can see them brave the ever-changing violence of the winds and the blind fury of the waters.' Enchanted Manorbier is one of those rare places that carries a living memory.

* * *

The tip of Pembrokeshire is the Welsh Land's End. 'St David's', reminds Gerald, 'is in a remote corner of the country', chosen for its location by men who 'wanted to live as far removed as possible from worldy upsets'. Here, he says, there are no woods, no rivers and no pastures. The soil is 'rocky and barren' and the peninsula is 'exposed to the winds and to extremely inclement weather'. This is the most western point in mainland Wales, further west even than Scotland's Cape Wrath. As you approach St David's along the Pembrokeshire Coast Path, successive headlands reveal long views of fearsomely ragged reefs and the ever-beating sea. At Solva, a miniature Norwegian fjord curls inland, offering a deep draught anchorage to sea-going vessels. At sheltered havens like this, bedragged pilgrims tottered ashore for the final walk to the shrine of St David.

The cathedral crouches in a hollow, hunching its shoulders against Irish gales and the memories of Viking raiders. Close to the iron-bound casket containing the Saint's relics is a carved stone effigy, hands pressed in prayer, face smashed off. The tomb is said to be that of Gerald. Nearby is an undamaged, armoured figure with a lined face and long moustache, reputed to be The Lord Rhys. Keeping the prince and author company are a motley crew of knights, priests and the odd Bishop.

St David's Cathedral: the focus of Gerald's dream to free the Welsh church from Canterbury.

On the mission's arrival, Peter de Leia, the Bishop of St David's, made sure that his fellow-travellers were well accommodated. Modern pilgrims lurching off buses at Britain's smallest cathedral city are greeted by the familiar range of urban services from espresso bar to delicatessen. Gerald gives the impression of an English archbishop who didn't want to hang about in a Welsh bishopric. Baldwin spent a night at St David's, celebrated early-morning Mass in the Cathedral, then 'hurried off through Cemais to meet Prince Rhys in Cardigan'. One of the things on the Archbishop's mind must have been the need to secure support for the crusade from the Prince of South Wales and his two sons, Gruffydd and Maelgwn.

Gerald stayed behind, apparently ordered by the Archbishop to 'preach to the people'. The tactic which worked so well in Haverfordwest – of preaching in French or Latin to a Welsh-speaking audience – did indeed persuade a large number of men to take the Cross. But this success was short lived, for an interpreter then translated Gerald's sermon into Welsh, and his new recruits abruptly changed their minds. The benefits of a trip to the Holy Land had clearly been lost in translation.

The nave, looking east past the arcades erected by Gerald's travel companion, the Bishop of St David's, Peter de Leia.

Gerald's stake in the journey changed at St David's. Since Hereford, the itinerary had been curiously autobiographical, allowing him to weave a narrative which linked his archdeaconery in Llanddew, his beloved Llanthony, his birthplace in Manorbier, and St David's, the object of his sublunary dreams. But from here, the journey would take Gerald off the edge of his mental map into lands beyond the control of the Anglo-Normans and their temperamental ally, The Lord Rhys.

\* \* \*

Gerald left St David's with his rival, Peter de Leia, who had been charged with accompanying the mission to the borders of Deheubarth. Riding against the flow of in-bound pilgrims, they took the uneven track into the badlands of west Wales. Their route led them through the heart of the cantref of Cemais, a particular hotspot for its Angevin lords. Cemais was ruled by the FitzMartin family, who had always struggled to keep the Welsh under control (an earlier FitzMartin, Robert, had been routed in battle at Crug

Mawr near Cardigan). Cemais was now under the lordship of William FitzMartin, who had taken the precaution of marrying the daughter of the Lord Rhys, but this had failed to settle the troubled district. Three years after Gerald passed this way, young William would find himself besieged in his castle by his Welsh father-in-law.

Gerald and de Leia probably spent their first night out of St David's at Nevern Castle, the FitzMartin seat. For the second night, they made it to St Dogmael's Abbey, just outside Cardigan, where Gerald was reunited with Archbishop Baldwin. In the morning, they rode to Cardigan, and the great castle of the Lord Rhys. It must have been here that Baldwin and Gerald learned that the most powerful prince in Wales would not be joining the crusade after all. According to Gerald, the Lord Rhys had arrived home from greeting the Archbishop at Radnor, and thrown himself into many days of preparation for the journey to the Holy Land. He'd collected pack-animals and saddles, raised funds and persuaded others to take the cross too. But his wife Gwenllian had 'put a sudden stop to his noble intentions by playing upon his weakness and exercising her womanly charms'. This was a great blow to the Archbishop, for the absence of Rhys would hardly encourage other Welshmen to take the Cross. Among those who did not, were the two sons of the Lord Rhys, Maelgwn and Gruffydd.

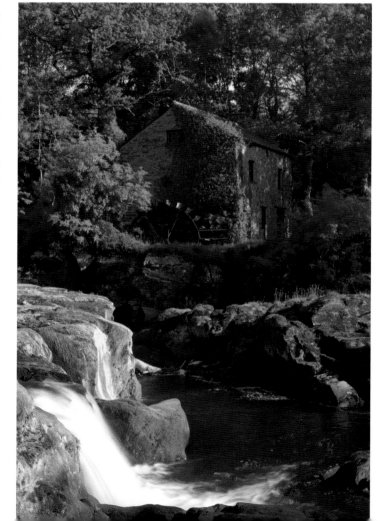

A medieval beauty spot: The falls at Cenarth. For the convenience of modern travellers, there is a car park.

Escorted by the Lord Rhys and his sons, the mission now left the coast for a detour into the interior. Way inland, by the rising of the River Teifi was a monastery that had recently been endowed by Rhys. Their guide was the river itself, and Gerald opens this riparian diversion at a delightful place he calls 'Cenarth Mawr'. He writes of a church, a mill, a bridge over the river with a fishing station, and a 'most attractive garden'. Salmon can be seen leaping up the falls here, 'about as far as the height of the tallest spear'. Cenarth has grown, and now has a couple of pubs and a coracle museum. Above the waterfalls, a footpath cuts through the woods beside deep, clear water. It was a lovely spot until a carpark was built on the rocks beside the bridge.

The Teifi seems to have released the natural historian in Gerald. So fullsome are the pages about the river and its creatures that it's as if he's describing the Garden of Eden. There is no river like it: the Teifi is 'better stocked with the finest salmon than any other stream in Wales', and the only river in Wales and England south of the Humber 'where you can find beavers'. He writes in detail of the salmon, and the astonishing contortions they have to perform in leaping up waterfalls, 'just as birds fly into the wind'. Sometimes, he says, 'in order to give more power to the leap, they go so far as to put their tails right in their mouths.' He describes how the beavers build their dams, and their 'castle-like lodges' in the river, their methods of 'carting timber' from the woods to the water, the nature of their teeth and the means by which they survive underwater. Hunted for their body parts, Gerald repeats an observation made in 'Eastern countries', that cornered beavers save themselves from death by cutting off their own testicles and throwing them down before the hunter's eyes.

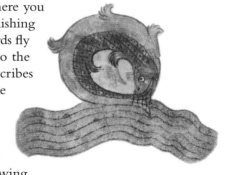

Salmon leaping, in a thirteenth-century manuscript of Gerald's *Topographia Hibernica*.

Repeatedly, Gerald conjures up landscapes of unimaginable beauty and natural diversity. Earlier in the journey, he describes Llangorse Lake, near Brecon, with its plentiful supply of pike and perch, trout, tench and 'mud-loving eels'. He writes of plagues of poisonous toads, tame jackdaws, of pastures full of cattle, and woodland 'teeming with wild animals'. Often, he mixes hearsay with his own, more factual reports. He includes in his description of Llangorse, stories of the lake's 'miraculous' ability to change colour from bright green to scarlet, and reports that the water had been seen 'completely covered with buildings or rich pasture-lands'. Elsewhere, he writes of immigrant Flemings who can foretell the future by reading the right shoulder-blade of rams. and of a rich man who got bitten by a viper after dreaming that he would find a gold torque if he put his hand in a hole by a waterfall. 'It seems to me,' rationalises Gerald, 'that dreams are like rumours; you must use your common sense, and then accept some but refuse to believe others.'

Llangorse Lake, where Gerald records sightings of floating buildings and orchards, and where the water could turn from bright green to scarlet.

He has a strong sense too of natural forces. In the Black Mountains, Gerald strives to explain the local weather system, arguing that the high rainfall is 'because of the mountains' The further east one travels, 'the more the sky above seems to be pure and limpid … because the wind which blows it clear is harsher and more piercing'. Conversely, the further west you go, the 'more cloudy and more thick' becomes the air. It's a fairly neat resume of the principle air currents which strike the British isles. He also stumbles across evidence of sea-level rise. Forced to cross the sands of Newgale Bay on the way to St David's, Gerald comes across a 'curious phenomenon' which had been first observed in the aftermath of a great storm twenty years earlier: 'Tree trunks … standing in the

sea, with their tops lopped off, and with the cuts made by the axes as clear as if they had been felled only yesterday.' To Gerald, this had been a 'forest grove, cut down at the time of the Flood, or perhaps a little later', which had then succumbed 'by slow degrees' to the waves 'which encroach relentlessly upon the land and never cease to wash it away'. By the late 1100s, sea-levels had been rising for nearly three hundred years, as the 'Medieval Warm Period' heated the oceans and increased their volume. Generations of Gerald's countrymen had grown up with tales of retreating coasts, inundations by water and drifting sand.

* * *

Thirty-five days after crossing the border into Wales, the travellers came to a dark gulf. Three times wider than any estuary they'd crossed so far, the Dovey was not just a dramatic natural feature, but a formidable border. This was the limit of the diocese of St David's, and the edge of Lord Rhys' domain. The Dovey, wrote Gerald, 'divides North Wales from South Wales.'

It must have been an uneasy moment for those in the party whose fate it was to cross the water. They had reached the point of no return. It would be less difficult to continue with their circumnavigation of Wales than to return the way they had come, and in any case, the Archbishop had undertaken to celebrate Mass in each of the Welsh cathedrals – which meant pressing on to Bangor and St Asaph. The Lord Rhys and Peter de Leia took their leave of the Archbishop and turned for their homes in the south.

Beyond the water rose ominously gloomy, forested hills. Over there was 'the territory of the sons of Cynan' – the brothers Gruffydd and Maredudd ap Cynan. Maredudd ruled Eifionydd, and Gruffydd held Merionydd and Ardudwy. On the far shore of the Dovey, Merionydd symbolised the untouchable interior of Wales. It was 'wilder and less accessible' than other regions and the 'rudest and roughest of all the Welsh districts'. Culturally, this was a foreign country, inhabited by Welsh men and women who had never been subjugated by the Normans, and who therefore spoke no French or Latin. Even their weaponry was different. In the north, noted Gerald, the weapon of choice was not the bow, but the long spear. Hurled like a javelin, at close quarters, it would pierce a cuirass of chain mail. Opportunities to recruit crusaders would be rare. The Dovey was Gerald's Rubicon. Sinister to many, the Dovey took its name from the Welsh word 'duf', for 'dark or 'black'. Depleted in numbers, the mission embarked upon boats and were rowed into the current.

* * *

As soon as they stepped ashore, the travellers knew that they had arrived in another land. Immense mountains crowded the coast, leaving little space for the road. Ominously, the ruler of Merionydd, Gruffydd ap Cynan, failed to greet them on the northern shore, though he would show up the next day, apologising 'humbly and devoutly'. They spent the night at Towyn, then continued north, confined between

Waiting at Traeth Maelgwyn for the boat over the Dovey, the most ominous gulf Gerald crossed.

Cadair Idris, the 'chair of Idris' (a mythical Welsh warrior) defends the southern approaches to Snowdonia.

the sea and the lower slopes of Cadair Idris. Never had the terrain looked so intimidating: 'The mountains are very high,' remember Gerald, 'with narrow ridges and a great number of very sharp peaks all jumbled together in confusion. If the shepherds who shout to each other and exchange comments from these lofty summits should ever decide to meet, it would take them almost the whole day to climb down and up again.

They reached another estuary, the Mawddach. No doubt recalling the quicksand incident on the Neath, the Archbishop and Gerald embarked upon a twenty-mile detour which allowed them to cross the much narrower waters of the Wnion and the Mawddach, far inland. Meanwhile, the prince's impetuous son, Maelgwyn ap Rhys, found a ford near the sea and rode across the mouth of the estuary. That night, the mission made it to Llanfair, but was confronted the next morning by yet another huge gulf of water, Traeth Bach, the last of the Cardigan Bay estuaries. Gerald's note-taking appears to have become patchy by this stage of the journey, and he fails to mention whether they rode across the sands at low tide, or enlisted the help of rowing boats at high tide. There are signs too that the author was confused by the unfamiliar terrain. Beyond the Dovey, geographical errors creep into his account. A couple of rivers are misplaced, and he appears to have moved a mountain pass from the Lleyn peninsula to the foothills of Snowdonia. After five hundred miles in the saddle, he was unquestionably tired.

Beyond Traeth Bach, the mission rode obliquely across the Lleyn peninsula to Nefyn on the southern shore of Caernarfon Bay. Nefyn was a long way off the mission's shortest route to Bangor, and a visit to this modest village today provides few clues to its medieval attraction. The forlorn churchyard is padlocked and has sheep grazing among the graves. What might be the motte of the medieval castle rises as a grassy pimple in the nearby childrens' playground. Why did the mission come here? A clue can be found on the Ordnance Survey maps. While most of the north is solidly mountainous, two areas are low lying. Eight hundred years ago, the Lleyn peninsula and Anglesey were fertile and populous, and one of the oldest Welsh settlements hereabouts was Nefyn. The main town for the region, it was also the princely court – a tradition that was said to reach back to the presence here of King Arthur's court. One hundred years after Gerald came this way, Edward II humiliated the defeated Welsh by staging at Nefyn an Arthurian Round Table of such extravagance that the floor collapsed. For the first time in the north, Baldwin preached. It was Palm Sunday, and the result appears to have been gratifying, for 'many people took the Cross'.

For Gerald, Nefyn produced an unexpected reward. The monasteries and churches that had been their way stations since Hereford were also the medieval equivalent of public libraries, and for Gerald these had provided moments of succour on a gruelling journey through a literary wilderness. Now, at Nefyn, Gerald found books, and in particular, an extremely rare manuscript, a work, he says which he 'had long been looking for.' Written in the 'ancient British language' the book was regarded with such awe by its custodians that it had been kept hidden at Nefyn for as long as anyone could remember. 'There,' recalled Gerald, 'I myself, Archdeacon of St David's, discovered the works of Merlin Silvester…' Not to be confused with the Welsh Merlin (Ambrosius) who was born of a Carmarthen incubus, Merlin Silvester (or Celidonius or 'Merlin the Wild' as he becomes in Gerald's *Conquest of Ireland*) came from Scotland and had dispensed prophecies from the great Caledonian Forest. It was Silvester who provided Gerald with the prophecy about fording the Ebbw on the south coast of Wales.

The route Gerald followed from Nefyn is unclear in the narrative, but obvious on the ground. A straight line from Nefyn to Caernarfon and Bangor takes the traveller through a notch in the crest of the only cluster of peaks on the Lleyn peninsula – the mountains of Yr Eifl. It's also the course taken by the Roman road which once ran from Nefyn to the fort at Segontium, the Imperial stronghold which has since been swallowed by the eastern suburbs of Caernarvon.

From Nefyn, the climb drags out for nearly seven miles, skirting a mountain flank high above the sea, then twisting through a valley, crossing a broad saddle and scaling a long ridge before tackling the pass itself. This was the longest, steepest climb on the entire circumnavigation, and it became the scene for the most amusing exchange Gerald records. 'Our road led us to a valley,' he writes, 'where the going was hard, with many steep climbs up and down.' As the Archbishop and Court Chaplain rode towards the pass, they must have been talking about their impending departure for the Holy Land, and the difficulties they would soon face. Climbing down from their horses, they began walking up the long, winding trail 'in intention at least rehearsing what we thought we would experience when we went on our pilgrimage to Jerusalem'.

Unused to walking, the exercise took its toll: 'We walked the whole length of the valley,' continues Gerald, 'and we were very tired by the time we reached the farther end. The Archbishop sat himself down on a convenient oak-tree, which had been completely uprooted and overturned by the force of the winds, for he needed to rest and recover

The modern village of Nefyn, on the northern shore of the Lleyn Peninsula, seen here from the beginning of the climb through the twin peaks of Yr Eifl.

On Bwlch yr Eifl, where the Archbishop joked about the hardships of travel in Wales; from here, the mission would have ridden their horses along the coastal Roman road to Caernarfon.

his breath.' Looking up, the Archbishop asked his exhausted retinue: 'Which of you, now, in all my company, can soothe my tired ears by whistling a tune?' Just then, a bird in a nearby coppice began to sing. Some of the travellers thought that it was a green woodpecker, others that it was an oriole. When one remarked that it couldn't be a nightingale, because such a bird wasn't seen in north Wales, the Archbishop quipped: 'If it never comes to Wales, the nightingale is a very sensible bird.' Then he added: 'We are not quite so wise, for not only have we come here, but we have traversed the whole country!'

When the weary travellers eventually reached the summit of Bwlch yr Eifl, they would have seen – if it was a clear morning – an astonishing view. So steep is the northern side of the pass that it appears to fall vertically to the fields one thousand feet below. Beyond the greensward, the long curve of Caernarfon Bay leads the eye to the flat pan of Anglesey, and, roaming to the right, a mass of seething peaks. This spectacular stage was to be the setting for Baldwin's final effort to persuade the Welsh to accompany him to the Holy Land.

Next morning in Bangor, the metropolitan see of Gwynedd, Baldwin took to the high altar and exerted the full weight of episcopal leverage. The Welsh Bishop of Bangor found himself 'hard pressed ... rather than persuaded' by Baldwin, but took the Cross, as did 'a number of other people'. It clearly wasn't a stampede. Then the crusaders took to boats and crossed the Menai Straits to Anglesey, where they held a series of open-air sermons 'near the seashore where the surrounding rocks form a sort of circular theatre'. This seems to have been a bluff called Cerrig y Borth, where an amphitheatre of rock can still be found among the trees. Evidently an enormous crowd had assembled, for Gerald claims the presence of 'all the inhabitants of the island and quite a few from the adjacent mainland'. The crowd included the Prince of North Wales, Rhodri ab Owain Gwynedd, and a contingent from his household. Confession was heard and then – with a local archdeacon translating into Welsh – Baldwin preached, followed by the Abbot of Strata Florida, Seisyll. The difficulties in Bangor were repeated. A 'band of youths' from Rhodri's household sat unmoved on a rock, despite the Archbishop and the other preachers 'exhorting them again and again'. Not one of them, remonstrates Gerald, could be persuaded to pick up their spears and march to Jerusalem. It was 'as if trying to extract blood from a stone'. Three days later, the young men were variously wounded or killed whilst pursuing a local band of robbers. Soon after that, Rhodri was dispossessed of his lands by his own nephews. It was, remarked Gerald, 'divine vengeance'.

For Baldwin, the episodes in Bangor and on Anglesey had been a cruel confirmation of Welsh indifference to a Holy War. After a night in Bangor, the mission turned towards the English border, 'the sea on one side and a steep cliff on the other'. Gwynedd had exposed the flawed core of both mens' aspirations. Baldwin could no more persuade thousands of Welsh to fight a Holy War in a faraway desert than he could whistle up a nightingale in Lleyn. And Gerald knew that a hollowness lay within the heart of his literary masterpiece. For days, the mission had been edging around a geographical feature whose physical scale was matched by its role in Welsh mythology; a feature so embedded in the British imagination that it appeared on maps drawn on the far side of England. On Matthew Paris's map of the late 1250s, Snowdonia is the only mountain range shown in Britain. The Mappa Mundi now hanging in Hereford was drawn thirty or so years later, and on this, Snowdonia is shown as a thirteen-headed massif occupying the whole of North Wales (curiously, there are fourteen peaks in Snowdonia higher than three thousand feet, so the mapmaker's symbol might not be quite as arbitrary as it first appears). Snowdonia shows up again (as a giant cogwheel) on the most important medieval map of Britain, the 'Gough map' of 1360. Among the Welsh, Snowdonia was a symbol of national reboutability: the resting place of Gruffudd ap Llywelyn, the only man ever to have ruled the whole of Wales; for seven extraordinary years, while Gerald was a young man, Wales had fallen under the compass of its own king. To the Welsh, these mountains are, explains Gerald, called 'Eryi', the haunt of the eagles; to the English they are the 'Snow Mountains'. When looked at from Anglesey, writes Gerald, 'they seem to rear their lofty summits right up to the clouds. They are thought to be so enormous and to extend so far that, as the old saying goes: 'Just as Anglesey can supply all the inhabitants of Wales with corn, so, if all the herds were gathered together, Snowdon could afford sufficient pasture.' Borrowing from Virgil, Gerald adds:

'And what they crop by day the
    shorter night renews,
Thus feeding all the flocks thanks to
    its cooling dews.'

Matthew Paris's thirteenth-century map of Britain, with 'Wallia' on the left and a compressed Scotland north of Hadrian's Wall. The only mountain range marked is Snowdonia.

By Snowdonia, it is finally apparent that this is not – as our author claims – a journey through Wales, but a journey around its periphery. Through sleight of the quill, Gerald has been playing a clever game of deception. As we ride with him around the Anglo-Norman edge of the country, he's been regaling us with tales of the Welsh interior. Hearsay and prodigous research allow him to penetrate the fastness that is out of bounds to those of Marcher blood. Gerald knows every river that reaches the sea, but has no idea of Snowdonia's scale or nature. 'At the very top of the mountains,' he writes, 'two lakes are to be found… One has a floating island, which moves about and is often driven to the opposite side by the force of the winds.' Shepherds, he adds, 'are amazed to see the flocks which are feeding there carried off to distant parts of the lake.' The second lake is even weirder. It abounds in eels, trout and perch, all of whom have only one eye (the right one). And of course, Gerald has been told the tale of Snowdonia's eagle, which assumes that war will break out 'every fifth feast-day' and so perches on a particular stone 'hoping to satiate its hunger with the bodies of dead men'. The stone has been pierced by the eagle cleaning and sharpening its beak.

In the medieval imagination, Snowdonia was the most spectacular, impenetrable geographical feature in Britain. Treading wearily along the cliff-shelf towards Conway, Gerald knew all too well that the real Wales was beyond his reach.

The ride back to Hereford was executed at a punishing pace. At the start of the journey over a month earlier, they had been dawdling along at an average of around twenty miles a day, but the hundred or so miles from Bangor to Chester were covered in just three days. Baldwin preached at St Asaph Cathedral, then the mission decided to carry on riding rather than stay the night. The travellers reached Chester the night before Good Friday and spent three fruitful days through Easter convincing the town's finest menfolk to fight for Christ. For the final leg of the

Gerald wrote of two lakes in Snowdonia, one of which had a floating island. Seen here from the summit of Y Garn, are Llyn Idwal and Llyn Ogwen.

journey, the daily average soared to an astonishing forty-five miles, although they were so tired by the time that they reached Shrewsbury that Gerald writes of the need 'to rest and recover our breath'. By then, they had been on the road for over six weeks. One final day in the saddle took them back to Hereford: 'We thus described a full circle,' concluded Gerald, 'and returned once more to the place from which we had begun this rather exhausting journey through Wales.'

\* \* \*

By the time Gerald returned from his great journey, his mental map of Wales was astonishly comprehensive. He knew the basic shape of the coastline, the location of the major mountain ranges and the courses of the principal rivers. He carried a score of castles in his head, and knew where to find every monastery and most of the churches. Had he committed his Welsh geography to vellum, he'd be hailed as the best mapmaker of his age. Late in life, Gerald did direct the drawing of at least one map. More of a picture than an exercise in cartography, it is a stylised depiction of Europe, with Rome at the top and Ireland at the bottom. The whole 'map' is intended to draw the viewers eye from Britain to Rome by way of a central corridor which connects the English Channel with Flanders, Paris, Lausanne, the Great St Bernard Pass, Pavia and Tuscany. In the British Isles, eight sees are elegantly depicted and labelled in red ink. Missing are Canterbury and St David's. It is impossible to imagine a more graphic insight into Gerald's state of mind.

The Third Crusade was a fiasco. Gerald got as far as Chinon before being sent back to England – with Peter de Leia – by the King. Baldwin and de Glanville were less lucky; both died in the Holy Land. Gerald wrote his own epitaph in the preface to *The Journey Through Wales*: 'This little work is like a clear mirror, reflecting the wild and trackless places we passed through. It likewise names each spring and rushing river, and records our witty sayings, the hazards of the road, and the various accidents that befell us. It describes the landscape, and the notable things that have happened there both recently and a long time ago, with occasional digressions about natural wonders: and it portrays the country itself, as well as the origins, customs and ways of the inhabitants.' Time has been the judge of Gerald. He once wrote that his purpose had been to 'rescue from oblivion ... the secrets of my own native land.' In that, his crusading mission was a triumph.

Full circle: Returning to Hereford, Gerald claimed that 'three thousand men were signed with the Cross, all of them highly skilled in the use of the spear and the arrow ... and only too keen to attack the enemies of our faith.'

A medieval scribe at work, from a c.1220 manuscript of Gerald's *Topographia Hibernica*.

# John Leland *1536–45*
## *The madness of maps*

LELAND'S ITINERARY
*of*
THE WEST COUNTRY

DIEV ET MON DROYT

N

W     E

S

0   10   20   30
MILES

Bath

*Mendip Hills*

Wells

Dunster

Simonsbath    Axford

Bridgwater

Glastonbury

*Somerset Levels*

South Cadbury

Bideford

Barnstable

*Exmoor*

SOMERSET

DORSET

Great Torrington

Crewkerne

DEVON

Crediton

Honiton

Lyme Regis

Boscastle

Tintagel

CORNWALL

*Dartmoor*

Exeter

Axmouth

Bridport

Padstow

Launceston

Oterton

Wadebridge

*Bodmin Moor*

Bodmin

Liskeard

Teignmouth

Mitchell

Lostwithiel

Totnes

St Allen

Fowey

Plymouth

St Austell

Dartmouth

Cape Cornwall

St Ives

Truro

St Mawes

Penzance

Helston

Penryn

*Carrick Roads*

*St Michael's Mount*

UNDERTAKEN
*in the years*
1536–45

✠    Abbey

- - - -    Leland's routes, identifiable from his *Itinerary*

⊕    Town or city

FOR THE best part of ten years, Henry VIII's antiquarian, John Leland, travelled the length and breadth of the kingdom in an attempt to record the treasures of its threatened monasteries, and to reinvigorate England's identity by restoring its Arthurian past. But Leland's fascination with the worked landscape turned his 'laboryeuse Journey and Serche' into a topographical audit on an unimaginable scale. Eventually he went mad, but his manuscripts have been a Tudor touch-stone for the last five hundred years. Among those who turned to Leland's journeys was William Camden, whose definitive county-by-county description of England and Wales, *Britannia*, became the standard geographical reference for centuries to come.

\* \* \*

The month was January. For weeks, the west coast of Britain had been battered by gales. Roofs had been ripped off, trees toppled. One of the gales had taken only two days to cross the Atlantic. But in the lull between each storm, the skies momentarily cleared, and it was on one of these days, in the harbour of St Mawes in Cornwall. that I hoisted the rust-coloured sails of a gaff-rigger and turned the bow towards open water. Beyond Carricknath Point, white horses flickered across the open sea. But in the other direction, inland, a vast expanse of uncluttered water glittered between sheltering hills. Some five miles long and stretching to two miles in width, the combined area of Carrick Roads and Falmouth Harbour are claimed locally to be the third largest natural harbour in the world. John Leland had no doubts about its significance. To Henry VIII's peripatetic topographer, this was the most important harbour in the land; 'very notable and famose, and yn a maner the most principale of al Britayne'.

Leland took particular trouble to describe the harbour's complex geography. He devotes more space to it than any other harbour in his *Itinerary*, noting the creeks and anchorages, the depth of the water in fathoms, the locations of noblemens' houses, churches, piers, bridges and woodland. This was, he concluded, a safe refuge for the 'greatest shyppes that travayle be the ocean'. Two years earlier, Henry VIII had begun constructing a pair of revolutionary artillery forts to protect the anchorage. Tacking to and fro through the swell, alternately I came in range of the gun-ports of Pendennis Castle and St Mawes Castle, the 'fortelet lately buylded by the contery for the defense of the haven'. Beside it, basking in unseasonable sun, were the pastel cottages and hotels of St Mawes, 'a poor fischar village'. Between the two castles, I passed the 'blynd roke', sited, said Leland, 'nerer the west syde of the haven then the east'. Today, it is

*Previous pages:* **Pendennis Point and Falmouth, from St Anthony Head.**

marked by an enormous, tapered warning beacon, for the rock is submerged at high tide – or, as Leland puts it – 'covered at ful see'. Here, at a glance, was Leland's Tudor harbour, immediately recognisable despite the passage of half a millenium.

*Opposite:* St Mawes Castle, protecting the entrance to Carrick Roads. Carved into the castle walls are inscriptions composed by Leland for Henry VIII.

\* \* \*

As the pale cliffs of Calais receded, John Leland may well have reflected upon the future he had seen. The year was 1529, and he had just boarded a ship on the coast of northern France. Three years earlier, he had arrived in Paris, the largest and most exciting city in northern Europe. Twenties Paris seethed with poets and printers, bibliophiles and mathematicians, and above all, with dangerous ideas. Here, a young man could immerse himself in what historians would come to know as the 'mighty surging of a new age', the Renaissance. Less a movement than a series of intoxicating tides which had been washing northward across Europe for over a century, the new age was changing the landscape of state, religion and culture, at an unprecedented pace. Continental cities teemed with self-aware Europeans whose quest for knowledge was encompassing the globe with voyages of discovery. The figurehead of early sixteenth-century humansim was Erasmus of Rotterdam. 'Immortal God,' Erasmus had exclaimed twelve years earlier, 'what a world I see dawning! Why can I not grow young again?'

Leland's ship bore him back to an island kingdom whose peripheral location had left it far behind the various revolutions which were overtaking the continent. Across the spectrum, from art and architecture, to mathematics and printing, England was half-a-century behind the times. But revolution of a home-grown kind was being unleashed. For a thousand years, virtually everyone on Europe's largest island had lived as Catholic Christians. Now, Henry VIII was about to prise his kingdom away from the papacy and trigger a process of national self-discovery. Stepping ashore in Kent, John Leland knew that he would play a role in England's rebirth.

From the coast, all roads led to London, a city whose population at the time was barely half the size of modern Cambridge. But in terms of status, it overwhelmed every settlement in the land: 'London is not said to be in England,' mused a visiting Swiss student at the time, 'but rather England to be in London.' Leland knew the city well. He had been born here in around 1503, and then been sent to St Paul's School, which had recently reopened under the Dean of the Cathedral, John Colet. Colet had made St Paul's the first school in the kingdom to teach Greek, and its first High Master, William Lily, had compiled a work which would become Henry VIII's authorised grammar book. Versed in the classics, Leland had graduated from Cambridge University in 1521 or 1522, then been appointed tutor to Thomas Howard, the Duke of Norfolk's son. After the Duke's death in 1524, a couple of unsatisfactory years at Oxford (where Leland had been unimpressed by the old-fashioned teaching) had been followed by a scholarship to study in Paris.

At the time, Paris was four times the size of London, a vast, bustling metropolis of 200,000, with a university which was

Leland's school was, wrote its founder John Colet, a 'house of stone' constructed 'in the Est ende of the Churchyard of Paulis'. Both the cathedral and the school building were destroyed in the Great Fire of London.

equalled in northern Europe only by Louvain. Unlike London, Paris was awash with books. Print, the medium by which Europeans were dispersing new ideas, discoveries, doctrines and forms of expression, had barely crossed the Channel. Between 1520 and 1529, England produced 550 books, most of them typeset, bound and sold by foreigners working in a small number of London presses, while Paris was printing thre hundred titles every year. Some of the most popular titles were chivalrous thrillers recycled from medieval legends. Along with *Quatre fils Aymon, Fierabras* and *Pierre de Provence,* each of which had appeared in nearly twenty editions by 1536, Leland may have dipped into romantic editions of *King Arthur* – although Arthur himself was seldom at the centre of the action; the only French romance which cast him as the hero was *The Knight of the Parrot* – a work which failed to take off on the English side of the Channel.

Where the French could marvel at the latest printed maps and globes, not a single map of any sort had been printed in England. Here in Paris, Leland may have run into some of the giants of the northern Renaissance, the Lutheran-leaning scholar Guillaume Budé and perhaps even Erasmus himself. Also in Paris at this time was one of Europe's leading mathematicians and topographers, Oronce Finé. A man of many disciplines (he was a leading cartographer, book illustrator, wood engraver and educationalist), Finé had been recently released from a long spell of imprisonment for charges related to the occult. His cartographic works included a heart-shaped map of the world, and an enormous map of France based on co-ordinates of latitude and longitude that Finé had determined for 124 cities, towns and villages. While Leland was in Paris, Finé was working on mathematical instruments, an astronomical treatise and dabbling in verse; the year after Leland left the city, he wrote a poem praising mathematics. Finé had – quite literally – put France on the map; his six-sheet masterwork was the first map of France to be compiled and printed in that country.

In coming back to London, Leland was not only returning to the city which had set him on the path of humanist learning. He was also returning to the court of King Henry VIII. Ultimately, destiny would link Leland to his monarch in the most pitiful manner, but in 1529, both were in the ascendant. Henry had succeeded to the throne

The brilliant French cartographer, Oronce Finé, was working in Paris when Leland arrived in 1526. Finé's map of the world was a *tour de force*, decades in advance of English mapmaking.

while Leland was still a small boy, and the first twenty years of his reign were building to a climax. With Wolsey's prosecution in the year that Leland sailed home, Henry had cleared the way for his marriage to Thomas Howard's niece, Anne Boleyn, and begun hacking at the thousand-year bond between England and the papacy. The King's hatchet-man was the son of a Putney black-smith, Thomas Cromwell. Manipulative, ruthless, with a background in money-lending and law, Cromwell was perfectly cut as a Henrican courtier. Already, he had assisted Wolsey in dissolving some of the smaller monasteries, the proceeds of which had been used to endow new colleges at Oxford and Ipswich.

With no apparent funds, nor an immediate family, Leland had to make the most of his court contacts, his fashionable education and his experience in Paris. He was familiar to Cromwell, and appears to have sought patronage from Anthony Denny, and the 'Master of the Posts' Sir Brian Tuke. Both were recipient of Leland's poems. Leland was soon appointed a royal chaplain and awarded an absentee living in the Marches of Calais. He also gained a post in one of the Royal libraries. In 1533, one of his poems was recited at Anne Boleyn's coronation.

It was in Leland's capacity as a humanist and as a librarian that he was granted the royal commission that would lead him towards the first great work of English topography. And towards madness. Specifically, he was (in the words of the great seventeenth-century Leland scholar, Anthony Wood) 'to make a search after England's Antiquities, and peruse the Libraries of all Cathedrals, Abbies, Priories, Colleges, etc. as also all places wherein Records, Writings and secrets of Antiquity were reposed'. To facilitate his quest, Leland was equipped with an official pass which was guaranteed to gain him access to all libraries.

\* \* \*

Leland began his bibliographic mission immediately. Riding from library to library, he picked through the shelves, compiling lists of books and manuscripts, and on occasion removing volumes for the King's own collection. Given that there were nearly 600 monasteries in the country, he had undertaken an enormous – and urgent – task. Many religious houses had already been dissolved, and under the new vicar general, Thomas Cromwell, reformation of the English church was accelerating. The act of 1536, suppressing all monasteries with an annual income of less than £200, was the beginning of the end for England's monastic tradition.

The passing of time has removed from the record all but fleeting glimpses of Leland during these years, but there are sightings of him in Somerset in 1533, and at St Albans in 1535. He must have felt that he was cantering through a nightmare. A patriot and a passionate upholder of the Tudor realm, he knew that the libraries he was frantically cataloguing would be

Henry VIII introducing Anne Boleyn at court. Leland's fatally-ambitious project to map Britain would not be realised until the reign of Anne's daughter, Elizabeth.

Holbein's portrait of Thomas 'hammer of the monks' Cromwell, whose dissolution of the monasteries put an intolerable strain on Leland as he hastened around the country trying to save their literary treasures.

thrown to the four winds, and he feared that England's bibliographic heritage would be plundered by foreigners. On July 16, 1536, Leland wrote to Cromwell, imploring the vicar-general to help him rescue books for the King's Library, where they 'would be a great profit to students, and honour to this realm; whereas now the Germans, perceiving our desidiousness and negligence, do send daily young scholars hither, that spoileth them, and cutteth them out of libraries, returning home and putting them abroad as monuments of their own country'. Leland's friend, John Bale, wrote to him from Ipswich, offering support and encouragement in their mission to preserve the glory of 'our England'.

Rievaulx, visited by Leland during his tour of Yorkshire, had been one of the wealthiest abbeys in England, but had been hit by border wars, plague and debt. When the abbey was dissolved in 1538, it was said to have had only 21 monks, but 102 servants.

The year 1536 transformed Leland into a reactionary. Not only were the monasteries being dismantled and their libraries stripped, but the very roots of Tudor legitimacy suddenly came under assault from an Italian historian. Published in Basle in 1534, Polydore Vergil's *Anglica Historia* re-wrote British history from a modern, humanist perspective. Out went the medieval legends which had allowed the Tudor kings to claim direct descent from King Arthur; in came revisionist vistas based – as Vergil put it – on 'a full rehersall and declaration of things don, not a gesse, or divination'. To Vergil, Geoffrey of Monmouth was a laughable fabulist who had embellished his 'histories' with 'most impudent lyeing', and who had 'concocted the great fable of King Arthur'. With a precise, humanist uppercut, Vergil floored Arthur, the Tudors – and Britain. Caught between his humanist reasoning and his nationalist pride, Leland was in an impossible position. In 1536, he responded to the *Anglica Historia* with an irate pamphlet which charactersed Vergil as conceited and ignorant.

The nature of Leland's bibliographic quest shifted in emphasis. As he hastened between the disintegrating monasteries, he began taking notes on the fabric of the country: the roads and towns, and the nature of each county. Initially, this may have been little more than the excited observations of a loyal subject, 'totally enflammid', as he would write to his king, 'with a love to see thoroughly al those partes of this your opulente and ample reaulme.' But in Leland's mind, at least, it soon became a formalised survey.

He outlined his plan several years later, in a report to Henry VIII called *The New Year's Gift*. His exhaustive travel notes, he explained, would form the raw material for a map. Thinking perhaps of Oronce Finé, and the incredibly-detailed printed maps then being pulled from presses in Paris and Antwerp, Leland understood that the best medium for geographical descriptions was the map rather than the printed word:

'And because that it may be more permanent, and farther knowne, then to have it engraved in sylver or brasse. I entend by the leave of God, within the space of xii. monethts follwying, such a descripcion to make of your realme in wryttinge, that it shall be no mastery after, for the graver or painter to make the lyke by a perfect example.'

It is a passage strewn with the seeds of failure. Leland was proposing to create a written, topographical description of the entire kingdom. Every river and bridge, hill and vale would be described, and its location identified using words alone. He would then present this extraordinary document to an engraver, who would try to visualise this textual landscape, and convert it into a map. or rather, and enormous number of maps.

Leland understood the pressing need for a detailed topography of England. He knew that monarchs and military leaders, the clergy and scholars, would all benefit from an accurate, comprehensive description of the kingdom. But words were the wrong medium. Unfortunately, he was fifty years too early. While geographers on the continent such as Van Deventer, Apian and Mercator were creating detailed, accurate maps using the latest methods of triangulation, in England such forms of surveying were barely known. Leland had set himself an impossible task. From 1538 or 1539, Leland resumed his travels with expeditionary zeal, taking to the road each summer, and compiling his notes through the winter. Later, he would claim to have travelled comprehensively throughout the entire kingdom of England and Wales.

Exploring the two countries with Leland's *Itinerary*, it's impossible not to cross his tracks, but there is one region which illustrates better than any other, the scope of his passions and the nature of his journeys. In May, 1542, Leland left London heading west for Somerset, Devon and Cornwall, three counties uniquely placed to shed light on our shadowy topographer. Not only are Cornwall and Somerset the most thoroughly described counties in the surviving *Itinerary*, but they have the most potent Arthurian connections. In the West Country, Leland revealed the essence of his age.

The map Leland failed to make: Christopher Saxton's county map of Somerset, engraved on copper thirty years after Leland lost his mind and died. Saxton's atlas of 1579 was the first systematic survey of the kingdom to be published.

\* \* \*

For modern travellers, the gateway to the West Country is the M4/M5 interchange, beyond the northern suburbs of Bristol. But there is another, far older, and rather more evocative spot due south of here. Right in the centre of the West Country, where the Dorset uplands plummet to the Somerset Levels, is a prominent hill of well-drained limestone, crowned by an enormous fort. Archaeologists reckon that the site was occupied for nearly four thousand years, right through to Saxon times. Running by the foot of the hill is the ancient highway between eastern England and the West Country, a route which can be traced back eastwards along high ground, of Salisbury Plain and the North Downs, all the way to the connecting point with the continent on the Straits of Dover.

The horizon was ablaze with a fiery sunrise when I squelched up the steep, deeply incised trackway between Cadbury's ramparts. Around the dark island of the deserted site were constellations of light: the torrent of silver and red streaming like tracer fire through a cutting on the A303; the linear dots of the runway lights at the Yeovilton airfield; solitary sparkles from isolated farms on the Somerset Levels. Pottering about among the grazing sheep, Leland found all the evidence he needed: the site itself was a on a prominent hill, 'wunderfully enstrengtheid of nature', and around its crest were '4. diches or trenches, and a balky waulle of yerth betwixt every one of them', which was breached by '2. enteringes up by very stepe way'. The size of the site was staggering; he estimated it to be twenty acres (it's actually eighteen). Poking through the turf, he found 'the fundations and *rudera* of walles', and reported that 'much dusky blew stone' had been 'caryid away' by 'people of the villages'. A large number of Roman coins had been found, and 'within living memory', a silver horseshoe had been discovered. To Leland, it was clear that the extensive ruins were 'sumtyme a famose toun or castelle'. Further evidence that this was indeed Arthur's seat of power

Cadbury Castle in Somerset, the hill fort identifiied by Leland as King Arthur's Camelot.

was provided by the names of surrounding villages associated with the word 'Camelot', and information from local people that King Arthur had 'much resortid' to the hilltop castle.

The procdeures Leland followed here were a triumph of pioneering fieldwork, and he was the first recorded person to link Cadbury Castle with Camelot. Medieval writers had settled on Caerleon and Carlisle for Arthur's court, but a West Country Camelot made more sense to Leland. The evidence he'd found on the ground established Arthur's power base as a real geographical location; the centre of British civilisation; the point of departure for chivalrous adventures.

Close to Camelot were three Somerset towns admired by Henry's topographer, yet ravaged by Cromwell. The categorist in Leland was always quick to identify towns by type; industrial centres would have their products listed; county towns would have their walls described, market towns their wares and so on. Here in Somerset, he had a trio of religious centres. Arriving in Bruton over Leland's 'est bridge' (with '3. archys of stone' still intact), I called at the home of the painter, Richard Pomeroy. From an upstairs window in his house, he can look across the Brue to a solitary tower on a rounded hilltop. In Richard's painting of the dovecote, it appears to float like a memory. The dovecote belonged to Bruton's abbey, dissolved in 1539 after one of Cromwell's emissaries – a priest named Richard Layton – discovered Catholic relics in the abbey. The abbey was sold to the Berkeley family, who converted it into their mansion. Leland was impressed by Bruton's ecclesiastical fabric, noting that the abbots had spent a small fortune on a splendid new market cross, and on 'almoste reedifiying' the abbey. Leland must have been in Bruton on his first trip to the West Country, a few years before the abbey was dissolved.

Wells too suffered at the hands of Cromwell. Behind the moat of the Bishop's Palace, the Great Hall now stands as a gaunt ruin surrounded by impeccable lawns. A latter-day Leland, Nikolaus Pevsner, regarded Wells as the 'most memorable of all Bishop's Palaces in England'. Even as a shell, it is overwhelming. The medieval ranges beside the gatehouse are imposing enough, but they are dwarfed by the eyeless wall of the Great Hall. Decorated with local sandstone, the hall's enormous windows were glazed, and it was floored with encaustic tiles. Gigantic timbers supported a roof of lead (the Bishops of Bath and Wells had a monopoly on the Mendip lead mines). A banquet held in the Great Hall in 1337 was attended by 286 guests, and had an industrial shopping list of 672 loaves, 349 pipes of ale, 86 pipes of wine, and a variety of fish, pike, eel, hake, salmon, plaice, bream

One of the more curious relics of Henry VIII's monastic purge: the building thought to be a dovecote, perched on a hilltop outside Bruton.

pollock and pickerell. A butcher produced a sheep, half a cow, ducks and chicken. Such was the power and wealth of a medieval bishop, and the riches of an abbey's estates. After Henry VIII died, one of his son's regents – Sir John Gates – stripped the Hall of its timber and lead, and the weather began to do its worst.

Leland passed through Wells on the eve of oblivion. He notes that the Great Hall is 'exceding fayre', and that the present bishop, William Knight, is busy building 'a crosse in the market place, a right sumptuus peace of worke'. Along the northern side of the market place, one of Knight's predecessors, Bishop Beckington, had built twelve 'right exceding fair houses al uniforme of stone high and fair windoid'. Only his death, laments Leland, prevented him from building a corresponding row along the south side of the market square. Had he accomplished it, Wells would have 'bene a spectable to al market places in the west…'

It was in the chained library that I felt for the first time that I had been brushed by Leland's cloak. It is a long room of creaking boards and ghostly browsers. Pools of daylight fall across the spines of books. This was the 'great librarie … having windowes on eche side of it', that had been built – so Leland tells us – by Thomas Bubwith, the Archdeacon of Wells. Strange it was to pause in one of those bays of leathery tomes, and look, just as Leland did, at wonder upon the wealth of accumulated literature: here was Livy and Homer and Tacitus … Thomas Aquinas, Sleidan's *History of the Reformation* … Downames' *Guide to Godliness*. But the spine which made the hairs on my neck tingle was the one which provoked Leland's fury in 1536. There, in the library in Wells, was the Basle edition, published by Simon Grynaeus, of Polydore Vergil's *Anglica Historia*. A very long time ago, someone had been through the volume page by page, carefully highlighting passages with a pencil.

To Leland, Wells was all that a town should be, 'al for the most part buildid of stone'; large, wealthy, beautiful and built to endure. Leland had to look no further than Wells to be frightened by the future. The town that he celebrated had been built by bishops of the old Church. He must also have wondered who would build the England of the future.

It was in the third of these Somerset towns that Cromwell's programme of 'visitations' wreaked a truly terrible outcome. 'From Welles to Glessenbyri about a 5. miles from north to south west,' noted Leland, as he rode between the two towns, logging every stone bridge, stream and meadow. On his first visit to Glastonbury, Leland appears to have been shown around the abbey by the Abbot, Richard Whiting. Among other details, Leland recorded that an earlier abbot, Richard Beere, had 'made a rich altare of sylver and gilt', and had founded an almshouse for ten or so 'poore wymen'. In 1539, three years before Leland returned to Glastonbury during his tour of 1542, Whiting was tied to a hurdle at the abbey gates, then dragged through the town and up the slopes of the Tor, where he was hanged. His head was hacked off and his body cut into quarters, one to be displayed at Wells, one at Bath, one at Ilchester and one at Bridgwater. The head was placed over the gateway of Glastonbury Abbey. In his notes of 1542, Leland failed to make any mention of the abbey.

Until Cromwell's avaricious eye fell upon the West Country, Glastonbury was the wealthiest abbey in the land. The source of that wealth was not actually the Abbey itself, but its vast land holdings. Glastonbury owned a huge swathe of property across the eastern part of Somerset, with outlying estates in Dorset and Wiltshire. Spaced across the estates were magnificent stone barns which acted as collecting centres for produce. Glastonbury's

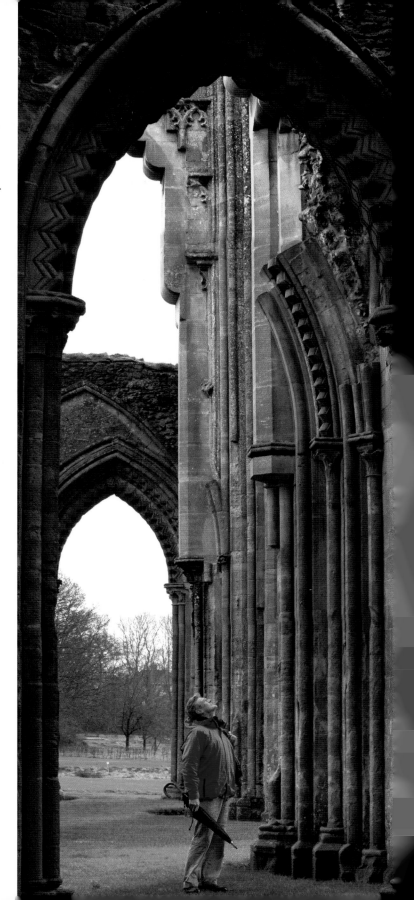

heartland estates were known as the Twelve Hides, and occupied fertile land less than a day's walk from the Abbey. Leland crossed the Twelve Hides more than once, and describes a mysterious lake which has disappeared from modern maps. According to Leland it was '4. miles in cumpace' during winter when water levels were highest, shrinking to two-and-a-half miles during dryer spells. Apparently it was 'a good mile yn lenght'.

So what happened to Meare Pool? And where precisely was it? Look at a modern OS map and there are clues in the alignment of field patterns and drainage ditches, as if the landscape has had to 'heal' around a feature which has been removed. There is also a hint of altered landscapes in the course of the minor road which links the hamlets of Upper and Lower Godney; at the western end of Lower Godney, the road just stops, as if it's collided with an invisible barrier. Using the field and dyke alignments, the Godney road and the absence of contours, it's possible to sketch out an approximate location for the Pool, which is corroborated on the map by a couple of features marked in the Gothic script which denotes 'Non-Roman Antiquities'. On what must have been the southern shore of the Pool are the 'Abbot's fish ho', and 'Lake Villages'.

Deeply curious, I headed off onto the Levels. Long, straight drainage ditches – locally called 'rhynes' – ran to the horizon, the exposed soil as dark as chocolate. At various times in my life, I've walked the East Anglian Fens, and the interminable floodplains of the Rhone and the Danube, but generally found them sinister places, stripped of humanity by industrial agriculture. Their flat, cloying, muddiness makes the miles crawl and the mind wander into frightening precincts. But the Somerset Levels are different: this is pasture land, speckled with cattle, and the comforting hills are always in sight.

At Lower Godney, a public footpath passed through a back-garden and onto the grassland of the Levels. After a mile or so, the footpath met a wide rhyne. A couple of hundred yards beyond it, the land began to rise, very slightly. This must have marked the southern limit of the Pool. A bridge crossed the dyke, and there was a tall stone building standing alone in a gently sloping field. Leland makes no mention of the

On the Levels: the largest area of low-lying wet grassland in Britain. After the dissolution, monastery lands were sold off and agriculture became more intensive.

building, but a source from around 1540 describes it as having a hall, a parlour and chamber, and being 'pretty'. The upper rooms contained living quarters, and were reached by exterior steps. This was the centre of operations for fishing in the Pool. The Abbey's fish were salted and stored here.

Standing in the dusk, I watched the mist rising as if gauze was being drawn imperceptibly across the grassland. From the upper floor, the mere would have shone in the moonlight; a black inland sea rimmed by ribs of upland. In a single year back in the 1200s, the Meare fishery caught 224 sticks of eels, thirty great eels, fifty-five pike, 200 bream and around 120 white fish. The Fish House was first recorded in 1344, so by the time Leland came by, it had been standing for a couple of centuries. With the Dissolution of the Monasteries, Glastonbury's lands were sold off, and the Meare was drained and turned into pasture.

Meare's medieval Fish House, now marooned in a field; Meare Pool once lapped close to its walls.

\* \* \*

The counties Leland recorded so meticulously have been reinvented many times over during the last five centuries. Of the tens of thousands of places he described, the survivors are the structures and shapes on the landscape that escaped the wreckers' ball and the plough. Their rarity means that it's hard not to alight upon the most humble of ruins, or recognisable descriptions, with a faintly ridiculous exuberance. Equally frustrating is Leland's virtual absence from his own narrative. We know he is there, for he scatters his *Itinerary* with his presence. Here he is, for example, on the road from Glastonbury, heading towards the heights of Exmoor:

> '…I went over Thone by a wood bridge… The way or I cam ynto Bridgwater was causid with stone more then half a myle… I passid over 2. notable brokes bytwixt Stowe and S. Audres that ran from the montaynes to the se.'

We can sense him, peering over hedges, pausing at road junctions, asking the way of passers-by. But we never meet him. We never find out what he is feeling, and we search his notes in vain for anything resembling a practical aside. Throughout the *Itinerary*, we learn nothing of the weather he endured, or the state of roadside hostelries. Where sixteenth-century humanists like Erasmus and Dürer left us with wonderfully detailed accounts of everyday travel, Leland feeds us not a tidbit on over-charging ferrymen or invonvenient plagues. Neither do we know much about his own circumstances as a traveller, although he does allude in *The New Year's Gift* to the human and financial burden of the enterprise, when he refers to the journeys 'sparynge neythger labour nor costes'.

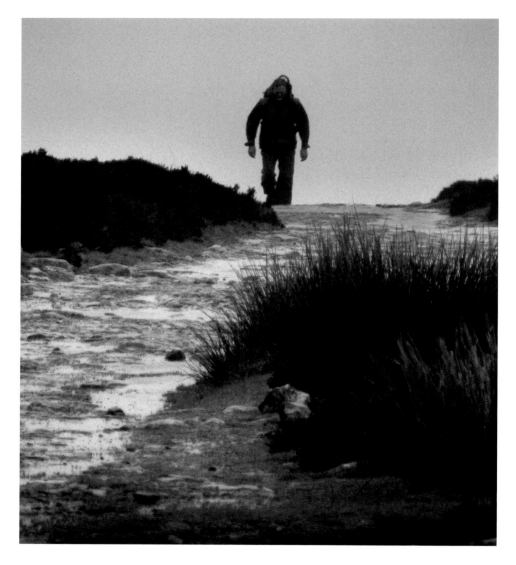

The rocky road over Dunkery Beacon, on Exmooor.

So we have to fill in the gaps ourselves. Very likely, he travelled with a small entourage which probably included a servant, a scribe and a horseman. Like Gerald of Wales, he would have employed the services of local guides when negotiating difficult rivers and estuaries, and perhaps stretches of mountain and moorland. On one occasion, in south Lancashire, he refers to a guide who helped him cross the dangerous swamps west of Manchester. On another occasion, in Nottinghamshire, he mentions that he crossed the Trent by boat, while his horse was ridden through the ford. Possibly the river had been in spate at the time, and the water too deep for Leland to risk fording the Trent himself. Frequently, it is all but impossible to divine which routes he took. His traverse of the 'montaynes' of Exmoor is tantalisingly abbreviated. He notes that the first part of the route to Exford was 'al hylly and rokky, ful of brokes in every hilles botom and meatly woddid' and that the second part 'was partly on a moore and sumwhat baren of corne, and partly hylly'. The least difficult route between Dunster and Exford would have been the direct line that takes you over the roof of the moor, by way of Dunkery Beacon. Since there are no outcrops or crags in the district, the 'rokky' nature of the route must refer to Exmoor's stony tracks.

Finding features Leland describes in the countryside is far harder than locating urban remnants of his *Itinerary*. Often, it's unclear exactly what he is describing, such as these 'hillokkes' on Exmoor:

> 'The boundes of Somerseteshire go beyond this streame [the River Exe] one way by north west a 2. miles or more to a place caullid the Spanne, and the Tourres, for ther be hillokkes of yerth cast up of auncient tyme for markes and limites betwixt Somersetshir and Devonshire; and here about is the limes and boundes of Exmore forest.'

So where are these 'hillokkes of yerth'? Well, Leland's dishevelled notes contain a second sighting of what appear to be the same 'hillokkes', in one of his descriptions of Devonshire:

> 'The partition of the shire a mile and more by northe west from Simon's Bath at the towres. The toures be round hillockkes of yerth sette for limites.'

Leland leaves a trail of clues which leads – eventually – to his hillocks. In Simonsbath, he mentions that 'ther is a bridge of woodde over this water'. Walk through Simonsbath today and you find that the bridge (no longer of timber) leads out of the village on the road which climbs to the moors. Over three miles (roughly equivalent to Leland's two Tudor miles), the road climbs to a cross-roads on a ridge at 1,500 feet above sea level. Turn right here, peer over the hedge, and there, silhouetted against the western skyline are some distinct hummocks. Cross the tussocks of Western Common, and Leland's 'hillokkes of yerth cast up in auncient tyme' turn into a series of Bronze Age burial mounds. On top of the highest mound, long-gone surveyors have left a concrete triangulation pillar. With binoculars and a 1:25,000 OS map, it's possible to spot other mounds, aligned roughly north-west/south-east along the crest

A moment of high excitement, as Leland's 'hillokkes of yerth' creep into view.

of the ridge. Just as Leland said, they follow the county boundary of Somerset and Devon. In one direction are the billowing grasslands of Exmoor, and down below in the other, the fields and farms of Devon. It's a very ancient boundary; a boundary between two types of landscape which evolved to separate two counties. Walking guides to Exmoor still refer to the ridge Leland called 'Spanne' and 'the Tourres', as 'Span Head' and 'The Towers'.

* * *

The scale – and hopelessness – of Leland's ambition becomes most apparent when you tread his laborious steps. The notes he amassed in his *Itinerary* were a topographical databank of unparalleled volume. When he eventually completed his travels, he was able to report to Henry VIII that:

> 'In so muche that all my other occupacyons intermytted, I have so traveled in your domynions both by the see coastes and the myddle partes, sparynge neyther labour nor costes by the space of these vi. yeares past, that there is almost neyther cape nor baye, haven, creke or pere, ryver or confluence of ryvers, breches, washes, lakes, meres, fenny waters, mountaynes, valleys, mores, hethes, forestes, woodes, cyties, burges, castles, pryncypall manor places, monasteryes, and colleges, but I have seane them, and noted in so doynge a whole worlde of thynges verye memorable.'

Leland's notebook sketch showing the Humber estuary, various rivers, and the Roman canal, Fossdyke.

And he wasn't exaggerating. The man left no stone untrodden; no significant feature unrecorded. But with every page turned, the reader of his notes cries out for a map; he left us hundreds of thousands of places in search of a location.

Leland was incapacitated by the absence of a measured survey. The geographical information in his notebooks carried no co-ordinates. They had been scribbled as words into notebooks, not plotted onto a mathematical grid. The Bodleian Library in Oxford holds a rare and fascinating sketch map prepared by Leland. He'd probably drawn it following his tour of the north-east in 1544. It's a painful illustration of the impossibility of his task. The map is an attempt to make sense of the drainage basin of the Humber and the Witham. Annotated tributaries squiggle across the sketch, which includes a rough representation of the coast running north from The Wash, past the Humber estuary to Hornsey. Stare at the sketch for long enough, and it becomes apparent that one of the twenty or so waterways is drawn as a straight line. Leland appears to be trying to work out the role played by Britain's oldest canal, the Fossdyke. The sketch neatly shows how the Fossdyke – which was built by the Romans – links the Trent with the Witham, thus allowing ships to sail inland to Lincoln. In his *Itinerary*, Leland describes Bishop William Atwater's attempt to 'clense', or dredge, the dyke in order to reopen Lincoln to shipping. Atwater started at a place called Torksey, where the canal joined the Trent, and his dredging operation reached halfway to Lincoln before he died in around 1520, and 'the work was abandoned. Leland's sketch reveals two attempts to place Torkey accurately.

The Bodleian sketch reveals the mind of a man who knew that he was ahead of his time. In 1533 – three years before Leland set off for the West Country – a scholar in Louvain had published the first printed description of the use of triangulation for surveying. While mathematical surveying took off in the Low Countries, it would be decades before the practice reached England. Leland was a poet, a librarian, an auditor. He was not a mathematician. Insomuch as they are arranged at all, the notes he left are organised around routes he travelled. A modern traveller could spend a lifetime trying to trace John Leland's footprints to and fro across England and Wales. But it would be a journey into madness, for Leland's journey had no end. His itinerary crosses and recrosses itself. He returns to places he has already visited, and describes them over again, slightly differently. With each visit, the *Itinerary* acccumulates more layers but less form.

The *Itinerary* is clearest when its author is depicting a town or city, or a specific location; and at its most murky when he attempts to describe the form of a coastline, or drainage basin, or the distribution of a district's settlement. Notes of mileages and place-names are no substitute for a map, but Leland's bibliographic instinct was to compile lists rather than to make a sketch. As a result, his mental map is frequently awry. Dropping down from the heights of Exmoor, you might expect – if you trusted Leland's geography – to follow the river Taw from its rising on the moor, all the way to Barnstaple on the coast. Leland had, after all, written that the Taw 'risith in Exmore south est from Berstaple'. But the Taw rises on Dartmoor, on the far side of Devon. In his maplesss world, Leland had been unable to place the rivers and moors of the deep interior. On the coast, it was a different matter. Here, his description of the Taw was far more accurate

In Barnstaple, the rush–hour still streams across the 'bridge of xvj. arches' Leland mentions. Leland was obsessed with bridges. To a Tudor traveller, a bridge was a measure of district's viability. Fords and ferries were inconvenient, hazardous, and a hindrance to trade. As assuredly as the printed page and brass astrolabes, stone bridges were emblems of the future.

With all the care of a government inspector, Leland recorded each bridge that he came across, noting the number of their arches, whether they were of stone or timber, and any associated tales. In Barnstaple, he learns that the causeway across the salt marsh at the northern end of the bridge had been financed by a London merchant called Stawford, who had watched a woman from the nearby village of Pilton drown after she had been caught on the marsh by the rising tide. Although she had cried out for help, no-one had been courageous enough to brave the waters.

Barnstaple Bridge and its carefully-counted arches.

Stawford had given the prior of Barnstaple funds to construct a causeway and a pair of bridges to span the river Yeo, which ran across the marsh into the Taw. The bridge at Bideford, seven miles to the south-west, has a tale, too. Here, Leland is told that its construction ('xxiiij. arches and a chapelle of our Lady at the farther ende'), had been inspired by a priest's vision. He also learned that a local guild provided a roster of men to keep the bridge clean of dung and refuse.

Both Barnstaple and Bideford lie on the huge, bifurcated estuary of the Taw and Torridge, at the innermost point of a huge bay terminated by the frightful capes of Morte Point and Hartland Point. In Leland's day, the Taw/Torridge estuary was the largest and most important haven between Bristol and Land's End, and he devotes considerable effort into creating a word-map of its features. Beside their notable bridges, Barnstaple and Bideford were admired by Leland for their stone-built houses. Bideford had a fine parish church and a pleasant street lined with blacksmiths, chandleries and shipbuilders; 'a praty quik streat of smithes and other occupiers for ship crafte'.

*Above:* **Near Hartland Point, a sailors' deathtrap which Leland takes pains to locate, several times. Had he compiled his great map, it would have been a significant feature.**

*Below:* **Any excuse to get in a boat: setting off from Barnstaple on the ebb tide. In Leland's day, the Taw estuary was one of the most important havens on the north coast of Devon and Cornwall.**

A stone's throw from the spot where the woman from Pilton drowned, I launched a canoe into the ebbing tide of the Taw, and set off to explore the estuary. Leland's summary of the Taw's geography is brief: 'From Berstaple to the very haven mouth a v. miles: and the very mouth of it is no large thing, and a litle without is a barre.' In a different part of the *Itinerary*, he adds: 'The haven entery is barrid with sande, and the enterie into it is daungerus.' Reassuringly, he notes that the tide at Barnstaple is relatively placid – 'no very mayne streame at the ebbe'. He didn't warn me about the wind, though. Snatched like a leaf by a gust, the canoe spun around and scooted away from the quayside so violently that the swell on the river nearly turned the thing upside down.

Tracing an old itinerary gives a unique sense of purpose to a modern journey. Led by an invisible, talkative guide, you find yourself gazing at landforms and places you'd normally miss. Leaving Barnstaple more-or-less upright, the canoe yawed and bobbed past the mouth of the Yeo and beneath the scaffolded towers of a new bridge being built to carry Barnstaple's long-awaited western bypass over the Taw. Leland would not have believed his eyes. Two hundred feet above the water, tiny figures in hard hats and high-vis coats performed indecipherable tasks above the abyss. Beyond an industrial estate, a spit of salt marsh ran out to Penhill Point. In Leland's day this stretch of water would have been busy with trading ships, barges and fishing vessels. On this wintry day, mine was the only boat in sight. The Taw has become another of Britain's secret wetlands: a discreet backwater for the Royal Marines to test amphibious kit; a serene interlude for hikers on the South West Coast path and cyclists on the Tarka Trail; a sanctuary for naturists and the rare Amber Sandbowl Snail. Travel the estuary by road, from Bideford to Barnstaple and Braunton, and your views of the estuary are limited to blurred glimpses of flat water; take to a boat and the Taw becomes a singular inland sea, rippling with enchantment.

Looking for a sandbar; Leland effectively invented fieldwork, a process which requires foot-slogging and methodical note-taking. And maps.

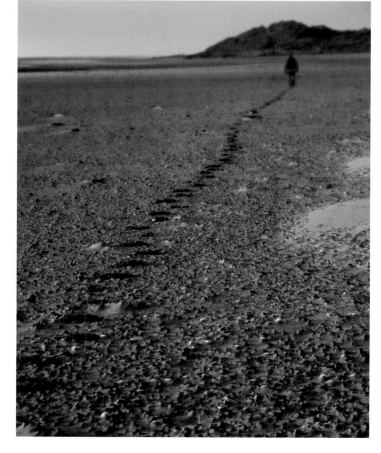

Leland reckoned it was five miles from Barnstaple to the bar at the 'very haven mouth'. The Ordnance Survey makes it eight miles. After six (OS) miles I reached the widest part of the estuary, where the Torridge empties into the Taw. Out in the stream, I felt very small indeed. From here to the mouth of the estuary, the north shore is fringed with the largest sand-dune system in the UK; ochre waves running towards the horizon. Ramming the canoe onto the sand at Crow Point, I refuelled with a quick sandwich taken beneath a windbreak of whispering marram grass, and then began the long tramp north-westwards, towards Leland's 'barre'.

Leland was as obsessive about sand-bars as he was about bridges. Shoved across estuary mouths by enormous tidal forces, sand-bars were the terror of Tudor shipping. At low tide, they would often be exposed, but at high water, when a ship had to break into – or out of – an estuary, they lurked beneath the surface, waiting to snag unwary keels. Wedged onto the sand, a sailing ship would quickly broach, then break her back. In recording the presence of estuarine bars, Leland had identified one of the most feared impediments to coastal trade. Not only had sand bars a habit of moving, but most were uncharted. The navigational charts circulating in Tudor Britain were one-off manuscripts and based on hearsay and observation, rather than survey. A mile or so along the sand, I came to Airy Point, and a range of enormous dunes. With binoculars, I could clearly see Leland's sandbar: a ferocious wall of tossing waves blocking the entrance to the estuary.

* * *

From Barnstaple, Leland continued south-westwards, towards the River Tamar. Few counties can boast such an emphatic geographical boundary, for the Tamar – as Leland points out – 'almost from the hed of it to the mouth devideth Devonshir and Cornewaule'. Extend the Tamar another three miles, and Cornwall would become an island.

In crossing the Tamar, Leland was straying into a foreign country. Cornwall was the least accessible county in the realm, and – as Richard Carew pointed out in 1602 – regarded by many of its inhabitants as 'a demi-island in an island'. In the early 1500s, the language of Cornish was still spoken in western Cornwall, and the county had long-enjoyed its own individual form of self-government, through the 'Stanneries'. Agriculturally, Cornwall was regarded by outsiders as 'sterile and without fecunditee', but its mineral resources and ports were known the length and breadth of Europe. For centuries, Cornwall had been the continent's chief supplier of tin, and since the Bronze Age, its havens had been bolt-holes for coastal traders.

To make matters even more daunting for a man with a King's commission, the Cornish were notorious rebels. Back in 1497, they had marched on London, where fifteen thousand of them were routed at Blackheath. Opposed to rule from London, and reluctant to adopt Protestantism, the Cornish were a rock in the Royal slipper. A few years after Leland's visit, their views on the new Book of Common Prayer, were put to the King: 'We,' they had written in a letter to the monarch, 'the Cornyshe men, whereof certain of us understande no Englyshe, utterly refuse thys newe Service.' Leland seems to have been briefed to pay particular attention to Cornwall, for his description of the county is one of the most comprehensive in the entire *Itinerary*.

The gateway to the county lay a ten-minute ride beyond the Tamar. Today, the town of Launceston is so out-of-favour with modern travellers that it doesn't even merit a mention in the Lonely Planet guide to England. The *Blue Guide* is slightly more forthcoming, conceding that this one-time capital of Cornwall is 'a pleasant town once known as Dunheved' ('hill-head'). There are actually two hills, one of which is crowned by the cylindrical keep of the castle. Gazing at its formidable battlements, Leland concluded that it was 'the strongest, but not the biggist, that ever I saw in any auncient worke in Englande'.

Recalcitrant Cornwall is hidden from readers of Leland's notes. Methodically, he records the size of the bridges, the agriculture, the location of tin mines, ports and markets. The Cornish gentry are logged in their various granite piles, but the Cornish themselves are invisible. Asides about the landscape allude to the difficulties of eking a living from such a barren, windswept landscape. Beyond Launceston, Leland rides across miles of 'morisch and hilly ground' where the 'great scarsite of wod' forces the inhabitants to use gorse and heather as fuel. Places treasured today for their quintessential Cornish beauty, are revolting and dilapidated. Leland's Padstow is an 'onclenly kept' Hideous-on-Sea, and Boscastle – another modern Cornish showpiece – is 'a very filthy toun and il kept'. Repeatedly, Leland comes across reminders of faded glory. Bossiney has slipped from being 'a bygge thing for a fischar town', blessed with 'great privileges' to a sad relic where 'a man may se there the ruines of a gret numbre of houses'. Tintagel – like Launceston – amazes Leland for its 'mervelus strong and notable forteres' and its 'inexpugnable' location on a 'high terrible cragge environid with the se'. But, like Launceston, most of Tintagel's structures 'be sore wether beten and yn ruine'. In this land of tottering masonry, Leland stumbled across the site of King

Launceston's awesome keep was built by the Normans to defend a town which grew to be the most important in Cornwall. Leland was impressed.

Tintagel castle. Leland's 'discovery' of Camelot, and his description of Arthur's last battlefield on the River Camel, built on Geoffrey of Monmouth's claims that Tintagel had been the birthplace of King Arthur.

Arthur's final stand. On the banks of the River Camel, he claims to have found Arthur's 'last feld', and by way of proof, he recounts that locals have ploughed up bones and horse harnesses. This is the end of the Arthurian trail which had begun for Leland at South Cadbury. Leland's discoveries neatly bracketed the West Country between Camelot and the site of the last battle. Here was Henry VIII's evidence that Cornwall was integral to his kingdom.

The Cornwall of John Leland is a place of physical decay, weathered by the ravages of weather and time, and visited by inexplicable natural forces. By the time Leland travelled this way, the 'Little Ice Age' had gripped Britain for the best part of two hundred years. Profesor Brian Fagan has charactereised the era as as a 'climatic seesaw that swung constantly backwards and forwards, in volatile and sometimes disastrous shifts', which could bring 'arctic winters, blazing summers, serious droughts, torrential rain years, often bountiful harvests, and long periods of mild winters and warm summers'. These cycles of extreme cold or excessive rainfall could last from one year to a decade. British weather was utterly unreliable: 'The pendulum of climate change,' observes Fagan, 'rarely paused for more than a generation.'

It was during one or more of these violently-erratic spells, that much of Tudor Cornwall got wrecked. Repeatedly, Leland comes across scenes of environmental havoc – usually caused by sand. Sand seems to have been strangling Cornwall's livelihood. Over twenty miles of the north coast, all the way from St Ives to Crantock, had been 'sore plagued … with sandes' to the extent that 'no notable thing on the shore for so farre' could be found. At the mouth of the Hayle river on St Ives Bay, an entire castle has been 'drounid with sand'. In St Ives itself, most of the houses were 'sore oppressid or overcoverid with sandes that the stormy windes and rages castith up there'. The pier at St Ives had become 'sore chokid with sande'. Apparently, this 'calamitie' had been a problem in the area for over twenty years.

On Cornwall's other, southern coast, the trading town of Helston was also a hostage to shifting sands. South-easterly storms had a habit of pushing sand across the mouth of the estuary, creating a dam, behind which a huge inland lake would develop. Each time this happened, Helston's water-mills ceased to function and townspeople would have to dig through the sandbar to release the water and restore power to the mills.

The tin workings also contributed substantially to the difficulties of Cornwall's coastal communities. St Erth, a mile up the Hayle, had been throttled of trade after sand washed down from tin workings blocked the harbour, preventing 'good talle shippes' from berthing. A similar problem had occurred at Lostwithiel, where sand from tin workings had washed down the Fowey from Bodmin Moor, and choked the bridge. Up at the headwaters of the Fowey, it's still possible to see the scars of tin 'streaming': parallel dykes over a hundred metres long, pooled with floodwater and flanked by marsh grass. In Leland's day this shallow valley would have been a teeming open-cast mine.

Intriguingly, Leland includes in his observations of landscape upheaval, a couple of reference to major changes in sea-level. Between Penzance and Mousehole, he finds that 'much land' has been 'devourid of the sea'. And in Mount's Bay, he records that

Exploring the scars of tin 'streaming' in a winter gale on Bodmin Moor. Cornish tinners were a tough breed.

'betwyxt the Mont and Pensants be fownd neere the lowe water marke rootes of trees yn dyvers places, as a token of the grownde wasted'.

By 'wasted', Leland meant eroded. Somewhere in Mount's Bay was what appeared to be a submerged forest. This was not the only time he stumbled across ancient forests. Near Manchester, the guide he hired to lead him across Chat Moss told him that the roots of fir trees could be found in the peat. And in Suffolk he was told of a large forest which had been engulfed by the sea at Dunwich.

Frustratingly, the passage describing the Mounts Bay forest is followed by a marginal note, which is partly torn: 'Ther be found from the inward part of the … yvers … re stones … wes and … ois v. miles … the se.'

Ask around Penzance, however, and people do speak of tree roots being seen out in the Bay. With four divers, I spent a day aboard the 40-foot dive-catamaran *Pamela P.* Several dives failed to produce any sightings of ancient timber, although one of the divers did report that he had seen cavities in the sand filled with fine, peaty silt – evidence perhaps that we were searching in the right area. That evening,

Searching for a sunken forest in Mount's Bay.

as I was walking away from *Pamela P*, along the harbour wall on St Michael's Mount, I was met by one of the staff. He was carrying a plastic carrier bag containing something angular and bulky. 'Thought you might be interested in seeing this…' he said, smiling. It was a large, twisted tree root. He had found it several years earlier, while walking on the beach near Penzance. 'They get washed clear in the storms,' he explained. 'Then another storm comes along and covers them with sand again. I haven't seen them for ages.'

St Michael's Mount has barely changed since Leland described it 500 years ago; the garden, jetties, steps, paths and chapels – and the causeway – are all still there.

\* \* \*

Leland appears to have extended his travels to the very end of England, for he provides a detailed description of Penwith, the 'toe' of Cornwall which protrudes westwards from Penzance. The coast down here, he writes, is 'withowt havyn or creke, savyng yn dyver places ther remayne capstaynes lyke engins as shyppes doth way ther ancres by, wherwith they draw ther bootes up to dry land, and fisch but yn fayr wether.' So I went looking for winches in the form of ships' capstans.

The coast path west from Mousehole runs like a rocky belvedere for mile after mile above the broken edge of the Atlantic. Every rock and chasm seems to bear a tale that has been encoded on the Ordnance Survey map: Merlyn Rock, Point Spaniard, Zawn Organ, Little Heaver … Coffin Rock. About halfway to Land's End, the path ducks into the little cove of Penberth, where a concrete slip has been laid across the boulders so that boats can be launched. And there, beyond the slip, I came across a gigantic capstan. Mounted in a walled enclosure of huge rocks, it had once hauled fishing boats out of the water, exactly as Leland described. Close by, two men were chatting beside a pair of beached fishing boats. Teddy and Matt had just returned from an abortive expedition to catch bass off Land's End. The swell had been too dangerous, and they'd been forced back to Penberth with empty boats. They specialised in 'handlining', a slow, difficult, unpredictable method of fishing which harks back to an age before trawling. Here were the very fishermen Leland had talked about, men who fished 'but yn fayr wether'.

Pressing on along the coast path, it ocurred to me that John Leland had embarked upon a never-ending journey. Beyond the major bridges, there were smaller bridges to list, and innumerable fords; after the big rivers, there were streams, and then streamlets. His notes are scattered with reminders to himself to go back and investigate the blanks on the map he could never complete.

I'd been heading in a general kind of way for Cape Cornwall, the promontory Leland mistakenly identified as being the westernmost point of Cornwall. It is one of only two places in Britain which merits the prefix 'Cape' (the other is Cape Wrath), and it's worthy of its name: a granite spear thrust into the shipping lane between the Scillies and Cornwall. But when I reached the Cape, and leant into the gale tasting salt on my lips, I knew that I'd been following a rarely-glimpsed wraith. He left his mark just once, in the artillery fort he'd seen being built at St Mawes. Chiselled into the stonework are a number of short Latin poems written by Leland for his King. One of them reads:

SEMPER VIVET ANIMA REGIS
HENRICI OCTAVI QUI ANNO 34 SUI
REGNI HOC FECIT FIERI

May the spirit of King Henry VIII,
who had this castle built in the 34th year
of his reign, live forever

Logan Rock, probably the location of a remote castle and 'promontory almost surrounded by the sea', described by Leland west of Mousehole. It's now one of the most spectacular sections on the South West Coast Path.

The fort was completed in 1543, the year after Leland left the West Country. He travelled on until 1545, by which time he had probably visited most – if not all – of the counties in England and Wales. By now the kingdom – and the king – were in awful shape. Famine had hit the population in 1545, and war with the French was crippling the country's fragile economy. Henry himself was crippled with leg ulcers, hugely overweight and ailing disgustingly. At the end of that year, Leland penned his *New Year's Gift* to the king, in which he set out his plans to produce a masterwork of improbable scale: a written topography of Britain which could be converted into the great map, a biographical dictionary of British writers, a history of England and Wales, books about the offshore islands, and more books on the British nobility. It was all a fantasy, quite beyond Leland's ability to complete, and too late for his king to see.

Henry VIII died on January 28, 1547. Some time during the following weeks, John Leland was struck by a severe mental breakdown. Although he lived for a further five years, he failed to resume work on his promised books and map. He left behind his list of every significant place in England and Wales; a list thousands of miles long, and spatially indecipherable. Had he been born fifty years later, he'd have realised that he needed to travel in the company of a surveyor, who would measure the distance between places and plot them onto a map. But surveying and mathematical map-making had yet to cross the Channel to England. It would not be until 1579 that the first detailed county survey of England and Wales would be published by an obscure surveyor from Yorkshire called Christopher Saxton. But the fieldwork Leland had promised his king remains one of the greatest treasures of the sixteenth century.

Cape Cornwall, thought by Leland to be the most western point in Cornwall. Leland reported that it was known as 'Penwolase', meaning 'furthest headland'. Despite its remoteness, the tip of Cornwall was well known to Leland for its association with Celtic saints. The ancient sanctuaries he visited down here dated back to the dawn of organised Christianity in England.

# Celia Fiennes *1698*

*On horseback through England*

My Great Journey

# CELIA FIENNES

to Newcastle and to Cornwall

**1698**

Scotland

England

Wales

Irish Sea

North Sea

English Channel

MILES
0 20 40 60 80

City, town or village ○
Hill, mountain or moor
Route, showing direction
Building of interest ◇

Gretna Green
Haltwhistle
Carlisle
Newcastle-upon-Tyne
Penrith
Durham
Windermere
Darlington
Richmond
Kendal
Lancaster
Harrogate
Preston
Leeds
Blackstone Edge
Liverpool
Wigan
Holywell
Manchester
Chester
Northwich
Beeston Castle
Newcastle-under-Lyme
Whitchurch
Derby
Wolseley Hall
Burton-upon-Trent
Shrewsbury
Lichfield
Peterborough
Norwich
The Wrekin
Leicester
Thetford
Ely
Kidderminster
Huntingdon
Bury St Edmunds
Worcester
Ipswich
Colchester
Gloucester
Cotswold Hills
Windsor
Bristol
Bath
London
Salisbury Plain
Exmoor
Wells
Newton Toney
Taunton
Winchester
Honiton
Salisbury
Launceston
Exeter
Dorchester
Bodmin Moor
Dartmoor
Wadebridge
Plymouth
Truro
Penzance
Land's End

ENGLAND'S most remarkable woman traveller took to the road at the end of the 1600s, a bare eighty years after the death of Queen Elizabeth I. At the time, Britain was being chilled by what is now known as the 'Little Ice Age'. Winters were longer and more savage than they are now, and the travelling season was correspondingly shorter and more temperamental.

Eclectic, and crackling with brusque asides, the highly person-alised travel journal of Celia Fiennes is regarded as the first compre-hensive overview of England to follow the late sixteenth-century *Britannia* of William Camden. It now appears that she was also the first recorded person to have travelled through every English county. The purpose of this epic undertaking was to excite her audience with England; to 'cure the evil itch of over-valueing foreign parts'

* * *

Crossing the River Esk on horseback finally convinced me that I was out of my depth. Celia Fiennes had ridden this way in 1698, fording the estuary with the assistance of a local guide. The estuary feeds into the Solway Firth, the enormous gulf which separates England from Scotland on the east coast. The crossing, she noted, 'is very broad and hazardous', with patches of quicksand exposed at low tide. Fortunately, I had an experienced guide in Penelope Mounsey-Heysham, whose home borders the estuary. Astride one of Penelope's race horses, I rode with her across the salt marshes, learning of the bones she had broken in riding accidents, and of the chances of being caught by quicksand, or swept out to sea if the tide misbehaved. 'Just follow me,' she repeated. 'The dogs will go in front, and if there are holes in the river, they'll find them first.' On our second attempt, we did find a safe crossing point. Mid-stream, with the tide lapping the horses' bellies and my riding boots filling with water, I was struck with two revelations: firstly, that I was probably going to reach the far bank alive, and secondly, that I could not have completed Fiennes' journey of 1698 on a horse.

Celia Fiennes was born in June, 1662 at Newton Toney, on the eastern edge of Salisbury Plain, near the rising of the River Bourne. Few places in southern England were quite as remote as this. Each side of the Bourne billowed gentle waves of empty downland. It was perfect horse-riding country. In this generous seclusion, Celia grew up in the fading aura of a once-powerful aristocratic family. Her grandfather, William Fiennes, the 8th Baron and 1st Viscount Saye and Sele, had been one of the English peers who had helped to undermine Charles I, while her father, Nathaniel, had fought

*Previous pages:* **Penelope Mounsey-Heysham (and the author), heading for the River Esk.**

*Left:* Celia's grandfather, William Fiennes, 8th Baron and 1st Viscount Saye and Sele, was a staunch Puritan who gained his nickname 'Old Subtlety' after fighting for Parliament, then opposing the execution of Charles I, and winning a pardon from Charles II.

*Right:* Her father, Colonel Nathaniel Fiennes, who had fought against the King during the Civil War.

against the Royalists during the recent Civil War. With the monarchy restored to power, Colonel Nathaniel Fiennes and his wife Frances had settled on the edge of the Plain and raised a family. Their first three daughters all died in infancy, but Cecilia (later to become Celia) survived, and so did Mary, born a year later. Of her relationship with her father, Celia Fiennes provides just one memory; a story he told her of a pre-war journey across the Alps, 'where the clouds drive all about and as it were below them, which descends lower into mists then into raines, and soe tho' on the top it hold snow and haile falling on the passengers which at length the lower they go comes into raine and so into sun-shine at the foote of those valleys fruitful the sunshine and singing of birds.' To the genetically footloose, there are few images more alluring than sudden transitions between differing worlds.

The Colonel died when Celia was seven, and from that point on, her immediate company was largely female. Frances Fiennes steeped her girls in Protestant dissent, appointing a nonconformist as her private chaplain, and holding illicit conventicles in her house. She was eventually fined for this in 1671. No record of Celia's education has survived, but it was normal at the time for well-bred daughters to have been taught to read and write at home, often with the aid of private tutors. Her familiarity with the homes of various relations dotted about England also suggests that she may have been sent away – like many of her kind – to accumulate knowledge in suitable households. Later, Fiennes opened the window – just a fraction – on the limitations of country-house life. While men could hold (or bore witless, as Fiennes implies) an audience with tales from their latest continental Grand Tour, women had less exotic material to occupy their minds. If women could travel too, mused Fiennes, it 'would spare them the uneasye thoughts how to pass away tedious dayes, and tyme would not be a burthen when not at a card or dice table, and the fashions and manners or foreign parts less minded or desired.' We catch a momentary glimpse of Celia – perhaps as a teenager – when she writes of the downs around Newton Toney being 'a fine Champion Country pleasant for all sports – Rideing, Hunting,

Courseing, Setting and Shooteing'. It is still lovely country, dotted with ancient tumuli and carpeted in shivering grass.

In winter, Salisbury Plain could turn into Siberia. It's difficult to imagine, in these days of an overheating earth, just how bitter the winters would have been. As a girl, Celia would have been used to snow lying on the ground for twenty to thirty days each winter, an unthinkable hardship in the days of Gerald of Wales. Since then, the growing season had shrunk by around a month. Surrounded by high ground, Newton Toney would have been cut off from the outside world for considerable spells. The English climate had begun its latest phase of misbehaviour in the 1590s, and with various short term fluctuations, the weather of the seventeenth century had been the coldest that Europe had experienced for seven hundred years. And the very coldest period of that chilly century began to bite in the 1680s, as Celia Fiennes approached eighteen. The Fiennes family were used to winters being snowy, restrictive, and potentially dangerous.

There was also a risk from highwaymen. In the aftermath of the Civil War, highway robbery had become an alternative source of income for those who had derived a livelihood from unsettled times. A century earlier, Camden had warned his readers that the Plain was 'but thinly inhabited, and infamous heretofore for frequent robberies'. While Celia Fiennes was growing up at Newton Toney, the Plain was being stalked by at least two notorious highwaymen: William Davis, the 'Golden' farmer, who once had the nerve to rob the wife of General George Monck, and a mysterious, well-born gentleman, who was thought by some to be the son of Sir Walter Biss of Bishopstrow, a village over on the west side of the Plain. Biss was Wiltshire's own Robin Hood, popularised for robbing the rich to favour the poor. Davis was eventually hanged at Tyburn in 1689, while Biss was hanged at Salisbury in 1695.

Isolated on her Wessex prairie, Celia Fiennes grew up with far horizons. Visiting a city, her relations or a medicinal spa, was an adventurous expedition. Travel excited her, and so did England. A horse's saddle was a slow-moving, extra-sensory viewpoint. She glided through the sounds and smells of town and country, overhearing conversation, peering over hedgerows. Pure intuition was her only navigational aid. There was nothing dull about seventeenth-century travel. Roads varied from belly-deep sloughs to ringing pitch. Villages were rural business centres, with cobblers, tanners, brewers, bakers, mills and inns. England had been enjoying a commercial boom since Celia's childhood. Market towns were stuffed

Fiennes grew up on the edge of Salisbury Plain during a climatic era known as the 'Little Ice Age'. Snow lay on the ground for twenty to thirty days each winter, compared with two to ten days during most of the twentieth century.

with produce, and innovative industries were springing up across the land. The landscape was racing through one of its periodic step-changes, and Fiennes was mesmerised.

Her first recorded ride was undertaken no later than 1682, and over the next thirty years she covered thousands of miles on journeys which ranged in duration from a few days to many weeks. Jotting notes as she travelled, she eventually compiled a fair copy of the experiences and observations that she had amassed on her seventeen most notable journeys. Of these, the longest, and most remarkable, was her last major ride, in 1698. But to understand the significance of that journey, we have to join her at around the age of twenty, still living at Newton Toney with her mother and sister. 'The Account,' she begins, 'off severall Journeys into severall parts of England with many Remarkes…'

\* \* \*

She began with the spiritual centre of the Plain. Salisbury itself is fairly run down, its ageing timber houses yet to be replaced by stone dwellings, and its streets running with rivers of filth. But the cathedral is 'the finest in England in all respects', and as the reader is led across its water meadow (learning on the way that the foundations are made from faggots and timber), we get a first inkling of Fiennes the writer, craning her head backward and observing that the spire 'appears to us below as sharpe as a Dagger yet is in the compass on the top as bigg as a cart wheele'. Unlike Salisbury's other buildings, the cathedral is 'all stone' and 'carved finely'. The enormous Chapter House is miraculously supported, notes Fiennes, 'by one small stone Pillar in the middle'. Chiselled for eternity, the cathedral's stonework is a masterclass in materials and craftsmanship. Before she leaves, Fiennes lists the cathedral's effigies, monuments and paintings, in a roll-call of lords and ladies, a duke, a doctor and a judge. By the time she rides out of this emblematic Christian city, we are left in no doubt that the future of England will be wrought by

 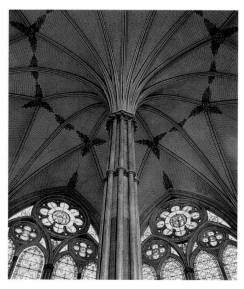

*Left:* Quarried from Chilmark, twelve miles outside Salisbury, the stone spire is both the first of its kind in England, and the tallest. 'The cathedral', writes Fiennes, 'lyes low in a watry meadow' and can be seen 'many miles off'.

*Right:* The chapter house of Salisbury Cathedral was built in the late thirteenth century. Its elegant geometry and exquisite stonemasonry contrasted with the squalid, ramshackle timber-built town.

every class, from nobleman to gentleman, merchant to artisan.

To Fiennes, Salisbury's spire is the centre of a compass, the hub of a wheel, from which all roads radiate. Her first three journeys, through her 'home' counties of Wiltshire, Dorset and Somerset, are packed with the thrills of discovery. She writes with an intimate, first-hand intensity, as if she has travelled halfway around the globe to explore a new and exotic land. On the edge of the Plain, Devizes is 'a very rich tradeing place for the clothing trade', and Warminster has 'Coale which is allmost as good as the sea-coale from New-Castle'. At Wilton, she discovers an earthly paradise:

On the recommendation of Inigo Jones, the gardens at Wilton House had been laid out by Isaac de Caus. Fiennes was enchanted by the water features.

'The Gardens are very fine, with many gravel walkes with grass squaires set with fine brass and stone statues, with fish ponds and basons with figures in the middle spouting out water, dwarfe trees of all sorts and a fine flower garden, much wall fruite: the river runns through the garden that easeily conveys by pipes water to all parts. Grottoe is at the end of the garden just the middle off the house, its garnished with many fine figures of the Goddesses, and about 2 yards off the doore is severall pipes in a line that with a sluce spoutts water up to wett the Strangers; in the middle roome is a round table, a large pipe in the midst, on which they put a crown or gun or a branch, and so it spouts the water through the carvings and poynts all round the roome at the Artists pleasure to wet the Company; there are figures at each corner of the roome that can weep water on the beholders, and by a straight pipe on the table they force up the water into the hollow carving of the rooff like a crown or coronet to appearance, but is hollow within to retaine the water forced into it in great quantetyes, that disperses in the hollow cavity over the roome and descends in a shower of raine all about the roome; on each side is two little roomes which by the turning their wires the water runnes in the rockes you see and hear it, and also it is so contrived in one room that it makes the melody of Nightingerlls and all sorts of birds which engaged the curiosity of the Strangers to go in to see, but at the entrance off each room, is a line of pipes that appear not till by a sluce moved it washes the spectators, designed for diversion.'

Fiennes' lines giggle with delight. Water at its most lucid and amusing would always lift her spirits. Wilton House was new. A triumph of Renaissance proportion and style, it had been rebuilt thirty years earlier by the 4th Earl of Pembroke to designs overseen by John Webb, a brilliant protégé of Inigo Jones. On the south coast, Fiennes found

Brownsea Island in Poole Harbour, the first industrial site Fiennes visited in her journal. General Robert Stephenson Smyth Baden-Powell held his experimental scout camp on the island in 1907.

herself equally transported by an industrial process. Taking a sailing boat out into Poole Harbour, she landed on Brownsea Island to investigate the production of copperas, or hydrated ferrous sulphate, a green-coloured compound used for dyeing, tanning and for ink manufacture:

> '…the stones being found about the Isle in the shore in great quantetyes, there is only one house there which is the Governours, besides little fishermens houses, they being all taken up about the Copperice workes; they gather the stones and place them on ground raised like the beds in gardens, rows one above the other, and are all shelving so that the raine disolves the stones and it draines down into trenches and pipes made to receive and convey it to the house; that is fitted with iron panns foursquare and of a pretty depth at least 12 yards over, they place iron spikes in the panns full of branches and so as the liquor boyles to a candy it hangs on those branches: I saw some taken up it look't like a vast bunch of grapes…'

Cathedrals, copperas and water-gardens were just the tip of the itinerary. In parallel with her mission to explore all that was new and worthy in her land, she had a recurring private quest. In the journal's introduction, Fiennes informs her readers that her travels 'were begun to regain my health by variety and change of aire and exercise.' Possibly suffering from the effects of an over-rich diet, Fiennes' attempts to sample new medicinal remedies led her further and further from home, and exposed her to situations alien to women of her breeding. On her second recorded journey, she tried out a new healing well in Somerset. Forced to spend the night in Castle Cary, she complained that there was 'no good accomodation for people of fashion', and that the locals were 'a clounish rude people'. In this hellish backwater, she struck off across the fields, for two muddy miles, to a small, stone-lined cavity in the ground, which bubbled with a strong upwelling of water. Since its discovery a decade earlier by a local minister, the saline waters at Alford had become known throughout the region for their extraordinary ability to relieve constipation. Within three years of its discovery, the well was drawing flocks of customers. The queues were infamous. By 1676, it was being bottled and sold throughout the West Country. Alford's spectacular popularity dried up after rumours spread that its waters were killing rather than curing; a Dr Pierce of Bath later recorded that indiscriminate consumption had led to patients 'dying almost on the spot'. Arriving some ten or so years after its discovery, Fiennes approached the well with understandable caution. Peering into the clear water, she noted that the bed of the well was composed of 'a sort of blewish Clay or Marle'. She does not record the taste (to an earlier visitor, it had been 'nauseous and bitter'), or how much she imbibed, but notes conclusively that 'it's a quick purger'. Clearly it had been a successful call.

The journey to Alford was immediately followed by a coach ride to Bath. Her description of the five baths is one of the longest in her journals, a reflection of her fascination with water treatments. Nothing seems to escape her eye, from the quality and temperature of the various waters, to the construction of the bath houses and the procedures for maintaining decorum. Fiennes approves of the voluminous all-in-one canvas bathing suits used by 'the Ladyes'. In these, 'your shape is not seen', quite unlike those worn by the 'poorer sort that go in their own linning', which tends to 'cling close' in a most inappropriate fashion. Fiennes' account of her exit from one of the baths is an exercise in synchronised de-robing:

'…you still ascend severall more steps, and let your canvass drop of by degrees into the water, which your woman guides takes off and the meanetyme your maides flings a garment of flanell made like a nightgown with great sleeves over your head, and the guides take the taile and so pulls it on you just as you

Bath: the King's bath, with the 'great Cross with seates in the middle' where 'many hot springs riseth'. The smaller Queen's Bath on the left was added in the 1570s so that women bathers could enjoy segregated faclities. Fiennes didn't like the way the baths made the town's air unpleasantly 'thicke and hot by their steem'.

rise the steps, and your other garment drops off so you are wrapped up in the flannell and your nightgown on the top.'

The Bath experience could not have been more removed from inhospitable, crude Alford. There are pleasant walks to be taken in King's Mead, the streets are clean and, as in London, there are chairs 'to carry the better sort of people'.

The opening tours through three counties revealed an England of astonishing diversity, and set the agenda for the next ten years of increasingly adventurous travel. The course of these early journeys may have been determined by the locations of relatives' houses and an urge to sample medicinal waters, but her observations were also guided by an ambition to reveal 'the nature of the Land, the Genius of the Inhabitants, so as to promote and improve Manufacture and Trade suitable to each and encourage all projects tending thereto.' On the road to Alford we learn that the nature of the land around Stonehenge is 'most champion and open, pleasant for recreations; its husbandry mostly corn and sheep, the downs though short grass the feed is sweet, produces the finest wooll and sweet meat though but small.' Somerset, however, is very different. Here, the land 'is very fruitfull for orchards, plenty of apples and peares', and yet Fiennes sees scope for improvement. The problem, she thinks, is that the orchard-owners are 'not curious in the planting the best sort of fruite'. This she continues, is a 'great pitty', given the excellent growing season and quantity of fruit the region can bear. Just as careless in their cider production, they 'press all sorts of apples together'. A more selective attitude, concludes Fiennes, would allow Somerset to match the quality of Herefordshire cider. Already, the England of Celia Fiennes is revealing itself as a deeply inconsistent place. Roads vary from Lyme Regis' vertiginous ascents, strewn with 'large smooth pebbles that make the strange horses slip', to the immaculate 'well pitched' streets of Bath. Dishevelled, timbered Salisbury compares unfavourably with 'neate stone built' Bruton. Buried in this vivid, wilful travelogue is a hint of methodical intent. Each time she crosses a county boundary, it is logged in her journal. But it isn't until her final 'Great Journey' of 1698 that the reason becomes apparent.

* * *

After the trip to Bath, Celia took two journeys with her mother into the heartland counties of southern England. Frances Fiennes was well into her sixties, and the itineraries bear an inescapable poignancy. The first of these two journeys took them back to the fortified manor house near Banbury in Oxfordshire that Frances had known as a younger woman. Here, her husband Nathaniel had grown up with his older brother James, and here, their father, the 1st Viscount Saye and Sele, 'Old Subtelty', had provided a secluded tower room for leading Parliamentarians to plot the downfall of their king. Today the house still floats upon its moat in magnificent defiance to the passing of time. In his wonderful revivalist guide, *England's Thousand Best Houses*, Simon Jenkins places Broughton alongside Wilton in the country's top twenty houses, but to Fiennes, its medieval core and centuries of accretions had produced an untidy outcome. Broughton, she notes, is 'an old house moted round and a parke and gardens, but are much left to decay and ruine'. She devotes far more space and enthusiasm to nearby Wroxton House, with its paintings of Queen Mary and Elizabeth, and its new rooms 'built all the new fashion way'.

The last journey Celia undertook with her mother occurred no later than the summer of 1691. Travelling east from Newton Toney to Nursted near Petersfield, they stayed with Frances' youngest sister Margaret, the last surviving member of her immediate family. Margaret and her husband Richard Holt occupied 'a neat new built house with brick and stone', and a garden with 'fine gravel walkes' and 'grass plotts'. From Nursted, they headed for Guildford ('a good town built with stone, the streets are broad'), and then looped around via London, Maidenhead and Cliveden House ('a fine building') to Reading. Here, Fiennes suddenly reveals that they have come to a place with a touching resonance for mother and daughter. 'Redding,' she tells us, 'which is a pretty large place, severall Churches, in one lyes buried one of my sisters that dyed.' It's a moment in the journal when this indefatigable topographer unexpectedly turns to face the reader with a reminder that every journey is guided to some extent by private forces. Ann was the third of Frances' daughters to die. She had been staying with her grandmother in 1675, when she caught smallpox. It's painful to speculate upon the scene, as the two women stood before Ann's 'monument of white marble'. The memorial can still be seen in the church. Of Frances' two surviving daughters, only Mary had married. Shortly after the journey to Reading, in December, 1691, Frances Fiennes died.

* * *

Following her mother's death, Fiennes embraced travel with the passion that many reserve for marriage. She was twenty-nine. A long ride through Buckinghamshire, Oxfordshire, Berkshire, Hampshire, Sussex ('much in blind dark lanes and up and down steepe hills') and Surrey, was followed by an even longer excursion westward to Herefordshire, and then a ride through the New Forest to the Isle of Wight. Returning through Portsmouth, she managed to be given a conducted tour of both the *Royal Charles* and *Royal James*; '…fine shipps,' she notes, 'the Roomes spacious for length and breadth but not high.' By the end of 1696, she had visited over a dozen of England's southern counties.

Broughton Castle, the family seat Celia Fiennes never really knew, was on the route of one of her ealier rides. She found it dilapidated and old-fashioned.

Then, in spring 1697, Fiennes conceived her most ambitious expedition to date. She called it 'My Northern Journey', and it would take her two-thirds of the way to Scotland. Probably accompanied by her cousin's two daughters, Susanna and Mary Filmer, Fiennes headed first to Cambridge, which she methodically compares to Oxford. The clear winner, incidentally, is Cambridge: Trinity College 'is the finest yet not so large as Christchurch College in Oxford', the library in Cambridge 'farre exceeds that of Oxford', while King's College Chapel 'is the finest building I had heard off'. Fiennes climbed to the roof of the Chapel, from where she could see 'a vast Country round', including the towers of Ely Cathedral – one of the places she would tuck away for a future journey.

As the women continued northward, Fiennes ticked off the county boundaries: Huntingdonshire, Rutlandshire, Lincolnshire… Nottinghamshire. No longer is Fiennes the twenty-something novice, peeking out from Wiltshire. Now, the journal is enriched with the armoury of comparison: just as Cambridge was weighed against Oxford, Huntingdonshire is described as 'good land and fruitfull and much like Oxfordshire', and Rutlandshire 'seems more woody and inclosed than some others'. Burghley House, 'eminent for its Curiosity', has the finest situation 'I ever saw' and Nottingham 'is the neatest town I have seen'. Nottingham would become Fiennes' benchmark town. With its lofty, yet 'delicate large', stone-built houses, well-surfaced streets, broad Market place, mile-long collonnaded "Pyaza"' and oustanding ale, was a symbol of urban aspiration, and worthy of comparison to London. Suddenly we are in the company of a veteran traveller; a woman who is amassing more first-hand views than Camden himself.

Where the M1 flings motorists northward at fifteen times the speed of a horse, Fiennes and her companions now found themselves meandering through the glades of Sherwood Forest and then joining 'a very heavy sandy way' out of Worksop. 'Musick,' she proclaims, 'wellcom'd us into Yorkshire.' It was Sunday, and the sound of bells carried across the lowlands of the Don.

The largest of the English counties by far, Yorkshire had a magnitude and novelty that made it appear almost like a foreign land. An inveterate browser of market stalls,

'The Prospect of Nottingham from Darby Roade on the West Side of the Towne', a copper engraving from 1677, after a drawing by Richard Hall. Daniel Defoe shared Fiennes' admiration for Nottingham, declaring that it was 'one of the most pleasant and beautiful towns in England'. Defoe notes with a literary wink that 'some in our company' enjoyed the 'excellent ALE … to a degree not fit to be made matter of history.'

Fiennes rushed from market to market with all the excitement of a child in a chocolate shop. At Ripon she marvelled at the price of veal and beef. Near Londesborough, she found a fresh salmon 'above 3 quarters of a yard long', which cost only eighteen pence. Beverley, where she was offered 'a large Codffish for a shilling and a good Pearch very cheape'. Here too, she ate 'Crabbs bigger than my two hands, pence apiece, which would have cost 6 pence if not a shilling in London, and they were very sweete'. A Londoner could live well in Yorkshire.

While the city of York had a disappointingly 'meane appearance' (Nottingham, she goads, 'is so farre before it'.), the county's waters were in a class of their own. She rode over to Scarborough to sample the mineral waters which seeped from the sands; and at Copgrove she found a bathing well as benefical as those at Bath. Here, at last, she discovered a cure for her headaches:

> 'I cannot but think it is a very good Spring being remarkably cold, and just at the head of the Spring so its fresh which must needs be very strengthning, it shutts up its pores of the body immediately so fortifyes from cold, you cannot bear the coldness of it above 2 or 3 minutes and then you come out and walke round the pavement and then in againe, and so 3 or 4 or 6 or 7 as many tymes as you please… I dipp'd my head quite over every tyme I went in and found it eased a great pain I used to have in my head.'

Fiennes enjoyed herself in Scarborough, taking a boat trip, walking on the sands, and seeing '70 saile of Shipps' pass by in convoy – Newcastle colliers protecting themselves from French warships. The 'Spaw Well' she sampled was 'on this sand by the Sea Shore'.

In Harrogate, she found four different mineral springs within two miles. It was one of these which extracted from Fiennes her most vivid description of hydrotherapy:

> '…the Sulpher or Stincking spaw, not improperly term'd for the Smell being so very strong and offensive that I could not force my horse near the Well, there are two Wells together with basons in them that the Spring rises up in, which is furr'd with a White Scumm… it has an additionall offenciveness like carrion or a jakes… its a quick purger and very good for all Scurbutick humours; some persons drink a quart or two – I dranke a quart in a morning for two days and hold them to be a good sort of Purge if you can hold your breath so as to drinke them down…'

'Jakes' being a lost word for 'privy', the reader is left reeling with admiration for a woman who can keep down half a gallon of carrion-and-khazi smoothie. I drank a small glass of it when visiting Harrogate's Royal Pump Room recently, and reeled into Valley Gardens with breath reeking of rotten eggs and drains. Apparently, it has the highest sulphur content of any mineral water in Europe.

Nearly two months after leaving London, Fiennes and her companions rode their horses southwards out of St Albans to join the route now taken by the M25 (clockwise). Near South Mimms motorway service station, they turned towards the celebrated spa of Barnet, and the capital. Fiennes however was not finished with travelling for the year. Before the summer was out, she was back on her horse for a five-day tour of Kent. It was during this ride that she came across both the finest river she had ever seen (the Medway), and a bridge (at Rochester) which she held to be 'the finest in England, nay its said to equal any in the world'.

That winter was one of the worst in living memory. In November, 1697, London was hit by severe frosts, and then sleet and snow. With occasional thaws, the sub-zero conditions lasted for a desperate six months. Deep snow drifts covered England, and rivers froze. In early February, sea ice eight inches thick was reported off the Suffolk coast. As late as May, 1698, heavy snow fell from Yorkshire to London. Even within the deep chill of the 'Little Ice Age', the spring of 1698 was the most retarded for forty-seven years.

While all outside was frozen, Fiennes was planning her final journey. It would be the longest and most adventurous by far of her rides, and it would take her through England's most extensive wetlands, its highest mountains, and its most feared moorlands. It would also take her to the greatest trading centre of the north, and to the two counties most distant from London. As it happened, none of these places could offer Fiennes the pleasures of the 'spaw'. It would be a hard ride.

Plotted on a map, her proposed route was shaped like an enormous, deformed figure-of-eight. On an epic scale, it touched upon the eastern, the northern, the western and southern limits of England. It was almost as if she was beating the bounds of her own nation. And yet this route had another, far grander, purpose. Her discreet intent had been concealed in a trail of clues throughout her journal:

'Nay the Ladies,' she had written in the journal's introduction, 'might have matter not unworthy their observation, some subject for conversation, within their own compass in each county to which they relate; and thence studdy how to be serviceable to their neighbours especially the poor among whome they dwell…'

William Camden's *Britannia*, and the list of counties Fiennes worked her way through during sixteen years in the saddle.

It took me many years to make the connection between her reference to 'each county', and the methodical logging during her travels of each county-boundary. What finally clinched it was her references to Camden's *Britannia* – the only book to be repeatedly mentioned in her journals. William Camden's county-by-county guide to England, Wales and Scotland was a gold-mine of historical, archaeological and geographical information. Within its encyclopaedic scope, readers could investigate matters as diverse as the wines of Gloucestershire, the origins of the 'The Picts Wall', and the number of arches under Padstow's bridge. First published in Latin in 1586, *Britannia* had been translated into English by Philemon Holland in 1610. A new edition, heavily revised and updated by Bishop Gibson, had been published in 1695.

Fiennes was using *Britannia* as a travel guide. The preliminary pages of *Britannia* include a section titled 'The General Heads of the Introduction, and Counties of England: A list of the tribes of Ancient Britain', and against them, the counties they occupied. At the time, there was some uncertainty about what exactly consituted a 'county', but Camden's definitive list totalled fifty-three, of which thirty-nine (plus a bishopric and some arsenals) lay in England. By the time Fiennes returned home from Kent in 1697, she had travelled through twenty-six of the counties on Camden's list. So, the peculiar, contorted route she devised for her final tour had been designed to connect, in a single ride, the remaining thirteen counties. These thirteen were grouped in three regions: East Anglia, the far north of England, and the West Country. In crossing the Tamar into Cornwall, she would become the first recorded woman to visit every one of England's thirty-nine counties. The enormous scope of this climactic ride was reflected in the title she wrote into her journal: 'My Great Journey to Newcastle and to Cornwall'.

* * *

Fiennes – like Defoe twenty years later – began her Great Journey with a loop through the counties of East Anglia. And like Defoe, she quickly discovered that she was riding through a region which had profited from the fertility of its soils and its proximity to London and the Continent. Dotted across the level cornlands were busy, heavily-populated market towns and centres of local industry. The coast was ringed with ports. But Fiennes didn't really enjoy East Anglia; it just wasn't very exciting. Where were the new, stone building styles of London and Nottingham? The mineral spas of Yorkshire? The natural wonders of Derbyshire? Elsewhere in England, she had already seen better cathedrals, longer bridges, wider rivers, and newer industries. And it all looked a bit of a mess. Colchester was still much 'ruinated' by the Civil War siege of 1648. Ipswich she found to be 'a little disregarded', blaming 'pride and sloth' for the town's failure to take full commercial advantage of its quayside. Why, she wondered, were colliers of three hundred tons showing up to deliver coal, then leaving with empty holds?

Short of riding a horse, which in my experience is a very hazardous practice, the closest a modern traveller can come to replicating the rides of Celia Fiennes, is to pedal a ladies' sit-up-and-beg bicycle.

Riding between East Anglia's towns was not easy, either. Beyond Ipswich, she entered a vague, wet land, where route-finding was difficult and the roads hazardous. Asking the way, she found that 'the people here are able to give so bad a direction that passengers are at a loss what aime to take, they know scarce 3 mile from their home, and meete them where you will, enquire how farre to such a place, they mind not where they are then but tell you so farre which is the distance from their own houses to that place.'

Then there was the weather. The appalling winter of 1697–8 had been followed by heavy rains. And in the flatlands of East Anglia, floods took a long time to disperse. When Fiennes eventually reached the county boundary separating Suffolk from Norfolk, she found 'a low flatt ground all here about so that the least raines they are overflowed by the River and lye under water, as they did when I was there, so that the roade lay under water which is very unsafe for strangers to pass, by reason of the holes and quick sands and loose bottom.'

Norwich was another East Anglian conundrum. Here, in the heart of the county of Norfolk, she found a 'vast place … 6 miles in compass', with markets for every product under the sun, and no less than thirty-six churches. The textile industry employed men and women 'in spinning knitting weaveing dying scouring fulling or bleaching their stuffs'. The whole city, she had to admit, 'lookes like what it is, a rich thriveing industrious place'. And yet Norwich was antique in its fabric. The medieval city walls were 'the best in repaire of any walled citty I know', but 'all their buildings are of an old form', constructed with timber, plaster and lathe, and 'none of brick except some few beyond the river which are built of some of the rich factors like London buildings'. An island in its own flood plain, Norwich seemed immune to modernity.

Norwich, England's second city after London, was a huge manufacturing centre, with an enormous population of thirty thousand, and a ring of medieval walls which had grown to be a symbol of security and diligence. This French plan dates to about 1650.

Getting out of Norfolk was almost as difficult as getting in. West of Norwich, the route to the Midlands was blocked by over a thousand square miles of impassable Fenland. So Fiennes rode south to Bury St Edmunds and then followed the higher ground across to Newmarket. Her first sight of the Fens came as she made the barely perceptible descent from Chippenham House to the River Snail: 'I passed over a low ground on each side,' she writes, 'deffended by the fendiks which are deep ditches with draines.' Looking about her, she observed: 'the Fens are full of water and mudd.' For centuries, Britain's largest wetland had been the scene of battles between the ingenuity of engineers and the ability of water to find its own level. The Romans had tried to drain this ancient wetland, and so had the Earl of Bedford, who, in the 1630s, commissioned dykes to be cut in a renewed attempt to turn water into pasture. But as the water drained from the Fens, the peat shrank, and the fields subsided below the level of the surrounding rivers. By the late 1600s, Nature was reinstating a wetland. Fiennes was amazed by the spectacle of such a vast, watery plain, with its arrow-straight dykes and rows of pollarded willows. It looks, she thought, 'very finely to see a flatt of many miles … but it must be ill to live there.'

The Fens. Flat, wet, and slightly mad. In Ely, Fiennes had to share a bedroom with frogs, worms and snails.

The only way to reach Ely was by riding along a seasonal gravel causeway. In winter, it was often flooded, forcing travellers to take to boats. In summer it should have been open, but so much rain had fallen that sections were now completely covered with water, and Fiennes could not see the edge of the embankment. As she floundered towards beleaguered Ely, she came close to disaster. Her horse, 'earnest to drinke ran to get more depth of water than the Causeey had, was on the brinke of one of these diks.' Horse and rider nearly toppled into the dyke.

Shaken, Fiennes found Ely 'the dirtyest place I ever saw'. The streets had 'not a bitt of pitching', and indeed the whole city was 'a perfect quagmire' and 'a harbour to breed and nest vermin in, of which there is plenty enough, so that tho' my chamber was near 20 stepps up I had froggs and slow-worms and snailes in my roome.' Not only was this the most disgusting city she had ever seen, but the Minster ('a curious pile of building') was littered with relics of 'Popery'. Ely, fumed Fiennes, 'has the most Popish remains in its walls of any I have seen, there still remaines a Cross over the alter the Candlesticks are 3 quarters of a yard high massy silver gilt very heavy.'

To gain an aerial view of this decrepit island, Fiennes climbed the eighty or so steps to the Cathedral's octagonal lantern. Looking about her, she appeared to be floating on a vast, inland sea. To the south, she could see Cambridge, 'and a great prospect of the country which by reason of the great rains just before laid under water, all the fenny grounds being overflow'd.' The only dry ground was the narrow bank of slightly higher ground on which Ely was built. Here, the farmers could drive their cattle to safety during the wet season. Bleakly, she summed up Ely's subsistence economy: she'd found no evidence of any trading in the town, and concluded that 'their maine buissiness and dependance is on draining and fencing their grounds and breeding and graseing cattle.'

Fiennes identified two causes of Ely's woeful state. The first was the absentee Bishop, who 'does not care to stay long in this place not being for his health … it's a shame.' An episcopal presence might have made Ely 'better ordered and the buildings and streetes put in a better condition.' The second was Ely's 'slothful' population. The land is so extraordinarily suited to cattle, she observes, that 'in case 6 or 7 wet yeares drown them all', one good year 'repaires their loss'. Why – with their 'vast allowance yearly' of 'at least 3000$\pounds$' – do they not keep the banks in good repair? 'I wonder,' she asks, 'they have not perfectly runn off the water, and so barracadoed it … they are all a lazy sort of people and are afraid to do too much.' For Fiennes, there was no natural obstacle so great that it could not be overcome by money, machinery and motivation. In the Fens, she happened to come across a community who – for the time being – were losing the battle.

Neither was her escape from Ely without incident. Ten miles west of the city, she found the bridge over the Ouse under water. The road was submerged too, and because its bed was 'so full of holes and quick sands', she was forced to detour to a ferry and pay two pence per horse to cross the flood. For the first time, the phrase, 'I durst not venture' escaped from her pen.

Riding through Leicestershire, Fiennes reached the seat of Sir Charles Wolseley, where she stayed for six weeks, resting and exploring the neighbourhood. She was also steeling herself for the most difficult section of her itinerary: the journey to the northern limits of England. When she eventually left Wolseley's moated house by the Trent, she headed north-westwards to visit the mineral spa at Holywell in north Wales, and then struck northward for Lancaster and the mountains. She was further from London than she had ever been in the past. Following Fiennes by bicycle up

Heading north in the summer of 1698, Fiennes left the coach road for Glasgow, and turned into the mountains of Westmorland.

through Merseyside and then Wigan and Warrington, the contrast between her landscapes and mine could not have been more extreme. Where Fiennes trotted through fields and villages, I was pedalling past chemical works and suburbs. So it was something of a relief when she turned towards the crenellated skyline of Westmorland. However, it wasn't the mountains that appealed to Fiennes.

At the King's Arms in Kendal, Fiennes had come across potted char. The fish was a fairly unusual speciality, even in the seventeenth century, and Fiennes – who reckoned it 'the best of any in the country' – asked the chef, Mrs Rowlandson, where the fish had been caught. She was told that the only place that char could be found was in the 'great standing water' of 'Wiandermer'. Ten miles of very narrow lanes led to Bowness and the shore of the lake. The char were out of season, but Fiennes was amazed by the sight of Windermere. This was the largest lake she had ever seen, and she gazed in wonder at the movements of its surface. 'This great water,' she wrote, 'seemes which seemed 'to flow and wave about with the wind or in one motion but it does not ebb and flow like the sea with the tyde, neither does it run' like a river.

Further along the lake, water again caught her eye, and then her ear. 'From these great fells,' she wrote, there are 'severall springs out of the rock that trickle down their sides, and as they meete with stones and rocks in the way when something obstructs their passage and so they come with more violence that gives a pleasing sound and murmering noise.' This is the same aquatic imagination which had woken to the sound of the water garden at Wilton.

To reach her next county, Cumberland, Fiennes had to cross the Kirkstone Pass, and, rather against her will, she had to confront for the first time the prospect of mountains. The crest of the pass, 1,489 feet above sea level, is approached from Windermere by a long, very steep climb known as 'The Struggle'. Forced to dismount, it took Fiennes an hour to reach the top, and a further hour to descend the far side. It wasn't a pleasant experience. 'I was walled on both sides,' she recalls, 'by those inaccessible high rocky barren hills which hangs over ones head in some places and appear very terrible.' After a night in a Carlisle brothel 'with a young giddy Landlady that could only dress fine and entertain the soldiers', Fiennes rode her horse through the quicksands of the Esk estuary so that she could put a toe into Scotland – just as she had with Wales.

Riding an antique ladies bicycle up Kirkstone Pass… Well, if Fiennes could do it three hundred years ago…

Windermere, the largest natural lake in England, was one of the most extraordinary sights Fiennes saw on her tour; today, the lake ranks sixth in UK tourist hotspots, with over a million visitors each year.

From Scotland, Fiennes crossed into Northumberland, the county most distant from London. Ahead of her was a long, hard ride over the roof of the Pennines. Troubled by the distances she was being given, she convinced herself that a 'mile' in Northumberland 'might be esteemed double the number in most of the countys in England'. The 'road' to Newcastle appears to have been little more than sets of hoof-tracks across the peaty hills, 'a sort of black moorish ground and so wet I observ'd as my man rode up that sort of precipice or steep his horses heeles cast up water every step and their feete cut deepe in, even quite up to the top; such up and down hills and sort of boggy ground it was.'

With night drawing on, and the distance to shelter uncertain, Fiennes found a local guide to lead them around the 'ill places'. But the trials of the day were far from over. Eventually, they reached Haltwhistle, but the owner of the only inn refused to provide hay for the horses, and when Fiennes' servants went out and bought some, the innkeeper got so angry that he ejected Fiennes into the night. 'I was forced to take up in a poor cottage,' she writes, 'which was open to the thatch and no partition but hurdles plaister'd.' Despite the fact that her host brought out her best sheets 'which serv'd to secure my own sheetes from her dirty blankets', Fiennes could not sleep for the smoke of burning peat.

As the riders closed on Newcastle, the roads improved. Newcastle fulfilled Fiennes' expectations of a modern city. It's a 'noble town', she writes, and 'it most resembles

On Fiennes' mental map, Newcastle-upon-Tyne was so far north that it might have been a port in the Arctic. It surpassed her wildest dreams.

London of any place in England.' Newcastle's 'lofty and large' buildings were mostly of brick or stone. The streets were 'broad and handsome and very well pitch'd', and many of them were furnished with water conduits 'for every bodyes use'. Stone pillars adorned public buildings, and a 'fine clock' topped the Royal Exchange. The shops, she enthused, 'are good and are of distinct trades, not selling many things in one shop as is the custom in most country towns.' There was a separate market for corn, and a market for hay. Down by the Tyne, Fiennes found the quayside 'soe full of merchants walking to-and-againe', while the river itself was 'full of ships'. This, she concludes, is 'a town of great trade'.

But Newcastle was not just her image of the ideal emporium. It was civilised, too. Fiennes came across a 'pleasant' bowling green, and a garden 'where the Gentlemen and Ladyes walke in the evening'. She also visited the Barber Surgeons Hall and inspected a display of skeletons and a stuffed man, used for anatomy lectures. Today, it's a bit crowded by a multi-storey carpark, an underpass, a flyover and railway lines, but the Hospital of Holy Jesus, was praised for providing '2 good roomes a piece' to fourteen widows of tradesmen. In front of the brick pillars which Fiennes walked beneath, is the 'large Fountaine or Conduite' for the use of the widows. On the Tyne, Fiennes had at last found a metropolis that could measure up to London.

* * *

As Fiennes made her way southward towards Leeds, she could congratulate herself on the success of her northern expedition. Since leaving Wolseley, she had visited seven new counties. She only had to visit another three – Shropshire, Devon and Cornwall – and she would have ticked all thirty-nine in Camden's *Britannia*. But a formidable barrier blocked her onward route.

In the seventeenth century there were only three major trans-Pennine routes. Fiennes' most direct means of reaching Shropshire and the West Country was to take the southernmost – and most difficult – trans-Pennine crossing, from Leeds to Manchester. The Pennines here are no more than ten miles wide, but the road lurched up to an astonishing 1,500 feet, crossed a moor, then plummeted giddily down the western side. 'Blackstone Edge...' jotted Fiennes, 'noted all over England for a dismal high precipice and steep in the ascent and descent on either end.' In February, 1698 – a matter of weeks before Fiennes headed north – the Yorkshire topographer and antiquarian Ralph Thoresby had been caught by the snows on Blackstone Edge, his horse had fallen, and his leg had been crushed. A few months before that, a travelling salesman had his horse shot by a highwayman. Modern motorists, thrumming along the six-lane M62 two miles south of Blackstone Edge, hurdle the Pennine backbone in a few minutes of effortless travel. But for Fiennes, this would be the most alarming road she had ever encountered.

The climbing began in earnest once she had crossed the packhorse bridge at Ripponden. Initially, the weather was 'pretty faire', but, as she followed the V-shaped cleft of the Ryburn valley towards the dark moors, conditions deteriorated. Even today, this is a bleak place. Half a mile or so after two columns of pylons stride across the A58, the medieval packhorse track can be seen cutting up a gully called Rag Sapling Clough. A few minutes up the Clough, the track suddenly steepens and loses

A few years before Fiennes embarked upon her 'Great Journey', a brilliant cartographer called John Ogilby published England's first road atlas. He depicted recommended routes in strips annotated with hazards. Fiennes never mentions that she has seen Ogilby's *Britannia*. If she had, perhaps Blackstone Edge would have been less of a shock. Ogilby features it at the top of the central strip.

itself in interminable peat swamps. It must have been around here that Fiennes noticed 'a sort of mist'. This was followed by 'small raine'. For over a mile, the track climbs up moorland which is completely exposed. There is not a building or a tree to be seen. Clearly apprehensive, Fiennes noted the 'very moorish ground all about', and was alarmed by the precarious nature of the 'very troublesome' causeway which carried the track across the bogs. More frightening was the mist, and the risk of losing her way. The spattering rain made her 'feare a wet day and that the aire would have been so thick to have quite lost me the sight of the Country.' Fear was not a familiar emotion for Fiennes.

At about 1,400 feet above sea level, the pack-horse track began to level. Off to her left, she would have seen the sombre cliff and tumbled rocks marking the high-point of Blackstone Edge. Beside her (although she doesn't mention it) she would certainly have noticed the Aiggin Stone, a medieval waymark to guide travellers over the moor. She does however record passing the massive cairn (a 'great heap raised up'), which is still there, and notes that it marks the county boundary separating Yorkshire and Lancashire. The passage which follows reads as a deliverance:

> '…the mist began to lessen, and as I descended on this side the fog more and more went off and a little raine fell, tho' at a little distance in our view the sun shone on the vale which indeed is of a large extent here, and the advantage of soe high a high[t] which is at least 2 mile up, discovers the grounds beneath as a fruitfull valley full of inclosures and cut hedges and trees.'

The transition from the appalling heights to the lovely lowlands took Celia back to her girlhood, 'and the account my Father gave of those Alps when he passed them and I could not but think this carryed some resemblance tho' in little, yet a proportion to that.' She had left the north behind.

Sunnier lands lay ahead, but Fiennes was mistaken if she thought that the dangers were over. Three days after crossing Blackstone Edge, she was riding through the rich cattle country of Cheshire when she ran into the kind of trouble that she must have been expecting for most of her travelling life. Earlier that day, she had passed through Northwich, where she'd spent some time examining the brine pits and learning of the recent discovery of rock-salt in the area. From there, she had taken the main route south across the Cheshire Plain, towards the prominent landmark of Beeston Castle, high upon its isolated sandstone crag.

At the crossroads below the castle, '2 fellows all on a suddain from the wood fell into the road…' Fiennes and her companions held their nerve, as the two men, 'truss'd up with great coates and as it were bundles about them which I believe was pistolls' began to intimidate them. For a while, the men shadowed the travellers, dropping back to mutter between themselves, then riding forward again. Fiennes must have asked their business, for she records that they 'did disown their knowledge of the way'. The men then attempted to isolate Fiennes from her companions, one of them riding in front of her and the other behind, jostling her horse in an effort to force it to one side. Fortunately, it was market day in Whitchurch, and the closer they drew to the town, the busier the road became. Frustrated, the troublemakers eventually lost patience, 'so at last they called each other off and soe left us and turned back.' Fiennes wraps up the incident in a characteristically cool fashion by observing that it had been the only time in her life that she 'had reason to suspect' that she had been 'engaged with some Highway men'.

The countryside below Beeston Castle, where Fiennes was intercepted by two troublemakers she took to be highwaymen.

And that wasn't the end of her trials. The roads in the borders were notoriously bad, and those of Herefordshire, some of the worst in the country. Campaigning here during the Civil War, fifty years earlier, the Earl of Leven had complained that Herefordshire's roads were so difficult to negotiate that his troops could only manage to march eight miles in one day. Rashly, Fiennes decided to take a long detour west from Worcester so that she could visit relations at Stretton Grandison, and see a new house at Stoke Edith. Again, the rains which had hit the country earlier in the year had made the roads – 'which are all lanes full of stones and up hills and down soe steep that with the raines the waters stood or else ran down the hills' – virtually impassable. 'This,' she concluded, 'is the worst way I ever went in Worcester or Herrifordshire.'

\* \* \*

Late that summer, Celia Fiennes crossed her final county boundary. 'Here,' she records, 'I entred into Cornwall...' England's most western county was still as remote to a Londoner as it had been in John Leland's day. And like Leland, Fiennes found herself describing Cornwall as if it were a strange, unexplored land. Having searched unsuccessfully for 'West Country tarts' as she rode through Somerset and Devon, she discovered in Cornwall 'the most acceptable entertainment that could be made me ... apple pye with a custard all on the top.' With lipsmacking approval, she records how they 'scalde their creame and milk ... and so its a sort of clouted creame as we call it, with a little sugar, and soe put on the top of the apple pye.' Travelling, however, was difficult. Ferries had to be used to cross long inlets of the sea, and the incredibly steep roads were either rocky, or filled with 'many holes and sloughs'. The shoes on her horses quickly wore thin and fell off on the stony tracks, and good blacksmiths were hard to find. Alternately battered by rain, hail and strong winds, she struggled on through the worst conditions she had known. At one point, her horse tripped in a flooded hole and 'had gotten quite down his head and all'. A lesser mortal might have turned back, but Fiennes was determined to investigate the unique Cornish industry that she'd read about in Camden's *Britannia*.

In the 150 years since John Leland had ridden these roads logging the distribution of tin mines, the extraction and processing of ore had become much more efficient. Fiennes chose a mine near St Austell to record an impression so vivid that the reader is left with ringing ears and stinging nostrils. Having hauled the ore to the surface, she watches them 'pound it in a stamping mill which resembles the paper mills, and when its fine as the finest sand, some of which I saw and took, this they fling into a furnace and with it coale to make the fire, so it burns together and makes a violent heate and fierce flame, the mettle by the fire being seperated from the coale and its own drosse, being heavy falls down to a trench made to receive it, at the furnace hole below; this liquid mettle I saw them shovel up with an iron shovel and soe pour it into molds in which cooles and soe

*The* Golden FARMER *and the* TINKER

Fiennes grew up on Salisbury Plain with tales of a highwayman known as the 'Golden Farmer'. The pair of losers who troubled her in Cheshire left empty-handed.

An empty road, and the shadow of a spinning wheel... Are there any greater pleasures? Well, perhaps. But not many. A bicycle propelled by a human in possession of moderately-functional legs can cover sixty miles a day.

they take it thence in sort of wedges or piggs I think they call them; its a fine mettle thus in its first melting looks like silver, I had a piece poured out and made cold for to take with me.'

With her pannier bags weighed with souvenirs of crushed ore and a tin 'pig', Fiennes continued her survey. From a single roadside vantage point outside St Austell, she was able to count no less than twenty tin mines. On the road to Tregony, she passed one hundred mines. This pocked, clamorous, smokey landscape teemed with activity; she estimated that one thousand men were employed night and day in the pits, furnaces and drainage mills. Excitedly, she noticed that the mills used to drain the mines were like those she had seen around London, Derby and Exeter, powered by water, and 'five tymes more good than the mills they use to turn with horses'.

Tin put Cornwall on Bronze Age trade routes, and Fiennes was determined to understand the full process of extraction and smelting. She left Cornwall with a tin 'pig' in her panniers.

Inexorably, Fiennes was led ever westward, past the River Fal (where she stayed in a relation's fine new house), to Redruth and Penzance ('it lookes soe snugg and warme'), until she was on a road as 'stone and barren as Darbyshire'. Finally, she saw the ultimate point of return: 'I came in sight of the maine ocean on both sides, the south and north sea, and soe rode in its view till I saw them joyn'd at the poynt…' She had reached Land's End. After a celebratory drink of 'very good bottled ale', Fiennes set off on foot for the furthest tip of land, 'a poynt or peak of great rocks which runs a good way into the sea'. This was the end of her journey. Beyond here, she quipped, her 'horses leggs could not carry me through the deep'. Like millions of travellers since, she was compelled to go right to the end, clambering over the storm-scrubbed rocks 'as farre as saftey permitted'.

\* \* \*

The journey home was tough. Fiennes was weary, and the days were growing shorter; 'the season of the year enclined to raine, and the dayes declineing'. The rains fell, the roads flooded. The day she crossed the border back into Devon was the wettest she had ever known. If she was lucky, she would find an inn with a fire, so that she could dry her clothes before supper. The rains followed her through Somerset, where one night's deluge 'put the cattle in the meddows swimming' and prevented her from going to church with her cousin, for fear that the water 'would have came over the windows of the Coach'. In Hampshire, overnight rain turned the chalky tracks to slippery gullies. In one of these sunken tracks, her horse's 'feete failed, and he could noe wayes recover himself'. Fiennes recalls how she was 'shott off his neck upon the bank'. Lesser riders would have been a bundle of broken bones. But Fiennes was unharmed, and her horse rolled himself upright and stood 'stock still' beside his remarkable rider.

Several days later, she was riding across Hounslow Heath, and into London. Celia Fiennes would continue to travel, to visit relations and spas, but by 1698 she had fulfilled her ambition. In twenty years of travelling, she had visited every English county listed by Camden on the Contents page of *Britannia*. She had seen every one of England's twenty-five cathedrals, sampled twenty-seven healing mineral waters and springs, and called at countless country houses. In sixteen years of travel, she had covered at least five thousand miles. She must have been one of the best-travelled Englishwomen of her generation.

Some four years after returning from Cornwall, Celia Fiennes decided to compile an account of her journeys. As a feat of authorship, it was just as impressive as her journeys, for the completed journal ran to well over one hundred thousand words. This was, she claimed, 'never designed, soe not likely to fall into the hands of any but my near relations.' A private document, it was intended to amuse and enlighten those close to her. And yet it is impossible not to conclude that she craved a wider audience. Not only does she refer to her journal as 'this book', but there are moments within it when she appears to be addressing both the nation and women in general. The loudest of these universal appeals appears on the opening page, when Fiennes urges 'all persons' to 'spend some of their tyme in Journeys to visit their native Land.' Two hundred years after she began exploring the English counties, her journal was published. It is still in print, urging new generations of readers to 'cure the evil itch of over-valueing foreign parts'.

Land's End. When Fiennes rode across the Tamar into Cornwall, she became the first recorded woman to visit every county in England.

# Daniel Defoe *1724-6*

*The secret tourist*

Conjectural Route through East Anglia Taken By

# DANIEL DEFOE

In 1724-6

ROUTE LOCATION WITHIN THE BRITISH ISLES

MAP SHOWING THE SUPPOSED ROUTE OF THE VARIOUS TOURS

Route & direction
Town or city

Norfolk

Wells
Blakeney
Weybourne
Cromer

Winterton Ness

Kings Lynn

Wisbech

River Yare

Norwich

Great Yarmouth

Downham Market

The Fens

River Ouse

Lowestoft

Ely

Cambridgeshire

Southwold

Bury St Edmunds

Dunwich

Suffolk

Cambridge

Newmarket

Woodbridge

Orford Ness

River Cam

Ipswich

Saffron Walden

Hadleigh

Essex

Harwich

Colchester

Walton-on-the-Naze

Hertfordshire

Witham

Epping Forest

Chelmsford

Maldon

Ingatestone

Wanstead

Barking

Canvey Island

Stratford

Dagenham

London

Tilbury

Thames Estuary

Greenwich

Gravesend

0    10    20
MILES

THE AUTHOR OF *Robinson Crusoe* is perhaps the most colourful writer ever to have saddled a horse and taken to the British byways. He is celebrated for bringing the 'realistic novel' to the English-reading world, and for being the father of modern journalism. Although he was a contemporary of Celia Fiennes, his description of eighteenth-century Britain could not be more different. *A Tour thro' the Whole Island of Great Britain* purports to be a record of seventeen 'Circuits or Journeys' undertaken by an anonymous 'Gentleman' who left London on a quest to reveal 'whatever is curious and worth observation' about his country. Published in three volumes, between 1724 and 1726, the *Tour* was lauded by the historian G.M. Trevelyan as 'an unparalleled survey of Queen Anne's England'. It is still Britains most spirited guide.

\* \* \*

Visit the scene of Robinson Crusoe's shipwreck and you will find a desert of sand backed by a mountainous range of dunes. In winter gales, blonde streamers of sandgrains wave on the beach like wind-blown hair. Even in summer, footprints are rare. At certain times of the tide, an ominous line of breakers can be seen extending far out to sea, as if the swell is tripping on an underwater obstacle. Daniel Defoe plotted the opening passage of *Crusoe* as if he was working from a map. The course of the ship and behaviour of the wind are nautically plausible, the fateful anchorage can be pinpointed on the Admiralty Chart, and the beach where young 'Bob' was washed ashore is on the Ordnance Survey 1:50,000. But why did Defoe wreck Crusoe off Norfolk?

Defoe's reasons for finding East Anglia the most dangerous, exciting region in Britain would emerge in 1724, three years after *Robinson Crusoe* was published. *A Tour thro' the Whole Island of Great Britain* also opened with East Anglia; at the head of the first chapter, readers were invited to step across the threshold of Britain by way of 'a description of the Sea-Coasts of the Counties of Essex, Suffolk, Norfolk, etc., as also of part of Cambridge-shire'. In subsequent chapters, Defoe would take his readers on a further sixteen journeys, or 'circuits', each contrived to describe a geographical region. In their entirety, they covered the whole of Britain, from the Highlands of Scotland to furthest Cornwall. But he started with East Anglia.

The trail which led Daniel Defoe from his birthplace in London to the byways of Britain is shrouded in estuarine mists. It is known that he was born in the London parish of St Giles, Cripplegate, probably in around 1660. His father, James, was a tallow chandler; an upright dependable merchant who belonged to a City livery company. His

*Previous pages:*
**Blackwater Estuary, Essex**

mother, Alice, has been described by a recent biographer as severe and unapproachable. Both were Nonconformists; Puritans who had learned since the Restoration of Charles II to the throne to live outside the established Church of England. As practising Dissenters, they suffered discrimination and suspicion from an Establishment which sought retribution for the indignities suffered during the Cromwellian Commonwealth. From his earliest years, Daniel was imbued with self-discipline, fortitude and the underdog's drive to succeed in the absence of privilege. He was educated at a special academy for Dissenters' children in Stoke Newington.

These were extraordinary times. Post-war Britain was in the throes of Restoration re-invention and multifarious catastrophe. Defoe was a boy when London was devasted by the Plague and the Great Fire, and he lived through wars with France and Holland, and through the worst storm to strike Britain. At the age of twenty-five, he fought in the rebel Duke of Monmouth's army at Sedgemoor, and he was in the wings during the 1707 Act of Union between Scotland and England. By the time he died in 1731, Defoe had produced over five hundred publications and adopted a multiplicity of causes, which he pursued with reckless passion. Reinvigorated Britain, with its ambitious economy, was an exciting playground for a chancer. Defoe was bankrupted twice, fined, pilloried and imprisoned. His 'occupations' ranged from breeding civet cats and running a brick factory to journalism and writing books. He borrowed money to buy a diving bell so that he could recover sunken treaure. At least once, he appears to have been aboard a ship smuggling tin to France, and for a while, he worked as a secret agent. He was a risk-taker and a survivor. And he was a man always on the move, as a soldier, merchant, fugitive, farmer, hack or spy. Habitually secretive, he laid a trail of biographical red herrings. He avoided writing first-person accounts relating to his own life, and often published anonymously (*Robinson Crusoe* was written – according to its title page – 'by Himself'). Subversively imaginative, he inserted invented passages into works of 'non-fiction'. The greatest of those supposedly-factual works was his *Tour*.

*A Tour thro' the Whole Island of Great Britain* was published when Defoe was in his sixties. And it was a characteristically risky venture. At a time when the literary world was metropolitan and classically-educated, low-brow Defoe headed off to the regions to write about places that were off the Establishment map. He knew that there was nothing quite like the scent of an untold story. Enormous in its compass and ingenious in its presentation, the *Tour* contained the accumulated wisdom of a lifetime's travel (and a scattering of passages recycled from Camden's *Britannia*). The journeys themselves were less the record of actual itineraries than a convenient narrative spine on which to hang his encyclopaedic observations. Defoe was clear that the *Tour* was not a geographical compendium. It was, he explained, 'particularly fitted for the Reading of such as desire to Travel over the ISLAND.' The *Tour* was a printed companion for travellers; a guidebook.

*Opposite:* Into the Pool of London with Thames waterman, Chris Livett, aboard the recycling and waste-management barge, *Tidy Thames.*

Defoe's London was a new metropolis, risen from the cinders of the Great Fire. 'The increase of the buildings here, is really a kind of prodigy,' he wrote of Piccadilly, Covent Garden and Soho. His *Tour* could begin nowhere else but here, in 'the great centre of England'.

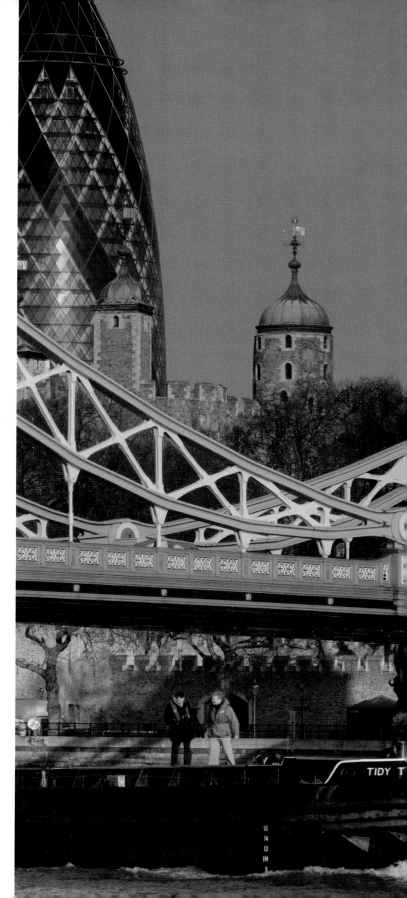

***

For Defoe, there was only one place where a journey through Britain could begin. London was the centre of trade; the capital of Protestantism; the heart of the Empire and the standard against which all other cities could be compared. Already the largest city in western Europe, it was growing by the day. Fifty years after the Great Fire of London, the city had risen from the ashes: 'New squares, and new streets,' rejoiced Defoe, 'rising up every day to such a prodigy of buildings, that nothing in the world does, or ever did, equal it, except old Rome in Trajan's time.' Over the course of several thousand miles of travel, Defoe would demonstrate that every village in Britain was connected by an economic umbilical cord to 'this overgrown city'. Feeding the capital, and therefore the rest of Britain, was the River Thames.

I joined Defoe on board a recycling and waste-management motor-barge moored just downstream of Tower Bridge. *Tidy Thames* is a neat little ship of around ninety tons, with polished brass in the bridge and a mahogany saloon fully-equipped with tea-making apparatus. In front of the bridge windows is a long, rectangular hold, half-filled on this particular day with miscellaneous urban detritus, from paint pots and beer bottles to industrial pallets and black bin bags. Viewed from the bow, *Tidy Thames* looks rather like an incongruous marriage between a rubbish skip and a Victorian conservatory. We untied from the pier as the rush-hour traffic stuttered above our heads, then Colin Murphy, the skipper, spun the spoked wheel and *Tidy Thames* tucked her bow into the ebb tide.

On board the barge was her owner, Chris Livett, a fifth-generation Thames waterman, who runs his company from a cramped suite of cabins below 'X' turret on HMS *Belfast*. Livett's family has worked the river since 1710. 'I came afloat when I was eight years old, with my grandfather,' he told me as Tower Bridge receded. 'I was apprenticed to the Watermens Company, to my father, aged sixteen.' Today, Livett's Launches operate ten pleasure boats and six barges. Livett's river flows through his conversation like a mysterious stream of energy and history, barely sensible to those who had not been born into the world of watermen. 'The smells and the sounds would have been intriguing,' he mused. 'Spices, sugar, tobacco … coal … all the different products coming in, the sounds of oars and flapping sails, the watermen running out, looking for business, throwing up their grappling hooks to the sides of ships, offering their services … quite a lot of banging and crashing as well. Remember the craft in those days were not particularly manouvreable. They were all dependant on the tide.' Livett's river was an inhuman force: 'The motto of the Watermens Company is "At command of our superiors". That's not the wife or mother-in-law, but the wind and the tide, and the forces that drive them.'

As *Tidy Thames* chewed a furrow downriver, Livett pointed to the scattered relics of London's one-time trading artery: the slimy timber 'campsheds' which had once supported barges at low tides; liver-coloured slipways, the renovated wharves, gentrified warehouses and mooring bollards marooned on riverside walks like abstract civic sculptures. Ours was the only vessel moving on a section of river which in Defoe's day was almost rafted with shifting decks. 'I have had the curiosity,' wrote Defoe, 'to count the ships as well as I could, *en passant*, and have found above two thousand sail of all sorts, not reckoning barges, lighters or pleasure boats, and yachts; but vessels that really go to sea.' Between Battle Bridge and Blackwall, he ticked-off three wet docks, twenty-two dry docks and thirty-three shipyards, and that was just for merchant ships. By the early 1700s, London's share of trade was greater than all other British ports put together, with fleets of ships plying the shores of Europe and new trade-routes to North America and the West Indies, Asia and West Africa. Today, explained Livett, the freight on the Thames is rubbish and road aggregate.

Beyond the serene glass stalks of Canary Wharf, *Tidy Thames* thumped past a place Defoe would recognise instantly. It is, he wrote in the *Tour*, 'the most delightful spot of ground in Great-

In this woodcut from 1684, a traveller waits for a ferry on the banks of the Thames. At the time, there was just one bridge over the Thames, and 40,000 watermen.

'That part of the river of Thames which is properly the harbour, and where the ships usually deliver or unload their cargoes, is called the Pool, and begins at the turning of the river out of Lime-house Reach, and extends to the Custom-house-Keys.' Three hundred years on, this is Butler's Wharf, on the south bank of the Pool of London. Today, there are just 1,000 Thames watermen, and the river's ferries have been replaced by thirty or so bridges.

Britain; pleasant by situation, those pleasures increased by art, and all made completely agreeable by accident of fine buildings, the continual passing of fleets of ships up and down the most beautiful river in Europe.' The fine buildings are still there: Queen's House, the Royal Naval College, Flamsteed House and the observatory. Defoe must have spent many contented hours on the waterfront at Greenwich, lapping up 'the best air, best prospect, and the best conversation in England'. It is one of the *Tour*'s many pleasures that its author's delight is so audible. Beyond the grubby mushroom of the Millennium Dome, our barge scooted between the polished cams of the Thames Barrier into less-protected reaches of the river.

Dagenham … Port bow … 1117 GMT … Here, announces Defoe, is 'the famous breach, made by an inundation of the Thames, which was so great, as that it laid near 5,000 acres of land under water.' An exceptional tide had broken the embankment in October, 1707, but repeated failures to repair it over the next ten years widened the gap and sucked 120 acres of Essex into the Thames, where it reformed as a gigantic mudbank threatening to block the river – and London's trade. It took the ingenuity of a Captain Perry, ho for several years had been employed, in the Czar of Muscovy's works, at Veronitza, on the River Don, to block the breach and clear the river. Episodes like this reveal Defoe as the kind of man who would read civil engineering pamphlets in the bath. It isn't just the *form* of landscapes which excite him, but the *processes* which shape them. Living through the depths of the 'Little Ice Age', Defoe's generation was used to extreme weather events such as catastrophic storms, floods, droughts and three-month frosts which froze the Thames.

Livett put me ashore at a concrete pier just downstream of Dagenham. In the early 1700s, this was uninhabited marshland. Today, the equivalent of forty million bin-bags of waste are brought every year to Frog Island, where Britain's first commercial-scale micro-biological treatment site shreds and sorts it all by weight, density and magnetism, then sells it on for recycling or fuel. Investing in garbage (Britain's waste sector is worth around £7 billion a year) would have appealed to Defoe; an impulsive venture capitalist, he lost a whopping £17,000 (over £500,000 today) when a flutter on shipping went wrong and led to his first bankruptcy.

Defoe's Hanoverian view was gloriously unclouded by environmental tipping-points. Poverty could be cured and wealth created simply by relieving the planet of its natural resources and processing them into products which could be traded at markets. The more hands each product passed through, the more money everyone would make. Earth was inexhaustible. The North Sea was overflowing with fish and there was enough coal to keep the country's furnaces and fireplaces glowing for eternity. Some may have warned that Britain's forests were being consumed by iron foundaries at unsustainable rates, but Defoe disagreed: 'I must own that I found that complaint perfectly groundless, the three counties of Kent, Sussex and Hampshire … being one inexhaustible source of timber.' Friends of the Earth would have found him tough to conscript.

The key players in this brave new nation were tradesmen, 'these circulators of goods, and retailers of them to the last consumer'. Trade was an ethical, civilising engine of far greater potency than Britain's capricious Navy. The 'rising greatness of the British nation' was not 'owing to war and conquests, to enlarging its dominion by the sword, or subjecting the people of other countries to our power; but it is all owing to trade, to the increase of our commerce at home, and the extending it abroad'. Applied with Puritan diligence, there could be no limit to British fortunes. In Defoe's mercantile world, tradesmen were 'the only gentry in England'.

* * *

For a vision of the future, Defoe's readers were invited to begin with the site of the 2012 Olympics: 'The village of Stratford,' he marvels, 'the first in this county from London, is not only increased, but, I believe, more than doubled in that time; every little vacancy filled up with new houses.' Take a look at the map, (Robert Morden's county map of 1695) and there is Stratford, three miles out in the countryside. Here, and in surrounding villages like Leytonstone, Wanstead, West Ham and Plaistow, property values and rents had soared by as much as a third in twenty years. East of the River Lee, greenfield sites were being gobbled up for housing; Defoe puts the figure at 'above a thousand new foundations' in the area, generally of 'handsome large houses', being let for £20–£60 a year, 'for the habitations of rich citizens, such as either are able to keep two houses, one in the country, and one in the city; or for such citizens as being rich, and having left off trade, live altogether in these neighbouring villages for the pleasure and health of the latter part of their days.' Exploring the packed terraces of E13 today, it's hard to imagine this as a rustic haven for second-homers. The fragments of green space which remain are mostly cemeteries.

East of Dagenham, Defoe's Essex changes character. Villages become more sparse, the marshes broader, and there are secrets to hide. Just before the Thames widens into an estuary, there is an ancient crossing point. On the southern, hilly shore is Gravesend, and on the northern, marshy shore, an isolated fort. In Defoe's day, the ferry between Gravesend and Tilbury made this one of the busiest crossings in the south east; the point at which the Thames intersected the land route between Dover and eastern England. Celia Fiennes was ferried with her horse across the Thames here en route to Canterbury and Dover in 1697, noting the 'fine fort' and 'a great flatt to the land full of watry ditches'. For ships about to leave England, this was where they were obliged to drop anchor for a 'second clearing' by customs officers. Failure to do so could lead to a volley of cannon-fire from Tilbury Fort.

Defoe guides his readers around Tilbury Fort with authority. It is, he says, 'the key of the river of Thames', defended on its landward side by a moat, and on its Thames frontage by a platform arrayed with 106 guns. Its bastions are 'the largest of any in England'. The fort is still intact, its stern angles rising in geometric cliffs over flat marshes slashed by dykes and pylon lines. Around the parade ground, field-guns of various eras have been deposited like items of military lost property. From the grassy rampart at the south-eastern corner of the fort, there is a clear view for three miles downstream.

There has been a fort here since the days of Henry VIII, but the massive structure Defoe described had been built between 1670 and 1683 in response to intermittent, costly wrestles with the Dutch over trade routes and domination of the seas. Three wars with our North Sea neighbours since 1652 had put the Thames and East Anglia in the front line. War in the east was never far from Defoe's mind. His verdict on Tilbury

Tilbury Fort, with Gravesend on the far shore of the Thames.

Fort (sensibly designed by a Dutch engineer who was intimate with both marshland and Britain's foe) was that 'they must be bold fellows who will venture in the biggest ships the world has heard of, to pass such a battery'.

One such 'bold fellow' was Defoe himself, for he describes in 'Letter 2' of the *Tour*, how he once sailed past the fort 'with some merchants in a large yacht bound to France.' On board, he said, was 'a great quantity of block-tin … and other goods, which had not been entered at the custom house.' The fog being thick, the captain decided that the ship would not be observed by the customs house. 'As for Gravesend or Tilbury-Fort,' reports Defoe with a smirk, 'they could see no more of us than they could of London-Bridge; and we drove in this fog undiscerned … and went clear away to Caen in Normandy without being visited.' Defoe fails to explain exactly what business he was conducting with the yachtsmen.

Smuggling was not the only questionable activity Defoe had engaged in here. Although he doesn't make any mention of it in the *Tour*, he owned a sizeable chunk of land right beside Tilbury Fort. At some point in the mid 1690s, he bought a freehold on these marshes and built himself a brick and pantile works. A map

A section of Chapman and André's map of 1777. Defoe's brick and tile works is thought to be the cluster of buildings between 'Ferry House' and 'Milk House', to the left of Tilbury Fort.

Publish'd as the Act directs Oct.r 1.st 1777. by John Chapman & Peter André.

printed in 1777 by John Chapman and Peter André shows only two clusters of buildings on West Tilbury Marsh, an area of a little over two square miles. One of them is marked 'Milk House'. The other – which appears to consist of three buildings just over half a mile from the fort – is thought to be Defoe's brick and tile works. The Court of Sewers Order Book reveals that Defoe was living on the water's edge; in 1698, he was ordered 'to cope 6 rods of ye sea wall next to Wickss marsh'. The year before, Celia Fiennes must have ridden right past Defoe's door. Though no record exists of an encounter between the two peripatetic Dissenters, one suspects that Fiennes would have regarded Defoe as a dodgy reprobate of the wrong class.

Having plotted bearings and distances from Chapman and André's map, I pedalled to and fro across this eerie polder searching for remnants of Defoe's marshland acres. His house and works must have stood between Ferry Road and an import terminal. Beside a glittering parade-ground of Korean cars, I eventually found a surviving pasture, still grazed by ponies. Perhaps it was Defoe's land.

'It was observable that great parts of the lands in these levels, especially those on this side East Tilbury, are held by the farmers, cow-keepers, and grazing butchers … and that they are generally stocked (all the winter half year) with large fat sheep.' Today, East Tilbury Marsh is stocked with large, fat automobiles.

\* \* \*

From Tilbury, Defoe followed the coast of Essex from one muddy estuary to another: from the Thames to the Crouch to the Blackwater. In winter, this can be a strange, deserted hinterland between the grey sea and London's frantic tendrils. I cycled the backroads between mudflat and field as if I was the last person on the planet. The land is so flat that it seems to merge imperceptibly with the sea. It's a coast with two personalities. At high tide the creeks and flats become blinding mirrors, and every unflooded object shines with reflected light. When the water recedes, wet mud sucks the light from the sky. Listen, and you can hear the gurgles and pops of dribbling water and escaping methane.

Defoe offered his readers two versions of coastal Essex. On the one hand, the low-lying marshes were 'justly said to be both unhealthy, and unpleasant', with a chronic impact on female mortality: 'I took notice,' he observes, 'of a strange decay of the sex here; insomuch, that all along this county it was very frequent to meet with men that had had from five to six, to fourteen or fifteen wives; nay, and some more; and I was informed that in the marshes on the other side of the river over-against Candy Island, there was a farmer, who was then living with the five and twentieth wife, and that his son, who was but about 35 years old, had already had about fourteen.'

Defoe's informant was 'a merry fellow' who claimed to have had about eighteen wives himself ('though I found afterwards he fibbed a little,' admits Defoe). Apparently, the men, being bred in the marshland, were adapted to its ills, but in a Darwinian response to their genetic survival, they'd taken to sourcing their wives from the hillier, healthier interior of Essex. These 'young lasses', related Defoe, would leave their uplands 'healthy, fresh and clear, and well', but once they reached the 'fogs and damps' of the marshes, they 'changed their complexion, got an ague or two, and seldom held it above half a year at most'. As each wife died, the bereaved husband would have to 'go to the uplands again, and fetch another'. Clearly a touch sceptical, and observing his informant's mirth, Defoe nevertheless had to agree that 'the fact, for all that, is certainly true'. In coastal Essex, he had noticed that he 'seldom met with ancient people among the poor, as in other places we do', and that a large proportion of the inhabitants had indeed migrated here from other parts of the country. A marshland 'ague' was actually malaria, which was so rife at the time that inhabitants of these estuarine shores had a death rate three times higher than those living inland.

But there was another Essex; an Essex which could make a man rich. This, explains Defoe, is what had attracted so many immigrants to the county. Here, amid the level, lush grasslands, a diligent worker could enjoy 'the advantage of good farms'. The climate was ideal for agriculture, and so was the location, right on London's coat-tails. Land and sea oozed with productivity: the Blackwater estuary provided 'the best and fattest, and the largest veal in England, if not in the world'. At the mouth of the Colne, fishermen took 'the largest oysters in England'. Essex estuaries provided London's markets with fish 'night and day'. Near Harwich, Defoe claims that he saw 'such shoals, or hills rather, of mussels that great boats might have loaded with them, and no

The malarial marshes of Essex. Long before Defoe, Camden had already warned in his *Britannia*, that the air here was 'none of the healthiest'. The Blackwater is now a Site of Special Scientific Interest.

miss have been made of them.' At Walton-on-the-Naze, copperas lay for the taking, strewn on the beach.

As a man who had tried to make his fortune from the marshes of Tilbury, Defoe knew a bit about turning mud to money. He had, he wrote 'examined into it critically in several places.' He does not however let on that he was using his East Anglian tour to further his 'examinations'. Having departed from London, he says, on April 3, 1722, documents have revealed that he agreed on August 6 to pay the Corporation of Colchester £1,000 for a 99-year lease on a farm and several hundred acres of land known as the 'Severalls', one mile north of the town in the parish of Mile End. The soil of the 'Severalls' was silty and sandy clay, with substantial stands of woodland. It wasn't a bad bit of real estate; far better in fact than his malarial swamp at Tilbury. (The brick and tile works had gone bust in 1703, when he was arrested for publishing an inflammatory pamphlet on Dissenting.) Colchester was home-turf for Defoe. A Protestant town in the Civil War, he had friends here, one of whom was the Rector of Mile End. William Smythies, a severe critic of the High Church, had retired from his post a couple of years before Defoe bought into Mile End, but William was succeeded by his very able son, Palmer. They would have been neighbours to Defoe, who had great plans for his new farm, intending to market timber for shipbuilding, and to produce cattle and corn, cheese and butter. Later, he used his Colchester estate as a base for trading oysters and honey, metal buttons, tanned leather and imported anchovies. Intriguingly, Celia Fiennes rode past the Severalls ('a sort of deep moore ground and woody') in 1698, as she made her way along the main road from Colchester to Ipswich.

Incomers with new money were changing the social profile of Essex. 'It is observable,' Defoe notes, 'that in this part of the country, there are several very considerable estates purchased, and now enjoyed by citizens of London, merchants and tradesmen.' He goes on to list an iron merchant named Weston, a wholesale grocer called Cresnor, a merchant named Olemus at Braintree and several others who had made a packet from trade. John Eyles, 'a wealthy merchant of London' had erected a 'noble stately fabric or mansion-house' outside Romford. 'I mention this,' continues

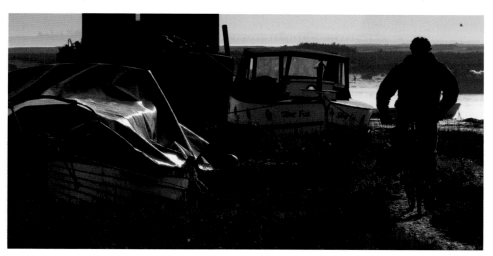

Mersea Island, the most easterly inhabited island in Britain. Defoe comments that he was 'not able to travel without many windings and indentures, by reason of the creeks, and waters'. The Essex coastline is the longest of any English county.

Defoe, 'to observe how the present increase of wealth in the city of London, spreads its self into the country, and plants families and fortunes, who in another age will equal the families of the ancient gentry, who perhaps were bought out.'

The incoming trading classes had adopted the Essex coast as their playground. Osea Island in the Blackwater estuary was 'well known by our London men of pleasure, for the infinite number of wild-fowl, that is to say, duck, mallard, teal and widgeon, of which there are such vast flights, that they tell us the island, namely the creek, seems covered with them, at certain times of the year, and they go from London on purpose for the pleasure of shooting; and indeed often come home very well loaden with game.' There was, of course, a risk associated with gallivanting in the marshes. It must be remembered, warned Defoe, 'that those gentlemen who are such lovers of the sport, and go so far for it, often return with an Essex ague on their backs, which they find a heavier load than the fowls they have shot.' Defoe claimed to be no fan of recreation. 'The tradesman that is the lover of pleasure,' he wrote in *The Complete English Tradesman*, 'shall be a poor man.' Osea Island is now the playground of a private landowner who keeps it out of bounds to the travelling classes, but neighbouring Northey Island has become a nature reserve and is currently home to 94,000 ducks, geese and wading birds. Both islands are connected to the mainland by ancient causeways which get inundated every tide; I lingered too long on Northey and pedalled from the estuary with panniers full of seawater.

Defoe's salt marshes are disappearing at an alarming rate; over one quarter of Essex's salt marshes have been lost since the 1970s, and projections suggest that by 2050, a further third will be swamped by rising sea levels.

* * *

The Britain portrayed by Defoe is a city state. All roads lead to London, and East Anglia is the pre-eminent province. The *Tour* is both a guidebook and an economic model intended to show 'how this whole kingdom, as well as the people, as the land, and even the sea, in every part of it, are employed to furnish something, and I may add, the best of every thing, to supply the city of London.'

A trickle-down effect from trading would bring wealth to the regions. London's booming population and markets needed 'provisions, corn, flesh, fish, butter, cheese, salt, fuel, timber, &c. and cloths also; with every thing necessary for building, and furniture for their own use, or for trades.' Towns not deriving an immediate income from trade with London benefited from servicing the capital. Brentwood, Ingatestone and Chelmsford all lay on the great road which cut diagonally across the county linking London and Colchester. These, observed Defoe, 'are large thoroughfare towns, full of good inns, and chiefly maintained by the excessive multitude of carriers and passengers, which are constantly passing this way to London, with droves of cattle, provisions, and manufactures for London.'

The key to shifting such vast volumes of produce and people was an efficient transportation network, but the roads were – as Celia Fiennes repeatedly discovered – in an appalling state. Rutted, pot-holed and periodically flooded, they were still preyed upon by highwaymen. Signposts were seldom seen and many rivers still required ferries, or fording. For much of the seventeenth century, road maintenance had been the responsibility of local populations, every able-bodied man being required to devote six days a year, unpaid, to repair work. It was a hopelessly inadequate system. As freight transport boomed, the country's roads disintegrated beneath increasing volumes of hooves and wheels.

At the time, just a scattering of turnpike trusts had been established, but Defoe was convinced that he had seen the makings of a road revolution. In Volume II of the *Tour*, he devoted his one appendix to turnpikes, opening his treatise with 'that great county of Essex', and the arterial highway linking London to Colchester, Ipswich and Harwich. It will come as a surprise to those who sit in tailbacks on the A12, biting their steering wheels, that Defoe rated this as the best road in England. Until the 1690s, this had been the worst road in the country, 'formerly deep' according to Defoe, and 'in time of floods dangerous, and at other times, in winter, scarce passable … the most worn with wagons, carts, and carriages; and with infinite droves of black cattle, hogs, and sheep, of any road (that leads through no larger an extent of country) in England.'

The Turnpike Act which transformed the 'Great Essex Road' was passed in 1695. Initially, toll gates were set up near Mile End, Romford and Ingatestone, which had the reputation (according to Defoe) for being 'the highest rated public toll in England'. Wagons were charged 12d, carts 8d, coaches 6d and single horsemen 1d. Defoe – whose new Colchester estate happened to border the turnpike – was thrilled: the Colchester road was 'now so firm, so safe, so easy to travellers, and carriages as well as cattle, that no road in England can yet be said to equal them'. In 2007, some four thousand drivers voted the A12 the worst road in Britain.

Defoe's tour through Essex ended at Harwich, whose harbour he reckoned to be 'one of the best and securest in England'. Defended from the Dutch by a fort and battery of guns which overlooked the only deep channel in the estuary, the harbour was strategically located at the busy end of the North Sea and, explained Defoe, 'of a vast extent … safe for all weathers … able to receive the biggest ships, and the greatest number that the world ever saw together; I mean, ships of war.' Defoe knew Harwich from earlier days. 'In the old Dutch War,' he recalls, 'great use has been made of this harbour; and I have known that there has been 100 sail of men of war and their attendants, and between three and four hundred sail of collier ships, all in this harbour at a time.'

*Above:* An engraving by Jan Kip from c.1700, showing Landguard Fort defending the entrance to Harwich Harbour. The town and the River Stour are on the left. Ahead is the River Orwell, leading inland to the port of Ipswich. The largest container port in the UK now occupies the right hand shore, between the fort and the mouth of the Orwell.

Gazing across the water from the old lighthouse on the east side of town, I tried to imagine what a flotilla of five hundred sailing ships would look like. While I was there, a wall of white steel slid across the scene. Turning with the slowness of a clock's minute-hand, a gigantic container ship moved with a low rumble towards the battlements of multi-coloured rectangles piled on the far shore. Today, Defoe's mega-harbour is the largest container port in the UK.

Defoe left Essex by boat, boarding a vessel at Harwich which would ferry him up the River Orwell into Suffolk, while his horse was taken around the estuary by land. As he sailed out into the broad expanse of the harbour, he left behind a county against which none could compare. Essex had it all: fertile land for corn and cattle, abundant fishing, villages suitable for traders and merchants, busy market towns, proximity to the capital, the best road in the country, one of the best harbours and the longest coastline of any county in England. Essex was the county of choice for merchants of fortune.

* * *

Out on the Orwell, in the space between two counties, Defoe lowered his mask for a moment. As the woods slipped by, the old man thought back to his early years, and the voyage he had taken from Harwich to Ipswich 'about five and thirty years before the present journey' (roughly 1687, then, before his bankruptcies and worst misadventures). Recalling how the Ipswich coal ships would get laid up each winter while the seas were dangerous and the nights long, he describes how the rigging and sails were carried ashore, the topmasts struck, and the vessels moored 'under the advantages and security of sound ground, and a high woody shore, where they lie as safe as in a wet dock'. It was, he reminisced, 'a very agreeable sight to see, perhaps two hundred sail of ships, of all sizes lie in that posture every winter.' Meanwhile, 'the masters lived calm and secure

*Right:* Tracking Defoe out of Harwich. He sent his horse around the estuary by land; *Clytie's* owners, Jo and Paul Masters, allowed me to park my bike in the cabin.

with their families in Ipswich; and enjoying plentifully, what in the summer they got laboriously at sea.' It was, he lamented, 'melancholy to hear, that there were now scarce 40 sail of good colliers that belonged to the whole town.'

Ipswich was still suffering the 'sloth' that Celia Fiennes had detected twenty-four years earlier, so Defoe set about providing a business plan for the port. The problem, paradoxically, was London, 'which sucks the vitals of trade in this island to itself'. If Ipswich could find 'some particular trade or accident to trade, which is a kind of nostrum to them, inseparable to the place', the town would have an independent source of commerce. By way of exemplars, he cited Yarmouth's herring fishery, Newcastle's coal trade, the Leeds clothing trade, Hull's corn trade, and Liverpool's trade with Virginia and West India. The solution for Ipswich, he decided, was Greenland. The port, enthused Defoe, was ideal for building and re-supplying whaling ships; the Orwell had plenty of space for 'the noisome cooker, which attends the boiling their blubber'; the town was conveniently close to the market for the oil; and the same wind which blew ships from the mouth of the Orwell, 'is fair to the very seas of Greenland'.

Fortunately for the local residents, Ipswich never did become Britain's blubber-capital, although the Novia Scotia yard did fit out two whale ships in the 1780s. Eventually, it was the Victorians who revived the port by dredging the river and excavating new docks. Today, Ipswich Docks are being reinvented yet again: the Victorian Customs House has survived, but the mills and warehouses have gone, and the malt house. In their place, tiers of apartments rise above the still water, with their bistro, brasserie and restaurant. Where sooty colliers moored deck-to-deck, glittering yachts nuzzle a pristine marina.

Eighteenth-century Ipswich just didn't get it right. Perhaps it was the wrong distance from London: it was less well placed than Essex to take advantage of London markets, yet too close to the capital to generate its own commercial identity. It is now thought that ship-building on the Orwell may have subsided because local builders were slower than those on the Thames and the Tyne to respond to the need for the longer, faster bulk-carriers copied from captured Dutch 'fly-boats'. Suffolk's

In Defoe's day, the wet dock was packed with coal brigs, or 'geordies', but by 1845, when the Customs House was opened, the wharves were lined with square-rigged grain ships. Today, two new marinas provide four hundred berths for a new generation of more frivolous seafarers.

commercial intuition seems to have been sharper inland. It was in this county, Defoe records, that the fattening of sheep and cattle on turnips was first practised, 'to the great enriching of the farmers', and it was Suffolk traders who invented a revolutionary waggon for the mass transportation of turkeys. Instead of marching the birds overland to the capital, the new horse-drawn, four-deckers could 'hurry away the creatures alive, and infinite numbers are thus carried to London every year'.

* * *

Travelling back to the coast of Suffolk, an undercurrent becomes detectable in Defoe's excitable economics. To find out why, his readers would have had to explore the first book Defoe wrote. Published in 1704, *The Storm* was Defoe's eyewitness account – corroborated by reports from various parts of the country – of what is still billed as the worst storm in British history. An extra tropical cyclone, it smashed into Britain on November 26, 1703. Over eight thousand people perished and Queen Anne declared that it was 'a Calamity so Dreadful and Astonishing, that the like hath not been Seen or Felt, in the Memory of any Person Living in this Our Kingdom'. Defoe was there. He saw it. The destruction was awesome. He writes of ships thrown together into tangled heaps on the Thames; of windmills catching fire because their sails were revolving so fast; of houses and churches dashed to pieces. Out at sea, there were countless shipwrecks, one of which Defoe would recycle for the opening passage of *Robinson Crusoe*. Once again, East Anglia had been in the front line.

The coast of Suffolk is low and friable, its soft cliffs alternating with muddy inlets and long banks of shingle dumped by the currents. The largest of these shingle banks is ten-mile long Orford Ness, 'a noted point of land,' informed Defoe, 'for the guide of the colliers and coasters.' The Ness suffered a Cold War takeover by the Ministry of Defence, who constructed a number of concrete 'pagodas' for testing nuclear firing mechanisms. It is one of the strangest places I know in the UK: a seemingly-barren stoney waste littered with military leftovers. It reminds me of a plain I once pedalled across in the north-western corner of the Gobi Desert. Historic maps show that the Ness grew in length by nearly three miles between the 1530s and 1600, but by 1736, it had mysteriously shortened to its sixteenth-century length. Defoe's 'dreadful tempest' had been so severe that it had wiped out three miles of shingle spit.

Sudden, catastrophic realignments of its shores are part of the East Anglian temperament. It was, after all, the last part of Britain to be connected to the continent by a land bridge. Further up the coast, Defoe called at ruined Dunwich, the Atlantis of the North Sea. Fable had embellished the scale of this disaster. 'Fame

Where the town of Dunwich once gazed down upon the ocean, there is now a bank of tide-washed shingle. In the last five hundred years, the shoreline has moved 500 metres further inland.

reports,' repeated Defoe, 'that once they had fifty churches in the town; I saw but one left.' Defoe was right about the nature of the loss, but not the detail. Dunwich once had eight churches (and three monastic houses), and back in the thirteenth century it had indeed been a thriving port, with a fleet of eleven warships, thirty-six trading ships and twenty-four fishing smacks. In a passage which displays Defoe's extraordinary ability to blend a local, topographic description with a broader, universal theme, he attributes the downfall of Dunwich to the fate which can overcome both places and people: 'towns, kings, countries, families, and persons, all have their elevation, their medium, their declination, and even their destruction in the womb of time, and the course of nature.' It's the kind of line which set the *Tour* centuries clear of Camden's and Leland's matter-of-fact topographies.

Dunwich, as it happened, had been built on sand. There is a new urgency along the coast of Suffolk these days: the lighthouse on Orford Ness is expected to topple into the sea in the next ten years, and the Victorian resort of Southwold (where Defoe had amused himself with conjectures on the flight paths of swallows) is bracing itself behind barricades of concrete and Norwegian granite. A mile away, a local resident called Peter Boggis has bulldozed 100,000 tons of sand and earth over the cliff in an attempt to protect the houses along the clifftop.

* * *

Defoe ritualised his arrival at Britain's extremities by dipping his foot – or the hoof of his horse – into the sea. Such dippings occurred at South Foreland and Selsey, Lands End and John O'Groats. But the first was Lowestoft, the most eastern point of mainland Britain.

Lowestoft is only seven miles from Yarmouth. The two ports are separated by a county boundary, and by feuding which goes back to at least the Middle Ages. At issue was competition over the market for herrings. The rivalry was frequently violent and caused many a head to be scratched in London. In 1596, Lord Burghley was petitioned by the seamen of Yarmouth for guard-ships, and at about the same time, Camden recorded that Yarmouth had become 'so rich and powerful, that they often engag'd their neighbours of Lestoff ... in Sea-fights'. Defoe of course found all this irresistible, relating 'a long and fabulous story' involving battles on land and sea

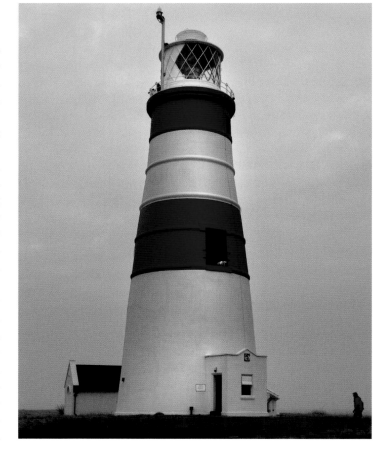

In the *Tour*, Orford Ness is 'a noted point of land for the guide of the colliers and coasters'. So fast is the shoreline eroding today, that the lighthouse – built in 1792 – is not expected to last more than another ten years.

THE WEST PROSPECT OF THE TOWN OF GREAT YARMOUTH IN NORFOLK

which culminate in defeat for Lowestoft and a terrible geomorphological reprisal: Yarmouth destroyed Lowestoft's trade by damming the mouth of the River Waveney to prevent it from reaching the sea. Instead, the Waveney takes a sudden turn to the north, and flows into the Yare. Defoe himself seems to have taken sides in the affair, failing to describe Lowestoft at all, yet heaping paragraphs of gushing praise upon Yarmouth. Could it be that Defoe, who had fought against the King at Sedgemoor, was swayed by the fact that, during the Civil War, Yarmouth had sided with Parliament and Lowestoft with the Royalists? Pedalling through Lowestoft looking for the docks, I found myself held up by traffic on Commercial Road, beside the boarded premises of 'Biggerland' and a hand-scrawled sign which read: 'SHOP CLOSED DUE TO FIRE PLEASE COME TO GRATE YARMOUTH'.

I spotted *Alert*'s thicket of aerials before I saw her. A Rapid Intervention Vessel, she is the latest ship in the Trinity House fleet, custom-built in Poland to keep Britain's sea-lanes safe and open. As we crashed through seas which periodically washed the bridge windows, the captain Roger Swinney, explained why the East Anglian coast was so lethal. It was, he said, a combination of factors: the shallow waters could create steep, broken seas; the sand banks had a habit of moving, so you couldn't trust your charts; and the shoreline was so low-lying that it was difficult to identify landmarks. In a small boat in big seas, you would only glimpse the land as you slid over the peak of a wave. Swinney pulled out an Admiralty Chart covering the Norfolk coast. 'Each of these circles is a wreck. Hundreds of them. There's an awful lot of metal down there.'

Defoe had no doubts about this coast. This was, he wrote in the *Tour*, 'one of the most dangerous and most fatal to the sailors in all England, I may say in all Britain.' The reason, he continues, is 'the great number of ships which are continually going and coming this way, in their passage between London and all the northern coasts of Great-Britain.' His impressions of the East Anglian coast had been formed in part

To Defoe, Great Yarmouth possesses 'the finest quay in England, if not in Europe', while merchants' houses lining the river 'look like little palaces, rather than the dwelling-houses of private men'. This engraving of the same era celebrates the port's commercial wealth.

Guardian of the sea: the Trinity House vessel *Alert*, passing through Yarmouth Roads, where the *John and Mary* lost her masts and almost foundered during the great storm of 1703. Off *Alert*'s starboard rail is Scroby Bank, notoriously exposed to north-easterly gales and covered by just seven metres of water. It is now the site of a windfarm which is expected to provide enough power for 41,000 homes.

from two terrible storms. The first, in around 1692, had wrecked (according to Defoe) 'above 200 sail of ships' and killed 'above a thousand people'. The second had been the far worse tempest of November, 1703. One of the most graphic descriptions to appear in Defoe's book about this extreme event came from the coast of Norfolk, where 'at least 400 Sail, being most of them Laden Colliers, *Russia* Men, and Coasters from *Lynn* and *Hull*' had anchored in Yarmouth Roads ahead of the 'intolerable Tempest'. The 'Roads' off Yarmouth were one of the most important anchorages on the east coast of England; a deep-water channel sheltered between the coast of Norfolk and an offshore sandbank called Scroby Sands. A haven in fair weather, Yarmouth Roads could be a deathtrap in the wrong wind. One of those caught in Yarmouth Roads that November night was the Master of the *John and Mary*, whose account bears an uncanny similarity to the first pages of *Robinson Crusoe*. The *John and Mary*'s skipper (who reckoned this coast to be 'the most dangerous Place between *London* and *Newcastle*') had anchored in Yarmouth Roads because a south-westerly wind prevented further progress towards the Thames. Hindered by an identical wind, the

Master of 'Bob' Crusoe's ship had done the same. The scenes are identical: the fleet of ships about them; the sudden freshening of the wind; the decision to strike the topmast and make 'all tite and fast upon Deck'; the setting of the sheet anchor; the breaking of the sea over the ship 'in such a vast Quantity'; the Mate's urgent requests to cut away the remaining masts … and the Master's eventual consent. The circumstances around them are similar too: other vessels being swept past, dismasted and sinking; ships firing their guns in distress; a longboat appearing from the maelstrom…

Till this point, Defoe is recording two parallel accounts; one tersely factual, the other grippingly fictional. Both come from the same source: the Master of the *John and Mary*. But with the appearance of the longboat, the two versions diverge. As the Master of the *John and Mary* recounts, what actually happened was that the longboat was swept from the night to collide with his ship, whereupon it was

Bob's longboat rows for the shore in *Robinson Crusoe*. Shipwrecks were as common then as car-wrecks are today, but far more catastrophic. In the storm of 1703, thousands of vessels were caught at sea. Defoe records that at least four hundred sailing ships were in Yarmouth Roads alone. One fifth of the sovereign fleet's seamen drowned.

'stav'd to pieces with the Blow' and its crew drowned. In *Robinson Crusoe*, the longboat somehow miraculously manages to rescue the entire crew of Bob's ship, and then to row them towards the shore of Norfolk.

Numbed 'partly with fright, partly with horror', Bob clung to the longboat as it was driven by the wind towards the shore 'almost as far as *Winterton Ness*'. On the sands, he could see figures running to assist the stricken boat as it was tossed towards land. But Bob and his shipmates were swept north-westwards, 'till being past the light-house at *Winterton*'. Here, observed Crusoe, 'the shore falls off to the westward towards *Cromer*, and so the land broke off a little of the violence of the wind.' In the lee of the Ness, the exhausted sailors were able to beach the longboat, 'tho' not without much difficulty'. Staggering ashore, they 'walk'd afterwards on foot to *Yarmouth*', where they were received 'as unfortunate men', and 'used with great humanity as well by the magistrates of the town, who assign'd us good quarters, as by particular merchants and owners of ships, and had money given us sufficient to carry us either to *London* or back to *Hull*, as we thought fit.' Crusoe, of course, headed towards London.

Out on *Alert*, it struck me that there is nothing comfortable, or scenic, about the North Sea in a Force Six. We were only a couple of miles off the coast, but I found it quite impossible to recognise any of the features I selected from my Ordnance Survey map. All I could see was a very thin, dark smear trapped between a vast expanse of lurching grey waves and an implacable grey sky. It was more reassuring to watch the instruments. On various screens, *Alert*'s location was being continuously-updated in 3D against the coast and the sea floor. Passing over the end of Scroby Sands, *Alert*'s scanners showed that the bank had shifted by fifty metres since the publication of the most recent Admiralty Chart.

Somewhere around 52 degrees 45 minutes north, Swinney turned *Alert* towards the coast. 'That,' he said, pointing towards the blurred shore, 'is Winterton.' Squinting through the spray out on the wing of the bridge, I could just make out Winterton church, poking like a piece of pencil lead above an indistinct skyline. I stuck my head back inside the bridge. 'Where's the Ness?' Swinney pointed over my shoulder: 'There. The surf.' Just a few hundred yards off our starboard beam was a long, dirty scratch across the chipped slate of the sea. Through binoculars, the standing waves looked big enough to flip a lifeboat. We were right above the spot where young Bob had been rowing for his life after watching his ship sink at the beginning of *Robinson Crusoe*. 'Have you ever run aground?' I asked Swinney. 'I have, yes,' he replied. 'Checking to find a shingle bank, and we found one. Quite successful really.'

Defoe found that the wreckage of ships was the main source of building material on the Norfolk coast. This is a housewreck at Happisburgh, on the north-east coast of Norfolk. As sea levels rise and storms increase, the winners and losers are being decided by Shoreline Management Plans. Some communities will be defended, others abandoned.

Viewed from the lurching deck of *Alert*, I could scarcely comprehend how sinister this coast seemed. I knew it well, but from the other side. When I was young, the place where Bob had stumbled ashore blinded by salt and fear was a perpetually-sunny paradise, with tidal lagoons for paddling and hours of sand to run across. I still go back, but it has changed. The cliff has moved so far inland that the cafe now hangs above an abyss, and the concrete tank obstacles which used to stand back from the cliff-edge are strewn on the beach like scattered dice.

Riding his horse along the shore from Winterton to Cromer wrenched from Defoe one of the most melancholic passages in the *Tour*. By the roadsides of this 'most dangerous and most fatal' coast, he found that 'the farmers, and country people had scarce a barn, or a shed, or a stable; nay, not the pales of their yards, and gardens, not a hogsty, not a necessary-house, but what was built of old planks, beams, wales and timbers, &c. the wrecks of ships, and ruins of mariners' and merchants' fortunes.' Defoe felt storms personally, for his first bankrupty had been triggered by the loss of goods at sea.

This shoreline of summery innocence is still on the front line. It was here, in 1953, that the sea broke through the dunes and drowned seven residents of Sea Palling. By the time the winds abated, the worst storm to hit Britain in the twentieth century had killed 307 people. The physical damage was colossal: 24,000 homes were damaged, gas works, power stations, oil refineries, cement works and 180,000 acres of land flooded. In Kings Lynn, the water rose by an astonishing 2.97 metres. With sea-levels rising, and the incidence of severe storms projected to increase, Crusoe's coast is horribly exposed to another catastrophe.

Darkness had fallen by the time *Alert* sailed slowly into the welcoming arms of Yarmouth's harbour moles. Unlike Lowestoft, Yarmouth's harbour is actually a two-mile section of river, lined on both sides by berths and occasional grand facades. Arriving from the black night of the North Sea, I could sense the source of Defoe's excitement. Here, running through the centre of this 'beautiful town', he found 'the finest quay in England, if not in Europe, not inferior even to that of Marseilles itself'. Tweaking the steering joystick with his fingers, Swinney eased *Alert* against the deserted quayside and the props fell silent. 'The ships ride here so close,' recorded Defoe, 'and as it were, keeping up one another, with their head-fasts on shore, that for half a mile together, they go across the stream with their bowsprits over the land, their bows, or heads, touching the very wharf; so that one may walk from ship to ship as on a floating bridge.'

\* \* \*

Nowhere in England were two trading centres of such importance so close together. Thirty-five miles up river from Yarmouth lay the city of Norwich. From all corners of Europe, ships could sail into the heart of Norfolk, and its teeming, industrious capital. Today, it is one of the calmest river journeys in Britain. For mile after mile, the river meanders in disorienting loops through a wetland of marsh and dyke and whispering reeds. Paddling a canoe, I was moving so slowly, so low on the water, that the land, that engineered platform crammed with buildings and highways, ceased to exist. Not a single road bridge crosses the Yare between Yarmouth and Norwich. Only fifty years earlier, I might have been overtaken by a freighter or two heading inland on the tide. Beyond Reedham, I had to drift for a moment while a raft bearing a couple of cars was hauled across the river. A sugar-beet factory sidled out of the fen. Eventually, I sneaked into Norwich past the football stadium, new apartment blocks and a derelict warehouse lined with grimy iron bollards. A flaking sign instructed ships' masters to take care with the wash from propellors.

Given that Norwich was second to London in size and importance, Defoe's description of the city is amazingly brief. But it seems there was a creditor to avoid. As it happened, Norwich was at the peak of its provincial success, with around twelve thousand looms and seventy thousand workers employed in the wool trade in and around the city. This was no cultural backwater, either. It was here, twenty years before Defoe peeped over the city walls, that the first provincial newspaper in the country appeared. By the end of the century, industrious Norwich, and flat-as-pancake Norfolk, would begin to succumb to the powerful water mills, cotton-spinners and coal fields of the north. But for the time being, Defoe can only see 'a face of diligence spread over the whole country'. It has all the virtues Defoe admires: Norfolk is densely populated, with 'great and spacious' market towns and farms 'exceeding fruitful and fertile, as well in corn as in pastures'. He is also thrilled to see large numbers of pheasants in the stubble, testimony, in his eyes, 'that the country had more tradesmen than gentlemen in it'. Gentlemen, you see, would have been wasting time shooting game. 'Indeed,' continues Defoe, 'this part is so entirely given up to industry, that what with the seafaring men on the one side, and the manufactures on the other, we saw no idle hands here, but every man busy on the main affair of life, that is to say, getting money.'

Out on the coast again, we pick up Defoe's hoof-prints at Cromer as he rides his horse 'on the strand or open shore to Weyburn Hope, the shore so flat that in some places the tide ebbs out near two miles'. Five hundred years after Gerald of Wales rode the sands of South Wales, some of Britain's 'coost roads' still ran below the tide line. Beyond Weybourne, he picked up the road to Cley ('where there are large salt-works, and very good salt made, which is sold all over the county, and some times sent to Holland, and to the Baltick'), to Wells ('a very considerable trade carried on with Holland for corn'). Out of sight of London, Defoe nods knowingly at 'the great trade' of smuggling between England and Holland. In Wells, he must have passed the new Customs House, which still has a wooden relief above the door depicting a customs officer with a drawn cutlass, leading his Revenue men in a charge towards a group of

The River Yare, Defoe's freight-route from Yarmouth to the heart of Norfolk, was used by sea-going ships until the 1960s.

smugglers unloading a smack onto packhorses. Throughout Norfolk, Defoe finds markets, industries and ports that are trading as never before. Records for the 'Glaven ports' of Blakeney, Cley and Wiveton show that the number of ships leaving for London each year had more than doubled between 1700 and 1722, from fourteen to thirty-four.

Up here in North Norfolk, there is a sense that Defoe has found what he is looking for: a level, productive land being tilled by diligent Puritans who feed the fruits of their labour to a network of active market towns and secure trading ports. His dreamscape was a world of visible endeavour. He liked his landscapes to seeth with motion and his coasts to be crowded with rigging. The landscapes he came to hate later in the *Tour* were the very ones which are treasured today for their undeveloped, natural state. Show Defoe a National Park, and he would have retched. Westmoreland is 'a country eminent only for being the wildest, most barren and frightful of any that I have passed over in England'. The horror he felt for Britain's uplands was exacerbated by the effects of the Little Ice Age, which frequently inflicted wintry conditions on travellers, even in high summer. Crossing the Pennines in August, Defoe was caught by a snowstorm. Riding past the Lake District, he miserably noted the 'unpassable hills, whose tops, covered with snow, seemed to tell us all the pleasant part of England was at an end.' The further south he is, the better his outlook.

John Speed's map of Norfolk, from 1610. Winterton Ness, the location of Crusoe's shipwreck, is shown as a pronounced promontory jutting into the shipping lane just north of Great Yarmouth. The River Ouse runs north through the Fens to the sea. In the corners are a city plan of prosperous Norwich, and a battle scene symbolising the periodic clashes between London's ruling elite and uppity Norfolk artisans.

A map drawn in 1725, showing the ground plan of Stourbridge Fair, which was developed in the early thirteenth century around a leper hospital close to 'Steers Bridge'. The chapel in the corner of the map dates from a few years before the birth of Gerald of Wales and can still be found below the embankment on Newmarket Road.

Defoe's coastal tour of East Anglia conveniently produces the perfect port. Kings Lynn is 'rich and populous and thriving'. It is 'beautiful, well built, and well situated'; it is militarily secure, and it has the best social scene in Norfolk: 'Here,' applauds Defoe, 'are more gentry, and is consequently more gaiety in this town than in Yarmouth, or even in Norwich it self; the place abounding in very good company.' (One wonders what Dan got up to in Lynn.) Above all else, Lynn scores higher than any other port outside London for its unique geographical location. Situated at the mouth of the River Ouse, it has 'a vast advantage in trade; namely, that there is the greatest extent of inland navigation here, of any port in England, London excepted. From here, a complex, dendritic system of navigable rivers squirmed far inland, supplying about six counties wholly, and three counties in part, with their goods, especially wine and coals.' Lynn had the reputation of bringing in more coal than any sea-port between London and Bristol.

From Kings Lynn, Defoe left the coast and followed the Ouse inland across the Fens to Cambridge, and the climax of his East Anglian journey. It wasn't the University which Defoe wanted to tell his readers about, but 'Sturbridge Fair … not only the greatest in the whole nation, but in the world'. Defoe devoted three times more space in the *Tour* to Stourbridge Fair, than he did to Cambridge and its University. Not even the international fairs of Leipzig or Frankfurt, or Nuremberg or Augsburg, could – Defoe crowed ('if I may believe those who have seen them all') – better Stourbridge Fair. Here on the meadows beside the Cam were arrayed 'goldsmiths, toyshops, braziers, turners, milliners, haberdashers, hatters, mercers, drapers, pewterers, china-warehouses, and in a word all trades that can be named in London; with coffee-houses, taverns, brandy-shops, and eating houses, innumerable, and all in tents, and booths.' Stourbridge was a lot more than an open-air superstore; this was Britain on exhibition; the trade fair and showcase for a modern economy.

The Fair can still be traced on the streets of suburban Cambridge. The Wool Fair and White Leather Fair are beneath the scrap yard and railway line by Swann Road. The Horse Fair took place on the southern side of Stourbridge Common. The Oyster Fair has been buried by the tarmac of what has become 'Oyster Road'. The main street which used to run through the heart of the Fair, is now a residential road named 'Garlic Row'. If the ghost of Daniel Defoe is to be found anywhere, it is here on the banks of the Cam, recording the fruits of diligence. He died in debt, and on the run, five years after the final volume of the *Tour* was published.

Trailing Defoe back towards London and the end of his first 'Letter', I found myself inspired by a man I'd once regarded as a contradictory, gifted loser. The *Tour* is a profoundly optimistic, imaginitive work written by an outsider who felt compelled to see the best in his country. He had survived more catastrophes than can usually be compressed into a single life, and he rode the shires with the joyful curiosity of a traveller who knew he was lucky. Britain's natural resources and entrepreneurial spirit appeared unlimited. In the golden dawn of the 1720s, anything and everything appeared possible for 'the greatest trading country in the world'. Defoe's dream came true. We dug, forged, manufactured and traded our way to economic supremacy. And then environmental exhaustion. Faced with the challenge to promote a sustainable economic system, this wonderful, tempestuous man would be sharpening his quill.

'I must not omit here also to mention that the river Grant, or Cam, which runs close by the N.W. side of the fair in its way from Cambridge to Ely, is navigable, and that by this means, all heavy goods are brought even to the fair-field, by water carriage from London, and other parts; first to the port of Lynn, and then in barges up the Ouse, from the Ouse into the Cam, and so, as I say, to the very edge of the fair.' The site of Stourbridge fair has partially survived as Stourbridge Common, in the north-eastern suburbs of Cambridge.

# William Gilpin *1770*

## *One man in a boat*

Map describing places associated with

# WILLIAM GILPIN'S

*"Observations on the River Wye
and Several Parts of South Wales, etc."
and showing route taken during his
tour of 1770*

WALES

N
W E
S

0   10   20   30
MILES

*Plynlimon
2467'*

*Severn*

Aberystwyth
*Rheidol*
Devil's
Bridge
Llangurig
Rhayadar
Builth Wells
*Wye*
Hereford
Llandovery
Hay-on-Wye
Brecon
*Black
Mountains*
Ross-on-Wye
Trecastle
*Dinefwr
Castle*
Llandeilo
Gloucester
Abergavenny
Monmouth
*Crickley
Hill*
Raglan
Castle
Tintern
Abbey
Neath
*Usk*
*Cotswold Hills*
Margam
Newport
Pyle
Bridgend
Caldicot
Castle
Chippenham
Cowbridge
Cardiff
Bristol
Marlborough
Bath

---

Ross on
Wye
From
Gloucester
Goodrich
Castle
Whitchurch
*Symonds Yat*
Lydbrook
*River
Monnow*
*Coldwell
Rocks*
Monmouth
*Forest of
Dean*
Whitebrook
St Briavels
Brockweir
*Tintern Abbey*
To
Monmouth
*Wynd
Cliff*
*Piercefield
Park*
Chepstow

0   1   2   3
MILES

## MAP OF LOWER WYE
### SHOWING THE COURSE OF
### GILPIN'S VOYAGE OF 1770

- - → Route by land
- - → Route by water
○ Town or city
Hill or Mountain
Castle
Abbey or
Cathedral
Forest

When the Reverend William Gilpin stepped aboard a rowing boat at Ross-on-Wye in 1770, he had no idea that his adventurous river voyage would lead to his ordination as 'The High Priest of the Picturesque'. The coldest period of the Little Ice Age had ended half a century earlier, the furnaces of the Industrial Revolution had just been fired, and Britain's landscape was entering an era of cataclysmic change. In shaping the taste for nature and for ruins, Gilpin accidentally became one of the most influential travellers of the eighteenth century. Published in 1783, *Observations on the River Wye* prepared the way for 'the Romantics', and allowed the Wye to stake its claim as the birthplace of British tourism.

\* \* \*

Ten days after seeing the Wye trickle from a spring in the mountainous heartland of Wales, I angled the prow of the canoe towards a dark arrowhead in the current and felt the hull surge towards the jaws of the gorge. Reefs of rocks reached out from each bank towards a space where the river appeared to fall over an edge. The little boat tilted and bucked. Water slopped inboard. Trees and rocks flashed by. Then all was calm. From somewhere in the sheer woods came the hollow knocking of a woodpecker. For two other-worldly miles, the Wye twisted through a green chasm. Each side of the river, tiers of foliage and rock scrambled skyward for six-hundred feet. There were no roads, and except for a couple of buildings and tracks, little sign of human presence.

You never quite know what you're looking for on a journey, but I knew just then that I'd caught a glimpse of my visionary guide. 'The first source of amusement to the picturesque traveller,' he had written, 'is the *pursuit* of his object – the expectation of new scenes continually opening, and arising to his view.' Gilpin's traveller was an explorer. He was searching for beauty. And the essence of that beauty could be found in nature. The more natural the landscape, the closer you were to the object of your quest. 'We suppose the country to have been unexplored,' he wrote. 'Under this circumstance the mind is kept constantly in an agreeable suspense. The love of novelty is the foundation of this pleasure.'

The man who'd brought me to the Wye has been caricatured as one of the most incompetent travellers ever to grace an English byway. In the course of his various misadventures, he topples into mud and water, mistakes a gentleman's house for an inn, is pursued by a bull, and gets tied to a tree by highwaymen. Memorably, he is duped into buying a blind horse, and of course he gets lost. 'Dr Syntax' was the creation of Thomas Rowlandson and Dr William Combe; in Gilpin, the old travelling elite could amuse themselves with the quaint notion that the middle classes had

*Previous pages:*
**Between Ross-on-Wye and Goodrich Castle**

discovered tourism. Syntax was well-meaning, sensible, and yet doomed to ridicule by the absurdity of his quest. That quest was to find the perfect view:

> *I'll make a* TOUR *– and then I'll* WRITE IT,
> You well know what my pen can do,
> And I'll employ my pencil too:-
> I'll ride and *write*, and *sketch* and *print*,
> And thus create a real mint;
> I'll *prose* it here, I'll *verse* it there,
> And *picturesque* it ev'ry where,
> I'll do what all have done before;
> I think I shall – and somewhat more.

Most who bought *The Tour of Dr. Syntax in search of the Picturesque* knew that the catastrophe-prone curate was based upon the one-time vicar of Boldre and 'apostle of the Picturesque'.

William Gilpin was born in a castle of blood-red sandstone in sight of the Lake District. Scaleby's gentle vale has been altered somewhat by Carlisle Airport and the M6, but if you know which roads to take, there are still corners of eighteenth-century tranquility. A third-generation artist, young Gilpin knew them well. Amid the copses and fields of barley and oats, Hadrian's Wall ran along the far side of Brunstock Beck, just a mile from the castle's dishevelled walls. Scaleby had been battered during the Civil War, and partially-restored by the time Gilpin was born in 1724. On a clear day, young William would have seen the southern horizon crinkled with Lake District peaks. He was schooled locally in Carlisle, then sent to the Free Grammar School at St

The Gilpin family home, Scaleby Castle, thought to have been constructed using stone liberated from Hadrian's Wall. When the Gilpins bought Scaleby after the Restoration, the castle was in a ruinous state. By the time William was born, in 1724, the south wing (seen here, facing the camera) had been restored. The moat was probably excavated in the fourteenth century.

Bees on the Cumberland coast, and finally to Queen's College, Oxford. Coincidentally, Gilpin left Oxford in the year – 1744 – that a young Welsh gentleman called Thomas Pennant matriculated at Queen's. Neither student appears to have drawn measurable benefit from University, Gilpin regretting the time 'squandered on the appearance of doing something more', while Pennant failed to graduate at all. Between them, this pair of drop-outs would play a leading role in forming a bridgehead between Britain's ten-thousand year history of exploration and the age of tourism.

Two years after graduating, Gilpin was ordained as a deacon and appointed curate of Irthington, the neighbouring village to Scaleby. It was an exciting time to move in ecclesiastical circles; the securities offered by the Toleration Act of 1689 had given Britons an extraordinary liberty of worship. A heretical spirit was sweeping the country, and Christianity was being exchanged for a new belief in the divinity of nature. In Gilpin's low-Church, liberal perspective, proof of God's existence could be found in the natural world, rather than through scripture alone. Like many of his age, he had been influenced by the amiable philosopher Lord Shaftesbury, to whom the universe exhibited all the signs of divine design. God, the artist-creator, had brought 'beauty' to Earth through harmony, proportion and order. Freed from the old rigidities of religion ahead of the game, Britons turned to their landscapes. In literature, the arts and design, nature would set the agenda for the next hundred years. Gilpin found himself in the midst of a spiritual revolution. One of the most exciting laboratories for landscape experimentation was a garden in Buckinghamshire.

Set in verdant farmland, Stowe's owners had created an incredible themed park dotted with classical temples, bridges, lakes and a 'Shrine of British Worthies'. Visitors were enchanted, and educated. Accessible from London, and vigorously promoted through its own guidebook and the engravings of Jacques Rigau, Stowe was a must-see for England's elite. Here, one's taste – and moral worth – could be improved and updated in a single, fashionable ramble through a terrestrial paradise. Stowe was a thrilling work-in-progress. When Celia Fiennes called by fifty years earlier, she had found Sir Richard Temple's new gardens pleasant, if unremarkable ('replenished with all the curiosityes or requisites for ornamental pleasure and use'), but between 1712 and the 1740s, Temple's son Viscount Cobham had devoted his wife's brewing fortune to transforming the estate. Cobham and his designer, Charles Bridgeman, broke all the rules, and invited nature into the garden. They achieved this with a ha-ha, an ingenious new type of barrier which allowed unobstructed views to be appreciated from a house through to the countryside beyond. Instead of fences and hedges, livestock was excluded from the man-made gardens by a hidden, steep-sided ditch. Cattle and sheep could be seen grazing in what appeared to be an extension of the gardens. At Stowe, the ha-ha was just the start. Cobham had banished all the formalities inherited from Versailles. Out went symmetry and manicured topiary; in came serpentine paths and constant references to the natural form of the landscape. The carefully placed monuments and temples expressed the ideals of his time. Stowe's head gardener since 1741 had been a Northumbrian called Lancelot 'Capability' Brown, who had been working with Cobham for several years on the 'Grecian Valley', an ambitious plan which included a grass amphitheatre and a Greek temple. Brown's 'great merit', Gilpin would write later, 'lay in pursuing the path which nature had

'A View to the Grotto of the Serpentine River in the Alder Grove at Stowe', from George Bickham's illustrated guide to the gardens, published in 1750. In the foreground on the right is the Temple of Contemplation. 'Water,' observed Bickham, 'is of as much Use in Landscape, as Blood is in a Body'.

marked out.' One of Stowe's many fans was the poet of the age, Alexander Pope, whose *Epistle to Cobham* made Stowe a focal point of the literary landscape. 'All gardening,' declared Pope, 'is like landscape painting.' For its genteel visitors, Stowe was a window on nature. Safely behind the ha-ha, the leisured classes could observe the form of the countryside without the risk of stepping in mud.

Gilpin soon found his way to Stowe, visiting the gardens in 1747, shortly after returning to Oxford for his MA. He left Buckinghamshire as an author and a visionary:

'Our Gardens for the most Part were laid out in so formal, aukward, and wretched a Manner, that they were really a Scandal to the very Genius of the Nation... But Stow, it is to be hoped, may work some Reformation: I would have our Country Squires flock hither two or three times in a Year, by way of Improvement, and after they have looked about them a little, return Home with new Notions, and begin to see the Absurdity of their clipped Yews, their Box-wood Borders, their flourished Parterres, and their lofty Brick-walls.'

Published anonymously in 1748, when Gilpin was just twenty-four, *Dialogue upon the Gardens of the Right Honourable the Lord Viscount Cobham at Stowe* was a sixty-page, trial airing of his views on the nature of landscapes.

Gilpin's 'new notions' were nourished over the next twenty years in the theatre of education, first as a teacher and then as headmaster of Cheam School for Boys in Surrey. Despite the fact that his *Dialogue* was re-published in 1749 and 1751, he seems to have been reluctant to return to print. Devoted to his family and his school, he preferred to circulate his various authorial 'amusements' in manuscript form among friends and relatives, rather than hawk his wares in the market-place. 'The hazard and expense,' he explained, 'had rather a formidable appearance.' When one of his fans, the Duchess of Portland, sent Gilpin a generous subscription of one hundred pounds, he squirmed free of her financial embrace: 'I could not accept her grace's kindness,' he recalled, 'as I was still afraid of an *engagement with the public.*'

Eventually, in 1768, aged forty-four, Gilpin was persuaded to send one of his manuscripts to the London publisher J. Robson. *An Essay upon Prints* was a remarkable little book. Confident, authoritative, and written with flair and clarity, it was the first English guide to print collecting, and one of the earliest publications to address engraving as a fine art. Again, Gilpin declined to put his name on the title page, and the preface – written apparently by a third party – is almost apologetic: 'The following work,' it begins, 'hath lain by the author at least fifteen years, in which time, as nothing had appeared upon the subject, he took the liberty to offer it to the public with whatever faults it might have.' Tip-toeing towards the art fraternity, he unfurled his intention to 'put the elegant amusement of collecting prints upon a more rational footing'. He began by listing the terms which should be used to describe prints: 'Composition', 'Design' … 'Expression', 'Effect', 'Spirit' … 'Manner' and 'Picturesque'. This was Gilpin's first use in print of the word. Until then, 'picturesque' had been taken to mean 'graphic' or simply 'pictorial'. A couple of years later, when Pennant referred to the 'picturesque and magnificent scenery' beside the river at Dundonnell, he meant that it looked like a picture. But to Gilpin, the word was fundamentally associated with the wonder of God's Creation; 'a term expressive of that peculiar kind of beauty, which is agreeable in a picture.'

In the pages which followed, Gilpin slashed and hurrahed his way through Europe's great masters. Rembrandt's landscapes had 'very little to recommend them'; Berghem had 'genius truly pastoral' when it came to cows; Sadler's landscapes were 'picturesque and romantic' although their manner was 'dry and disagreeable'; Piranesi was unbeatable for his ability to capture 'a defaced capital, a ruined wall, or broken fluting'. Claude Lorraine may have been surprised to learn that his etchings were 'below his character'; his talents, opined the Reverend Gilpin, 'lay upon his palette'. Who, then, won the 'landskip' contest? Well, it was Anthonie Waterloo. 'Waterlo,' announced Gilpin, 'is a name beyond any other in landscape.' The Flemish etcher had come closer to nature than anyone: 'His subjects are perfectly rural,' enthused Gilpin. 'Simplicity is their characteristic... A coppice, a corner of a forest, a winding road, or a stragling village... Every object that he touches, has the character of nature.'

*An Essay upon Prints* was a runaway success. Translations into French, German and Dutch followed, and Gilpin's 246-page guide became a standard reference for print connoisseurs. A copy even made its way into the library of Thomas Jefferson. Fashionable society seemed ready for some rules.

\* \* \*

In this print showing a ruined estate on a riverbank, Gilpin's favourite printmaker, Anthonie Waterloo, produced a study of picturesque detail, a full century before Gilpin took to the water.

Tourists on the road, in a pencil sketch by Paul Sandby (1725/6–1809), a topographical artist who is now recognised as the first in England to experiment with the aquatint process, later used by Gilpin's nephew, William Sawrey Gilpin, to illustrate *Observations on the River Wye*.

Gilpin took to the road the summer that his bestseller began pouring from London bookshops. In 1768, he toured Kent. In 1769, he toured Essex, Suffolk and Norfolk. Then in 1770, he headed west, to the river Wye and south Wales. Other tours covered Cumberland and Westmorland, the Scottish Highlands, south-west England and Wales.

Britain was now in the throes of unprecedented change. The Industrial Revolution had kicked into gear in the 1760s and – encouraged by a surge in food supply and mass production of everyday necessities – cities and towns were expanding fast: between 1750 and 1800, the population would soar from around 6–7 million to 9 million. As James Cook set sail for the Antipodes, and Thomas Pennant sailed off to explore the Highlands of Scotland, England discovered tourism. With much of the continent a war zone, the Grand Tour of Europe was being spurned in favour of domestic adventures. England offered brisk, low-risk, affordable encounters with an exciting range of unfamiliar landscapes.

The new 'tourists' were driven by the thrill of exploration. 'We travel for various purposes,' explained Gilpin, 'to explore the culture of the soils, to view the curiosities of art, to survey the beauties of nature, and to learn the manners of men, their different politics and modes of life.' On the itineraries of these summer tours of enlightenment would be Benedictine ruins and megalithic stones, industrial works, natural wonders, houses and gardens. Typical among these pioneers was the Honourable John Byng. After twenty years in Guards' regiments, he landed a second career with the Inland Revenue, which gave him the chance to take two- or three-month tours each summer. Byng lived for his travelling: 'Oh, that I had stayed in London till this day,' he exclaimed after six weeks on the road, 'and that now my holidays were to begin, for this was a summer's day, with a high and blue sky.' Gilpin's journeys may be remembered as 'art tours', but they were also great fun.

Conditions for travel in England had never been better. The Little Ice Age had thawed in the early 1700s, and the travelling season was longer than it had been for Fiennes and

Defoe. The road network was enjoying an unprecedented makeover, with the four middle decades of the eighteenth century seeing an explosion in turnpike trusts. When Defoe was travelling in the 1720s, the average number of turnpike acts passed each year by Parliament was a little over eight. In the twenty years from 1751, the annual figure rose above forty. Provincial cities like York and Exeter, which used to be three or four days' travel from London in the 1720s, were suddenly little more than twenty-four hours away. The rate at which horse-drawn coaches could travel also increased with the introduction of Arab bloodstock, while comfort (and speed) was increased as flexible steel springs gradually replaced leather braces. With improving roads came better inns and a range of travellers' aids. 'We are tolerably well accompanied,' observed Byng as he set out in June, 1781, 'with touring, road books, maps etc.' It is a measure of just how far and fast you could travel that Gilpin undertook his 1770 tour of the Wye and south Wales in just a fortnight, during which time he covered around four hundred miles.

Gilpin returned from these short summer tours with copious notes and sketches which he assembled into finished manuscripts. *On the Lakes and Mountains of the Northern Parts of England* grew into an eight-volume monster containing 830 pages and 249 sketches. He was a publisher's nightmare: 'I have not the most distant idea of printing them,' he informed London publisher William Mason, the man who would eventually tease Gilpin into print again. Mason encouraged Gilpin 'to make an essay in a smaller work of the same kind'. The 'smaller work' Gilpin chose to present to Mason was the account of his journey of 1770 down the River Wye. Included with the text were fifteen prints derived by Gilpin's nephew from original sketches. Nevertheless, it wasn't until 1783 that the first one appeared (the date on the book's title page is 1782, but publication had been delayed due to problems with the aquatint illustrations). *Observations on the River Wye and Several Parts of South Wales, etc. Relative Chiefly to Picturesque Beauty* would change the way Britons viewed their landscapes.

More Grampian than Cambrian: an aquatint that appears in the early pages of *Observations on the River Wye* to illustrate Gilpin's picturesque rules.

\* \* \*

Gilpin's quest for the picturesque began at Heathrow: 'Crossing Hounslow Heath from Kingston in Surrey,' he writes, 'we struck into the Reading road…' With pauses to condemn the 'heavy' beeches dotted around Capability Brown's park at Caversham House, and to scrutinise views of the Thames ('nothing very interesting'), he passed through Oxford and began the long, gentle climb westward on the Gloucester turnpike through the Cotswolds until the land abruptly fell away to reveal a breathtaking panorama. Here, on Crickley Hill, Gilpin presented his readers with a prospect of the journey ahead.

The landscape which amazed Gilpin with its 'singularity and grandeur', seen from his vantage point on Crickley Hill. Beyond the Vale of Gloucester are the border uplands surrounding the Wye.

Crickley Hill had been a vantage point for thousands of years before Gilpin peered over its brow. A sharp, triangular promontory formed from Jurassic coral beds, it juts west from the scarp slope of the Cotswolds, hovering 600 foot above a vast green vale. The remains of Stone Age ramparts – scattered with arrowheads and carrying evidence of a burned palisade – lie beneath one of the highest surviving Iron Age bulwarks in Britain. By the 1770s, the view from Crickley Hill was familiar to any on the London–Gloucester coach road who'd dared to snatch a glance from the window before tipping over the edge and skidding alarmingly into the Vale of Gloucester. But few would have dismounted and asked themselves what they were looking at. 'I know not,' gasped Gilpin, 'that I was ever more struck with the singularity and grandeur of any landscape.'

Gilpin recognised the Cotswolds as an unusual landform. Where many hill ranges had slopes of equivalent gradient on both sides, the Cotswolds were different. The

Gloucester, viewed from the hilltop at Over, looking back across the West and East Channel of the Severn. The scarp of the Cotswolds can be seen running along the horizon, with Crickley Hill rising directly behind the cathedral. Crossing the foreground on Over Causeway is the new turnpike that Gilpin followed as he left Gloucester bound for Ross-on-Wye.

beds of hard limestone which overlay this part of England had been tilted downward to the east and south-east, and raised in the west, where the underlying softer rocks had been eroded to create an asymmetric hill range. When nature, explained Gilpin, 'raises a country through a progress of a hundred miles, and then breaks it down at once by an abrupt precipice into an expansive vale, we are immediately struck with the novelty and grandeur of the scene.' You only have to compare his emotional response to Gloucestershire's geology with that of the Honourable John Byng to see the novelty of Gilpin's viewpoint. Arriving at the same spot eleven years later, the retired Lieutenant Colonel reacted rather differently: 'This is a truly fine prospect,' he conceded, 'yet prospects please me but for an instant, for they fatigue my eyes and flurry my nerves, and I always wish to find myself in the tranquil vale beneath.'

In an age before aerial views, it was the sheer immensity of the panorama which so moved Gilpin. 'Perhaps nowhere in England a distance so rich,' he avowed, 'and at the same time so extensive, can be found.' What he could see was perhaps a twenty- or thirty-mile stretch of the Vale of Severn. 'The eye was lost in the profusion of objects which were thrown at once before it, and ran wild over the vast expanse with rapture and astonishment…' Two or three miles to the north, the town of Cheltenham lay spread beneath their boots. Far up the vale rose the twin eminencies of Bredon Hill and the Malvern Hills, and between them Tewkesbury's church, 'bosomed in wood'. On a clear day, fancied Gilpin, one might even spy the towers of Worcester. To the west lay Gloucester, also between two hills. But the furthest and most inviting objects in this enormous prospect were far to the west, where 'a distant forest-view' and a thin line of Welsh mountains united the '*determined form*' of a slender, yet discernible, body of water; 'an arm', ventured Gilpin, 'of the sea.'

This Cotswold scarp was England's Darien peak; the natural barrier dividing the waters of the Thames from those of the Severn. Crossing the watershed, Gilpin clattered down the turnpike into Gloucester, where he took a quick look at the cathedral, and then pressed on towards the river which had lured him from London.

* * *

Those of watery sensitivities still lose their hearts to the Wye. Geology and climate have given it beauty, and the currents of human affairs have given it a story to tell. Although Gilpin's tour concentrated on a thirty-eight mile section of the lower Wye, he managed to include the entire river in his book, by recycling a description from a borrowed journal. The river rises just a couple of miles from the Severn, in the heart of Wales on 'vast, wild, and unfurnished' Plynlimon.

Tumbling through Llangurig and Rhayader to Builth Wells, it takes a sudden turn towards England at Llyswen, after its southerly flow is blocked by the Black Mountains. Gilpin

The Wye rises near the 2,467-foot summit of Plynlimon, just two miles from the source of the Severn. 'The two springs,' observes Gilpin, 'are nearly alike, but the fortunes of rivers, like those of men, are owing to various little circumstances, of which they take the advantage in the early parts of their course.'

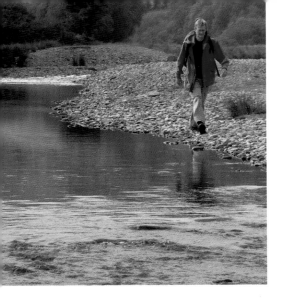

wondered whether this upper section of the river might be the most beautiful part of the entire Wye, and in many ways, he was right. Until it turns to skirt the Black Mountains, the river still behaves like a mountain stream, running fast and clear through wooded clefts. When it's not jostling over shingle, or falling over lips of bedrock, the river tends to pond into black pools where salmon rest in the shadows of overhanging trees. I have never seen trees like the oaks on the Wye; they seem as old as the river itself, with immense, complicated crowns which seem to reflect the Wye's own, infinitely-complex, dendritic basin, fed by ever-smaller tributaries which reduce to invisibility somewhere in the Welsh heartland. It is in his depiction of trees, writes Gilpin in his *Essay upon Prints*, that his great hero, Anthonie Waterloo, 'particularly excels'.

The character of the Wye is changing by the time it ripples across the border at Hay, and begins to meander uncertainly eastwards past Clifford Castle and Merbach Hill, to the red-brick bridge at Bredwardine. After cutting under the precipitous cliff known as 'The Scar', even lazier loops unravel past Capability Brown's park at Moccas, to Hereford, where another change of direction sets the Wye on a collision course with a band of limestone, and a spectacular rejuvenation.

When Gilpin first caught sight of the river, that summer's day in 1770, the Wye was a little-known backwater. Gerald of Wales described the course of the river so accurately from its source on Plynlimon, past the castles at Hay and Goodrich to the Forest of Dean ('full of deer and where iron-ore is mined'), that he seems to speak from first-hand knowledge. But Celia Fiennes never saw the river, and Daniel Defoe

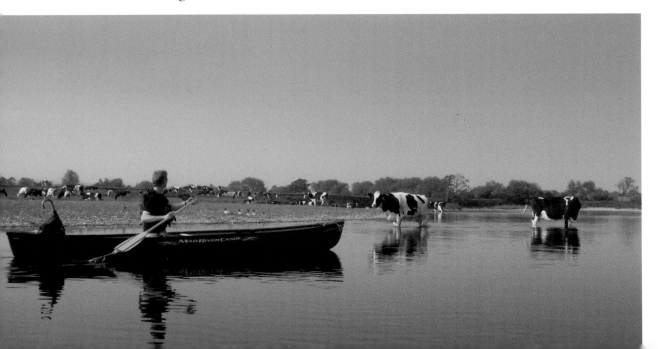

had been unable to reach the Wye on his great tour because of 'the badness and danger' of the ferries over the River Severn. Instead, he had relied on memories from an earlier visit; and those memories were not going to trigger a rush of well-heeled sightseers. 'Hereford,' he warned, 'is truly an old, mean built, and very dirty city, lying low, and on the bank of the Wye, which sometimes incommodes them very much, by the violent freshes that come down from the mountains of Wales.' The Wye's huge drainage area of 1,609 square miles, and various constrictions, cause wildly temperamental water-levels; droughts can reduce the river to a placid stream, while downpours in the Welsh hills can fill myriad tributaries to brimming and turn the Wye into a solid, brown torrent. Bridges over the river are infrequent, and high-arched. In Leland's day, there were no bridges at all between Builth Wells and Hereford, and only one – at Monmouth – between Ross and the sea; Chepstow's timber bridge had been torn away. Despite the roads revolution, the borders were an infamous brown hole on the transport map. Packhorses, rather than wagons, were still being used to shift goods across Herefordshire, and most of the roads were medieval sloughs. When the agricultural writer Arthur Young came this way shortly before Gilpin, he warned that the roads from Chepstow were 'mere rocky lanes, full of hugeous stones as big as one's horse, and abominable holes'. Another traveller, attempting to reach Tintern Abbey overland from Monmouth in the late 1700s, complained of 'hollow and uncouth tracks, seldom attempted by any carriage but those of the natives'.

The town which would soon claim to be the tourist capital of the Wye was small but strategically situated on the main road between the cathedral cities of Gloucester and Hereford. Ross-on-Wye had developed and prospered around one of the few bridging points on the river, and in the 1720s, it became one of the first market towns in England to be connected by turnpike to a city. Ross, recorded Defoe, was renowned for its cider, its iron-ware, and for its 'monstrous fat woman' whose waist measured three yards. Defoe – who could never resist a revolting aside – added that Ross-on-Wye's giantess 'was obliged to have a small stool placed before her, to rest her belly on, and the like'. Reading Defoe, eighteenth-century travellers could be forgiven for thinking that the Wye was the home of the grotesque, rather than the picturesque. But Defoe had missed the town's star turn. If he'd managed to reach Ross during the travels which formed the basis of his great *Tour*, rather than used recollections from an earlier visit, he'd have met an extraordinary man called John Kyrle. Immortalised as 'The Man of Ross' in 1732 by Alexander

Morden's 1695 map of Herefordshire, showing the mid-section of the Wye, as it meanders from Hay on the Welsh border, generally eastward through Hereford, and then south to Ross and beyond. In Gilpin's day, the two most important transport arteries in the county were the new turnpike from Gloucester to Hereford, and the Wye.

John Kyrle's 'heav'n directed spire' rising above Ross-on-Wye. The little wharf in front of the Hope and Anchor is still a point of departure for the 'Wye Tour'.

Pope, Kyrle had died in 1724, the year Defoe's *Tour* was published. Kyrle had devoted himself to the welfare of Ross, distributing alms, improving the education of children, arbitrating in squabbles, embellishing the town with gardens, and aiding the construction of a new, taller church spire. Admirers of Pope's *Moral Essays* knew Kyrle as the standard bearer for civic philanthropy. In an era of broadening spiritual perspectives, Kyrle had unwittingly laid the foundation stone for Christian tourism on the Wye.

When Gilpin's coach rumbled along the turnpike into Ross in 1772, the landmark he first spotted was Kyrle's slender church spire rising like a beacon above the flood plain. In the footsteps of Pope, Gilpin walked through the churchyard to Kyrle's 'Prospect' and gazed for his first time upon 'an easy sweep of the Wye'. Modern visitors making the same pilgrimage will be disappointed: The viewpoint on The Prospect is structurally unsafe, and inaccessible behind temporary fencing; elsewhere, roofs and trees block all but broken glimpses of the Wye's famous meander. Actually, Gilpin wasn't that impressed, anyway. While conceding that the churchyard commanded 'many distant views', and that they were 'indeed very amusing', the outlook was 'not picturesque'. The problem was that the view contained 'no characteristic objects' and that it was 'broken into too many parts'. The most commendable feature was Pope's 'heav'n directed spire'.

Poke about on the banks of the Wye at Ross at you can still find reminders of its one-time role as the launch-slip of the 'Wye Tour'. On the outside curve of the horseshoe bend are fragments of old wharf, and in one place, the ribs of an old boat. In front of the Hope and Anchor, concrete steps lead down the bank where timber skiffs once waited for customers.

By the time Gilpin came down to the water, the Wye Tour had been growing in popularity for some years. In 1745, a local rector called Dr John Egerton had constructed a sightseeing boat so that he could take his guests on summer trips down the river. Egerton's boat rotted in the mud after he left the borders in 1756 to become Bishop of Bangor, but around 1760 a local basket maker called James Evans had begun hiring out boats. By the 1760s, the river had been spotted by the scribe of the gardens movement, Thomas Whateley. His descriptions of New Weir and Tintern Abbey were published in *Observations on Modern Gardening*, which appeared in 1770, the year Gilpin headed west.

Gilpin hired a covered boat, with a local crew of three men. His plan was to use the boat for just one day, disembarking twenty miles downstream at Monmouth, where a chaise would be waiting to take him on by road to Tintern and Chepstow. Gilpin quickly found himself in a riparian paradise. The early moments of a river journey can be enchanted with a kind of magical incredulity. Left behind is the tumult and visual chaos of road travel, with its discomforts and unwanted decisions. In its place is a gentler, simpler form of movement. Pause on the oars, and the silence can turn a boat into an innocuous leaf, borne upon the current. Landscapes glide by at a rate which permits appreciation, and there are no options to weigh, for there is only one, and it ends at the sea.

When you take to the lower Wye in a small boat, the first thing you notice is the height of the banks. Set deep between sharp, parallel edges, the watercourse could have been carefully excavated by a cosmic trowel. Gilpin needed no further evidence of God's handiwork: 'The channel of no river,' he announces shortly after boarding at Ross, 'can be more decisively marked than that of the Wye.' Here in Herefordshire was evidence of Creation: 'A nobler *water-course* was never *divided* for any river than this of the Wye,' he continues, 'we see a channel marked with such precision, that it appears as if originally intended only for the bed of a river.'

Ross, viewed from Wilton, the one-time home of Luke Hughes, who won fame in the eighteenth century for paddling his coracle all the way down the Wye and then across the Bristol Channel to Lundy Island. And back. Gilpin wove the story of this 'adventurous fellow' into his book, remarking that when Hughes paddled back up the Wye, 'the account of his expedition was received like a voyage around the world'.

Gilpin introduces his picturesque system cautiously, explaining that nature works, 'no doubt harmoniously', on such a vast scale that it is 'beyond human comprehension'. In the meantime, the artist 'is confined to a *span*' and 'lays down his little rules, which he calls the *principles of picturesque beauty*, merely to adapt such diminutive parts of nature's surfaces to his own eye as come within scope'. More remote than the intensely-stirred emotions of the Sublime, the Picturesque was intended to rationalise the appreciation of nature.

The first few miles from Ross were a calm prelude to the spectacle soon to erupt from the river banks. Gilpin used this stretch of river to rehearse the Picturesque's 'little rules'. The perfect river-view, he explains, is composed of 'four grand parts': the river itself in the foreground, the two 'side screens' formed by the opposing banks, and finally the 'front screen', which is the onward view of the 'winding of the river'. Perspective would be led by the pair of side-screens. Amplifying himself, Gilpin points out that a long, straight Dutch canal would have no front screen, while its side screens would taper to a point. What makes the Wye so unusual is the extraordinary diversity of its screens. Such is the 'exceedingly varied' nature of the river that one bank can be lofty and precipitous, while the other can be level. Or both can be precipitous, or both flat. Further variations are created by 'the folding of the side-screens over each other', which have the effect of hiding from view the onward winding river, the 'front screen'. Lest readers think it's too simple, Gilpin then describes 'complex' variations, where one of the side-screens may be composed of both lofty and level banks. And that is just the start.

To the compositional screens, he continues, can be added four types of embellishment which he terms 'ornaments'. These are ground, wood, rocks and buildings. All will be revealed in the first couple of hours on the river. 'Ground,' explains Gilpin, can range 'from the steepest precipice to the flattest meadow', while a sub-category of 'broken ground' offers a wide range of surfaces from 'naked soil' to waterfalls

Gilpin's 'rules' of the Picturesque divided any view into four 'screens', which could be embellished by four types of 'ornament'. The varied geology and rich history of the Wye, together with its pattern of woodland and pasture, provided countless permutations of screens and ornaments.

and dry, stony channels. Bald downland is particularly unattractive, and drystone walls 'the most offensive separation of property'. The colour of broken ground is a significant picturesque element too, and the Wye can produce a palette which ranges from 'the yellow or the red ochre, the ashy grey, the black earth, or the marly blue', while the 'intermixtures of these with each other, and the patches of verdure, blooming heath, and other vegetable tints, still increase the variety'.

The other three ornaments are defined in similarly specific terms. Unaware of the havoc about to be wreaked on the countryside by the Industrial Revolution, Gilpin sees the destruction of woodland through rose-tinted eye-glasses. The Wye's woods, he states, are made more picturesque by the partial felling for the 'many works carried on by fire', which lead to 'a kind of alternacy' in the tree cover. Industry itself can be picturesque: 'One circumstance attending this alternacy is pleasing. Many of the furnaces on the banks of the river consume charcoal, which is manufactured on the spot; and the smoke issuing from the sides of the hills, and spreading its thin veil over a part of them, beautifully breaks their lines, and unites them with the sky.'

The third ornament, rock, is an element rare to large English rivers. Gilpin was no fan of rock in its 'bleak, naked and unadorned' form. Put him in a raft down the Grand Canyon, or on a ledge in Yosemite, and he'd have been appalled by the ugliness. Tint the same rock with mosses and lichens however, and you have 'a degree of beauty'. Adorn it with shrubs and 'hanging herbage', and 'you make it still more picturesque'.

Gilpin's list of picturesque buildings includes abbeys, castles, villages spires, forges, mills, and bridges. The lower Wye is rich in this ornament: 'One or other of these venerable vestiges of past, or cheerful habitations of present times, characterise almost every scene.' Buildings, thought Gilpin, were not necessary for us to appreciate the full wonder of a natural landscape; forests and lakes, rock and mountains were more than enough to 'furnish an inexhausted source of pleasure'. But once such views were contained within a frame, some types of buildings became important: 'Indeed the landscape painter seldom thinks his view perfect without characterizing it by some object of this kind.' Unacceptable buildings included industrial sites and profusions of whitened houses.

So much for the theory. The reality was rather more testing. Shortly after Gilpin left Ross, it began to rain. This was not what the Reverend had planned. In another age, he might have logged onto the Met Office website from an hotel in Ross, and departed accordingly. But he was two hundred years too early, and he was in for a soaker. 'I must, however, premise,' he apologises, 'how ill-qualified I am to do justice to the banks of the Wye, were it only from having seen them under the circumstance of a continued rain, which began early in the day, before one third of our voyage was performed.' Having followed Gilpin's wake down this wonderful river beneath a

A colour chart from William Gilpin's *Hints to form the taste and regulate ye judgement in sketching landscape.*

Mediterranean ceiling, I can sense the anguish in his words. Of his own bad luck, Gilpin can only offer a plaintive line upon the effects of falling rain on the picturesque: 'It is true, scenery at *hand* suffers less under such a circumstance, than scenery at a *distance*, which it totally obscures.' It must have been absolutely pelting down.

In that first hour or so before the first drops of rain pocked the river surface, his boat slid downstream to the rhythmic creak and plash of heavy, wooden oars. Just before Pencraig, the river twists through a double-bend, and Gilpin was able to observe the picturesque effects of the river surface: 'The bank,' he notes, 'soon began to swell on the right, and was richly adorned with wood. We admired it much; and also the vivid images reflected from the water, which were continually disturbed as we sailed past them, and thrown into tremulous confusion by the dashing of our oars.' Reflections, like memories, had a beauty of their own: 'A disturbed surface of water endeavouring to collect its scattered images and restore them to order, is among the *pretty* appearances of nature.'

Almost anywhere he looked, Gilpin could find elements of beauty. 'Even the rain gave a gloomy grandeur to many of the scenes,' he noted, 'and by throwing a veil of obscurity over the removed banks of the river, introduced, now and then, something like a pleasing distance.'

In the course of his two days on the river, Gilpin would muse on many views, but three of them stood out as exemplars. Four miles downstream of Ross, the first 'grand view' began to appear in the distance. Resting on the oars, they paused to watch a fractured tower rise above the trees. 'A reach of the river, forming a noble bay, is spread before the eye,' observed Gilpin. 'The bank, on the right, is steep, and covered with wood; beyond which a bold promontory shoots out, crowned with a castle, rising among trees.' Hastily, he sketched the scene: 'This view, which is one of the grandest on the river, I should not scruple to call *correctly picturesque*, which is seldom the character of a purely natural scene.'

Goodrich ticked the boxes: the 'parts are few; and the whole,' concluded Gilpin, 'is a simple exhibition.' Visiting the same spot in a canoe, I spent an energetic hour or so criss-crossing the river, then wading upstream hauling the boat against the current, in a futile attempt to match Gilpin's aquatint with the actual landscape. Gilpin's Goodrich has an elegant, eroded profile, with a staircase of battlements ascending to a pair of noble turrets. Below the gaunt walls is a formidable cliff adorned with vegetation, and a massive, sculptural rock reflected in the still, deep-looking waters of a narrow river. It looks a bit like a gorge in the upper Rhine, decorated with a borrowed Byzantine citadel. The effect is undeniably pleasing, but untrue. Gilpin

The aquatint of Goodrich Castle, from an original sketch that Gilpin made in mid-stream, adjacent to the ferry crossing. The practice for Wye tourists was to alight at the ferry landing, and then climb up through woods of oak and elm to the ruined castle. The rain was so heavy when Gilpin reached this spot, that he was advised not to attempt the landing.

re-engineered the castle, invented the cliff (and the rock) and halved the width of the river. 'I am so attached to my picturesque rules,' he admitted to an indignant William Mason, 'that if nature gets it wrong, I cannot help putting her right.' Gilpin never meant his hasty sketches to be factual representations: 'I did all I could to make people believe they were general ideas, or illustrations,' he explained.

The rain was now so relentless that Gilpin was unable to land and climb to the castle. Having travelled down the river from its source in the Welsh mountains, I was beginning to mistrust the picturesque concept. Among the images I'd collected were a dead sheep hanging in a tree, various utilitarian farm buildings, and a thundering water-extraction pump. The sense under greatest assault was hearing. On the slopes of Plynlimon, where I uncovered the Wye beneath a sponge of sphagnum moss, the air was rent periodically by fighter-bombers, and by rally cars being tested on mountain tracks. Lower down the Wye, trucks and cars are a frequent soundtrack. The whole way from the southern slopes of Plynlimon to Llyswen, the river is shadowed by the A44 and then by the A470. For precious miles north of Builth, the 470 is forced away from the river, but it is a rare segment of tranquility. From Kerne Bridge, the river acts like the slow lane on the B4234. Motor vehicles flash past unconcerned herons. The picturesque depends on selective use of a single sense: sight. Gilpin's idealised views tell you nothing of the true state of nature: the pollutants in the water, the collapsing salmon population, the anguish that can attend modern farming.

An hour or so after leaving Goodrich, Gilpin's boat rounded a sweeping, right-hand bend and he was confronted by his first sight of modern industry: 'All has thus far been grandeur and tranquility,' he muses. 'It continues so yet; but mixed with life and bustle.' The source of this activity was the long wharf on the outer bend of the river at Lydbrook, where coal from the Forest of Dean was shipped out to Hereford and beyond. Horses and carts were grinding up and down the long diagonal roadway cut into the river bluff between the moored vessels and the mines. The novelty of fossil-fuel extraction appealed to Gilpin: 'Here the scene is new and pleasing,' he writes. 'The contrast of all this business, the engines used in lading and unlading, together with the variety of the scene, produce all together a picturesque assemblage.' Separated from the sweat and curses of the toiling men by the river, Gilpin was able to view the scene with Breughelesque detachment.

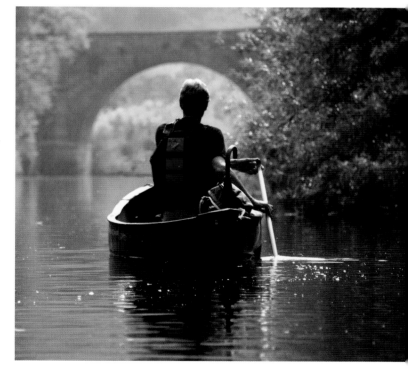

Kerne Bridge, close to Goodrich. Built in 1828, it has five, high arches to allow the passage of flood waters.

\* \* \*

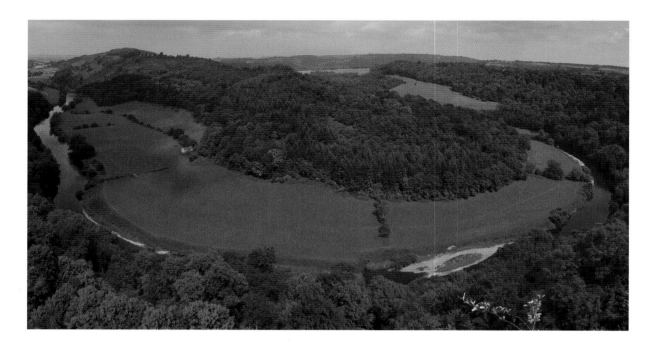

The greatest physical spectacle on the Wye begins as a tease. Gilpin describes their approach as if he's unveiling his 'screens': the front screen appearing as a wooded hill, 'swelling to a point' and then changing again into a lofty side-screen, 'while the front unfolds itself into a majestic piece of rock-scenery.'

They had reached the 'Yat', or gate.

At Coldwell Rocks, the river performs one of its most extreme meanders, taking a four-mile loop northward out of the hills, only to return to within five hundred yards of its earlier course. Gilpin had intended to disembark at Coldwell, and to hike over the steep ridge at the 'neck' of the meander. He'd been promised 'very noble river-views' from the top of the climb, but once again, the rain forced him to stay on the boat. He'd have found the climb quite an adventure. Seventy years later, Louisa Anne Twamley recorded 'toils and tumbles' as she climbed up to 'the platform of rock crowning the narrow ridge'. Today, a footpath scrabbles upward through the foliage to a vast car-park furnished with public conveniences and a cafe. Yat Rock, once a precarious slab poised above the abyss, is now rimmed with a stone wall and polished by millions of shoe-soles. On summer weekends, it looks like the deck of a cruise ship entering port. The view is still astonishing: far below, the river unwinds through a wooded chasm which opens like a flower into decorated farmland.

Denied his aerial view, Gilpin emerged from his four-mile detour to be confronted by the river's greatest natural wonder, 'the second grand scene on the Wye'. Since picturesque viewpoints had to be taken low down, he had missed little by failing to reach Yat Rock:

'The river is wider than usual in this part; and takes a sweep around a towering promontory of rock; which forms the side-screens on the left, and

The view north-eastwards from Yat Rock, the river flowing from right to left. The Wye is the most wooded protected landscape in Britain, and reaches 48 per cent woodland cover in the Lower Wye Gorge. Gilpin found the Wye overburdened with trees, and complained that they tended to block the view, and to disturb a sense of distance. Particularly problematic were clumps of trees on the riverbank, and trees 'immediately in the foreground'. These, he stipulated, 'cannot be suffered'.

is the grand feature of the view. It is not a broad fractured face of rock; but rather a woody hill, from which large rocky projections, in two or three places, burst out; rudely hung with twisting branches and shaggy furniture, which, like mane around a lion's head, give a more savage air to these wild exhibitions of nature. Near the top a pointed fragment of solitary rock, rising above the rest, has a rather fantastic appearance; but it is not without its effect in marking the scene.'

Gilpin was reminded of a description in Virgil's *Aeneid*. From the hamlet on the bank facing Yat Rock, 'volumes of thick smoke, thrown up at intervals from an iron forge, as its fires receive fresh fuel, add double grandeur to the scene'. Beneath the gauzy precipice is, continues Gilpin, 'a circumstance on the water.'

Approaching the rapid at Symonds Yat in a canoe, you are aware of an odd shift in the river's perspective, as if the scene has been scissored in two and then incorrectly joined. This was probably the first rapid Gilpin had shot:

> 'The whole river at this place makes a precipitate fall; of no great height indeed, but enough to merit the name of a cascade; though to the eye, above the stream, it is an object of no consequence. In all the scenes we had yet passed, the water, moving with a slow and solemn pace, the objects around kept time, as it were, with it; and every steep and every rock which hung over the river, was awful, tranquil, and majestic. But here the violence of the stream and the roaring of the waters impressed a new character on the scene: all was agitation and uproar; and every steep and every rock stared with wildness and terror.'

This was as wild as the Wye could get. For a few seconds, the Reverend Gilpin was tossed about as the timber rowboat bucketed down the cataract. Whether it really was the rock which stared with 'terror', or Gilpin himself, is hard to say. In the 1700s,

The aquatint of New Weir in *Observations on the River Wye*. The sense of spaciousness has been created by the artistic felling of obstructive trees.

shooting rapids was not standard practice among clergymen. Today, running the Yat's rapids is literally childs' play; during holidays, Gilpin's 'precipitate fall' is alive with coloured kayaks.

It is below the rapids at Symonds Yat that the river takes its secretive, two-mile excursion away from humanity. Allowing the current to take the boat, I drifted with the river, suspended in a kind of painful tranquility. After days of exploring, I had – so I thought – come upon a moment of pure beauty. Gilpin had compared the quest for the picturesque to the 'pleasures of the chase'. We can tramp and paddle every landscape, but never quite touch our quarry: 'Every distant horizon promises something new; and with this pleasing expectation we follow nature through her walks. We pursue her from hill to dale; and hunt after those various beauties, with which she everywhere abounds.'

Sliding downstream, I knew beauty would slip her bonds; I'd seen the map. And sure enough, the sounds of the A40 soon began to stain the murmuring stream. The last two miles into Monmouth were miserable. My arms ached, the canoe seemed to be dragging a sea anchor, and all the while the road roared above my right shoulder.

By the time Gilpin's crew of weary boaters floated down the interminable straight into Monmouth, the sun had set. Their chaise was waiting for them, but when Gilpin inquired about the road route to Chepstow, he abruptly changed his plan. It seemed that the river would provide better 'amusement' than the road. A new agreement was negotiated with the boatmen, with the intention of sailing next morning for the third and final 'grand view'.

* * *

Fortune favours the opportunistic traveller, and Gilpin's decision to stay on the water repaid him with serene weather: 'the sun shone; and we saw enough of the effect of light in the exhibitions of this day, to regret the want of it the day before.' As it happened, the day I travelled this section of the river, it rained so heavily that my canoe kept filling up like a bathtub. Below the gloomy forest, Berghem's inscrutable cattle watched my passing with no obvious signs of compassion.

The river here looks much as it did in Gilpin's day. As the Reverend says, the banks 'consist almost entirely either of wood or pasturage'. This suited Gilpin's vision of the picturesque, for there was nothing less helpful to a painter than arable farmland. 'Furrowed lands and waving corn' were 'charming in pastoral poetry', but 'ill accommodated to painting'. A picturesque landscape had to reflect the glory of God's creation; it had to 'approach as nearly as may be to nature'. And that meant grazing land: 'Pasturage not only presents an agreeable surface; but the cattle which graze it add great variety and animation to the scene.'

Along with the ghastly sight of arable farmland, Gilpin was selectively enthusiastic about industry. The day he left Monmouth, he floated down one of the main arteries of the awakening industrial revolution. The Wye had all the requisites for heavy industry: accessible coal reserves in the Forest of Dean, fast-running streams for power, plentiful timber for fuel, and a river to ship raw materials and finished products. When Gilpin refers to other boats on the river, 'whose white sails passing along the sides of woodland hills were very picturesque', he's glancing at the surface of the scene. These were industrial barges, and in side valleys such as Whitebrook, paper-mills were thundering.

Within years of Gilpin's voyage, the Wye Tour was a highly organised excursion. This is Thomas Roscoe, writing in the 1830s: 'My 'light bark' was not much unlike a gondola, when its tarpauling cover was spread over the framework; but being favoured by a radiantly bright morning, I preferred sitting under the skeleton and enjoying the charming scenes around me. A table in the centre of the part allotted to passengers, and cushioned seats around, made this small floating parlour a most commodious conveyance.'

The old wharf at Brockweir, a transhipment point for goods being taken down the Wye. It's a pleasant place for a picnic now, but in the eighteenth century, this was one of the Wye's more boisterous villages, with several pubs and a population of watermen who unwound after a long day on the wharf, by drinking and cockfighting.

At Brockweir I landed with difficulty on an old cobbled slipway inches deep in gelatinous mud. Beside the slipway, a short stretch of dressed stonework led past an unsightly rubbish skip to a flight of steps leading back down to the water. It was an old quayside. This perhaps, was one of the riverside sights Gilpin had meant when he wrote of 'harbours in miniature, where little barks lay moored, taking in ore and other commodities from the mountains'. He took these sights as indicators that his river was changing character once again: 'These vessels,' he continues, 'designed plainly for rougher water than they at present encountered, shewed us, without any geographical knowledge, that we approached the sea.'

There was one other indicator of the approaching ocean here, though Gilpin seems to have missed it. Between Monmouth and Brockweir, the river becomes tidal. The mud dumped all over Brockweir's slipway had been left by the last tide, and while I was wandering about the old wharf I was able to watch the bizarre spectacle of the small rapid beneath the nearby road bridge, change directions. One moment, it was a clear cataract flowing southward, and the next it reversed into a brown flood, heading north.

The climax of the Wye Tour was hidden a mile beyond Brockweir. From water level, it's impossible to see 'the most beautiful and picturesque view on the river'. And landing here is not easy, for the ferry slipway has been replaced by a near-vertical flood defence. On all fours, I clawed up a wall of slimy mud and lurched like a chocolate-coated puppet into a huge carpark.

Gilpin's initial reaction to Tintern is that of a pilgrim who has stumbled by chance upon the holiest of shrines. The abbey looked absolutely enormous, even in its ruinous condition. Dwarfed by eight-hundred foot hills, it rested like a shattered reliquary on a velvet pasture beside the streaming Wye. The Cistercian principle that

*Opposite:* Tintern Abbey, and the gables Gilpin didn't like. 'The way to enjoy Tintern Abbey properly, and at leisure,' explained the Hon. John Byng in 1781, 'is to bring wines, cold meat, with corn for the horses. (Bread, beer, cider, and commonly salmon, may be had at the Beaufort Arms.) Spread your table in the ruins; and possibly a Welsh harper may be procured from Chepstow.'

abbeys should be founded 'far from the concourse of men', in 'a kind of second paradise of wooded delight' are echoed by Gilpin's delight that Tintern should be so well 'hid in the sequestered vale'. The composition is made perfect by the river, as it 'winds its course' through the view. At Tintern, Gilpin finds the perfect expression of God's wondrous design. Enraptured by the scene, he drifts off momentarily in monkish reverie: 'Every thing around bears an air so calm and tranquil, so sequestered from the commerce of life, that it is easy to conceive a man of warm imagination, in monkish times, might have been allured by such a scene to become an inhabitant of it.'

Tintern is not quite perfect, though. The all-important 'ornaments', are present and correct, among them ivy 'in masses uncommonly large', and mosses 'of various hues', together with lichens, maiden-hair, penny-leaf 'and other humble plants' which 'had overspread the surface, or hung from every joint or crevice'. With some in flower and others in leaf, the effect 'gave those full-blown tints which add the richest finishing to a ruin'. The only thing which spoiled an otherwise perfectly-picturesque ruin was the state of the abbey itself. The fact that the tower had collapsed, had removed 'form and contrast' from the surviving buttresses and walls, leaving 'the whole ill-shaped'. Particularly offensive were the remaining gable ends, which 'hurt the eye with their regularity, and disgust it by the vulgarity of their shape.' Gilpin had a solution: 'A mallet judiciously used (but who durst use it?) might be of service in fracturing some of them; particularly those of the cross-aisles, which are both disagreeable in themselves, and confound the perspective.' The image of a middle-aged Reverend knocking lumps off Tintern Abbey with a mallet was a gift to eighteenth-century caricaturists.

As he wandered about the exterior of the abbey, Gilpin eventually settled upon a viewpoint close to the rutted road which passed down the vale. The actual spot is now blocked by the second-storey bedroom of an hotel, but it seems that

Gilpin was standing on what is now the small lane cut into the hillside behind the hotel. From this point, he sketched the abbey, removing with his pen what he wished to do with a mallet. Gilpin's Tintern is missing two of its gables. And he omitted the neighbouring iron works.

As Gilpin steps through Tintern's shattered west wall, beauty and horror become inseparable: 'But when we *enter* it we see it in most perfection…' The scale of the abbey church is staggering. The west front soars skyward like a fretworked cliff, its slender bar tracery thickened with centuries of ivy. Everywhere there are columns, 'noble columns', rising from a carpet of close-cropped turf to meet a long-gone roof. The eye, gasps Gilpin, 'was above measure delighted with the beauty, the greatness, and the novelty of the scene.' Lurking in the ruins were the abbey's wretched inhabitants, foul-smelling and ragged, begging for alms. Their shelters were scattered about the crumbled church and cloisters, 'little huts, raised among the ruins'. One of these impoverished souls, a woman, led Gilpin and his companions to the monk's library. 'She could scarcely crawl,' observes Gilpin, 'shuffling along her palsied limbs and meagre contracted body by the help of two sticks.' Through an old gate 'overspread with nettles and briars', the old woman revealed her shelter. 'I never saw so loathsome a human dwelling,' continues Gilpin, who describes it in detail: 'It was a cavern loftily vaulted between two ruined walls, which streamed with various coloured stains of unwholesome dews. The floor was earth; yielding through moisture to the tread. Not the merest utensil or furniture of any kind appeared, but a wretched bedstead, spread with a few rags, and drawn into the middle of the cell to prevent its receiving the damp which trickled down the walls. At one end was an aperture, which served just to let in light enough to discover the wretchedness within.' The Picturesque wasn't equipped to deal with the awfulness of human existence, but Gilpin's own humanity obliged him to find the words for this distressing vignette in his book. There are no hovels or beggars in the aquatint.

Gilpin's 'improved' view of Tintern, without the offending hovels and gables. Tintern was the climax of the Wye Tour. Byng also felt that the site could be improved: 'At some trifling expense,' he suggested. 'the surrounding cottages and orchards might be removed, and then the abbey would stand nobly backed by woods and open to the water: at present it is shamefully blocked up'.

Just before the tide turned, I left Tintern on water the colour of oxtail soup. Rafts of debris glided upstream as if carried on an aquatic conveyor-belt. The canoe's hull bumped against knotted tangles of foliage and dead wood. A table passed by, legs skyward, and then a dead salmon, as thick as my arm. Rain had begun to fall and the river was stippled with dark roundels. Mist seethed through the thick trees on the valley sides. Rounding a bend, a flight of six herons took to the air, flapping like pterodactyls towards the seeping vapours. Presently the tide rested, and the debris slewed to a halt. The river was very quiet, and enormous. Clamped between walls of smoking jungle, I felt as if I had paddled through a spatial warp into an Amazonian backwater.

Gilpin's voyage down the Wye finished close to this spot. He disembarked beneath the 700-foot wall of the river's final gorge, at a place called Piercefield, a 300-acre estate owned by a Mr Valentine Morris. 'We pushed on shore close under his rocks,' writes Gilpin, 'and the tide being at ebb, we landed with some difficulty on an oozy beach. One of our bargemen, who knew the place, served as a guide; and under his conduct we climbed the steep by an easy regular zig-zag.'

Traces of the 'regular zig-zag' can still be seen, though once again I found myself clawing upward coated in the Wye's peculiarly sticky mud. Piercefield was – as

The tidal Wye, between Tintern and Piercefield.

The grounds of Piercefield, oriented with east at the top. Gilpin's boatmen landed him at the foot of the woods on the first bend in the river. Having climbed the zig-zag path, he was able to join the three-mile walk along the lip of the cliffs. The Giant's Cave is marked above Martridge Meadow.

Gilpin noted – 'generally thought as much worth a traveller's notice as anything on the banks of the Wye.' Along with Mount Edgcumbe, Stowe, Stourhead, Hagley and the Leasowes, it was a compulsory sight for modern tourists. The procedure for gaining admission to these gardens took the form of an eighteenth-century right-to-roam. D.C. Webb noted in his *Observations and Remarks during Four Excursions*, published in 1812, that 'the only ceremony required being that of setting down your name and address in a book kept for that purpose at the Porters Lodge.' After this minor formality 'you are permitted to stroll through the park and grounds'. While other gardens were embellished with grottoes, Chinese pavilions and Gothic alcoves, Piercefield's attraction lay in a range of artfully-devised views which could be enjoyed from a series of paths and belvederes constructed along the edge of the precipice. Poor Mr Morris had got it wrong, though the views themselves were 'enchanting', and 'extremely romantic', but Gilpin could not, he decided, 'call these views picturesque.' The vantage points were too high; the planted shrubbery interfered with 'the grand beauties of nature', and the paths were marked by 'a degree of tediousness'.

Panting up through the strangling foliage, I found myself longing for a tedious path to follow. Piercefield today has been reclaimed by nature, and is a Grade I Registered Historic Park and Garden. The precipice path is still in daily use by dog-walkers and ramblers, but the ornaments Morris constructed are crumbling or hidden by undergrowth. The Grotto is throttled with laurel, and the dam, where a hydraulic ram pumped water into a pool, is lost to sight in new woodland. Only the Giant's

Cave, where a cannon was sited so that tourists could experience echoes, is in its original, rock-cut condition. Morris's great house is a precarious shell, stripped of its stone staircase and choked with rubble. In this ruined, semi-natural state, perhaps Gilpin would have been more lenient with Piercefield.

Gilpin's summer tour continued through south Wales, but it was his two days on the Wye which came to define the picturesque 'movement'. By the end of the century, the forty miles of river between Ross and Chepstow was one of the most celebrated landscapes in Britain. Among those who followed were J.M.W. Turner, Paul Sandby, Thomas Hearne and William Wordsworth, whose 'Lines, written a few miles above Tintern Abbey' came to define the poetic response to the Wye. Fleets of boats were operating by then, some of them bearing twenty passengers at a time, on cushioned seats. Awnings protected them from the worst of the weather, and tables were provided for the maps and books, barometers and telescopes. And the Gilpin-effect spread far beyond the Wye. Through his simple system of aesthetic appreciation, he removed the wall of incomprehension which had previously surrounded 'untamed' Britain, and replaced it with a virtual ha ha. Where Defoe and Pennant wrote through fear of mountains that were 'horrid and frightful', or 'naked, rugged' and 'dreary', Gilpin's looking-glass perspective insisted that there were 'orders of architecture in mountains as in palaces'.

Gilpin was not the first to gaze up at Goodrich, or to shoot the rapids at Yat Rock, or to gawp at Tintern, but his simple, accessible 'rules' provided the first generation of English tourists with the means to detect 'that peculiar kind of beauty' which can make a traveller smile or cry. Gilpin took the terror out of wilderness, and replaced it with wonder. The reverence he placed on picturesque views helped train a nation to value its landscapes. His rules are still in everyday use, in picture postcards and paintings, in planning departments, and in our choices when we plan holidays and choose homes. The Picturesque never could describe the real landscape, but in identifying its most pleasing features, Gilpin seems to have touched a craving deep in all of us.

There twice a day the
   Severn fills;
The salt sea-water
   passes by,
And hushes half the
   babbling Wye.
And makes a silence in
   the hills.

Tennyson, *In Memoriam*

# Thomas Pennant * 1772 *

*Highlands and islands*

# Thomas Pennant's
## VOYAGE TO THE HEBRIDES
### ← 1772 →

Cape Wrath

Ledbeg

Dundonnell
An Teallach
Gairloch
Duntulm Castle
Loch Maree
Dunvegan Castle
Skye
Talisker
Loch Hourn
Canna
Rhum
Tobermory
Staffa
Iona
Ardmaddie
Gulf of Corryvreckan
Colonsay
Jura
Islay
Benn an Oir
Gigha
Island of Bute
Greenock
Campbeltown
Arran
Ailsa Craig

SCOTLAND
Perth
Montrose
Ardmaddie
St Andrews
Greenock
Edinburgh
Coldstream
Newcastle-upon-Tyne
Richmond
Downing
Skipton
Manchester
Warrington
Chester
WALES
ENGLAND

10  20  30  40  50  60  70
### MILES

— — — Highlands & Islands route
– – – Route and direction taken by sea
– – – Route and direction taken by land
⊙   Town or settlement
◇   Building of interest

THE planet's wildest places remained secret till the last. In Britain, that wilderness lay in the far north-west, where mountains, sea and climate conspired to make travel – and existence itself – extremely challenging. As late as the eighteenth century, the highlands and islands of Scotland were a mystery to most who were not natives. Thomas Pennant's journey of exploration in 1772 opened the door to tourists like Dr Johnson, who claimed that Pennant was the 'best traveller' he had 'ever read'. Packed with insight, danger and uncomfortable truths, *A Tour in Scotland, and Voyage to the Hebrides; 1772* is the work of an explorer and natural historian who found himself on a mission to alleviate the suffering of an oppressed population.

\* \* \*

One evening last autumn I followed Thomas Pennant's route up Beinn na Caillich on Skye. The 'hill of the old hag' is a massive, curved bulwark which occupies the full width of the island above Broadford. To Pennant, on the deck of his ship, Beinn na Caillich was 'one of those picturesque mountains that made such a figure from the sea'. He liked his mountains to be rounded, or 'mamillary', as he put it. Today, few mountaineers give this 2,400-foot hummock a second glance as they speed along the coast road rowards the chiselled spikes of the Cuillins. Pennant climbed from the east, an energetic scramble up tongues of scree and heather, with no apparent path and plenty of opportunities for twisting an ankle. I couldn't help wondering whether I had got the right mountain, but once the gradient eased and the stones thinned to gale-rubbed turf, I recognised Pennant's summit, 'flat and naked, with an artificial cairn, of a most enormous size'. With the wind rattling my jacket, I dropped my pack at the foot of the cairn and turned to the four points of the compass. Northward, an arm of platinum sea ran between Raasay and the Applecross peaks towards The Minch. Southward, I could just see the island of Rum, a boulder resting on polished slate. To the east, lights were beginning to twinkle on the darkening mainland. But westward, backlit by a bleeding sun, a ferocious palisade of ancient rock was ripping low-flying cloud into tattered streamers. 'The prospect to the west,' Pennant had written with awe, 'was that of desolation itself; a savage series of rude mountains, discoloured, black and red, as if by the rage of fire.' There are parts of Scotland that have not changed for thousands years.

You only have to look at the emergence of Scotland from the last Ice Age to detect a spectacle in the making. The glaciers pulled back to expose tottering walls of rock, serrated ridges and immense U-shaped valleys streaming with meltwater. Vast areas of the far north had been levelled by the ice into polished plateaux of bedrock, strewn

*Previous pages:* **The Inner Sound, Skye.**

The last frontier: the mountains, lochs and bogs of northern Scotland are a formidably tough human habitat. Terrain such as this requires specialised survival skills, and can take four times longer to traverse than the drier, flatter lands of southern England.

with rubble. This frigid tundra was gradually colonised by hardy little shrubs such as juniper and willow, and wandering herds of bison, wooly rhinoceros, giant elk and mammoth. Scotland's first trees were birch, followed by hazel and then the big pines, elm and oak. As the forests rooted and thickened, the lumbering beasts of the tundra were squeezed into extinction, and new species of quicker, smaller animals – wolves and wild boar, bears and deer – stalked the glades. Red squirrels bounced among the boughs and freshwater lakes filled with fish. But of all the species to colonise post-glacial Scotland, the most successful by far was a nomadic hominid.

The humans who undertook the first seasonal treks into these northern lands were the greatest explorers to have trodden British soil. With its impassable cliffs, lethal cataracts and dense forests, Scottish terrain was as tough as it gets. But it was also a gigantic game park, and there is evidence that the highlands and islands of the far north were being explored within a couple of thousand years of the ice sheets melting. Near the outfall of a river on the east coast (at a place now called Cramond, on the north-western outskirts of Edinburgh), some of these pioneering hunter-explorers left the remains of a temporary shelter, and a dump of hazelnut shells which have been radiocarbon dated to around 8,500BC. At the time, there were probably no more than 2,500 people in the whole of Britain, so the total number of hunters in Scotland would have been counted in hundreds. They knew better than any of their descendants how to live with the land. Their axes, hammers, bows and arrows were fashioned from carved wood and knapped stone. They knew where to find caves for overnight shelter, or they constructed bivouacs from timber and skin. Some of them built seagoing boats capable of braving the fierce tides and winds of the west coast, and paddled to the Orkneys and to many of the islands of the Inner Hebrides. As early as 7,500BC, they reached Rum. On the island of Oronsay, archaeologists have found Mesolithic stake holes which may have supported windbreaks around open hearths.

For the best part of eight thousand years, the highlands and islands released their secrets with extreme reluctance. Snippets appeared in the work of early Greek and Roman writers, but the first real insight into this isolated, extraordinary land was written by Cornelius Tacitus in around AD 98, compiled from stories brought back to Rome by the victors of the battle of Mons Graupius. For the Roman army, the conquest of Scotland was both a military necessity and a journey of exploration. 'These remotest shores,' proclaimed Tacitus, 'were now circumnavigated, for the first time, by a Roman fleet, which thus established the fact that Britain was an island.' Tacitus wrote for Romans who believed they had found a new land, rather than invaded an old one: 'The farthest boundary of this land, which they only knew by report or rumour, we hold in our grasp with arms and fortresses. We have both explored and conquered Britain.'

The Scotland of Tacitus was unlike the rest of Britain. For the Romans, the isthmus between the Clyde and the Forth separated two lands. North of this 'narrow neck of land' was, wrote Tacitus, 'virtually another island'. Tacitus doesn't even begin to comprehend the form of this distant land. It's merely 'a huge and shapeless tract of country, jutting out to form what is actually the most distant coastline and finally tapering into a kind of wedge'. In this land of extremes, the shores were 'beaten by a wild and open sea' and the hinterland was rendered all but impassable by 'the perilous depths of woods and ravines', and an obstacle course of 'marshes, mountains, and rivers'. In the eve-of-battle speech by the Caledonian commander Calgacus, the Romans are caricatured as 'a scanty band, scared and bewildered, staring blankly at the unfamiliar sky, sea, and forests around them'. The Highlands are a labyrinth known only to her native warriors, who had 'hidden away in her most secret places'.

'We, the most distant dwellers upon earth, the last of the free, have been shielded till today by our remoteness and by the obscurity in which it has shrouded our name. Now the farthest bounds of Britain lie open to our enemies; and what men know nothing about they always assume to be a valuable prize. But there are no more nations beyond us; nothing is there but waves and rocks, and the Romans…' The eve of battle speech by Calgacus, before fighting the Romans on Mons Graupius.

An explorer's map of north west Scotland. This is Timothy Pont's attempt to make sense of the wildest corner of Britain, the unmapped wilderness between Eddrachillis Bay and Cape Wrath. Pont's map is oriented with west at the top. To make best use of his paper, Pont filled blank spaces with sketches of unrelated districts. Close to the right edge of the map (covering the area from Loch Inchard to Cape Wrath), Pont has written 'Extreem Wildernes'. Pont travelled the length and breadth of Scotland between 1583 and 1596, and his sketches eventually formed the basis for the first atlas of Scotland, published in 1654 by Blaeu. Pennant appears to have been familiar with Pont's work.

Tacitus' fearsome description of northern Scotland – revived during the Renaissance – informed prejudices for 1700 years. Other writers did little to encourage colonisation. In Donald Monro's sixteenth-century *Western Isles,* the myriad islands are depicted as a hunter-gather's paradise, but a seafarer's nightmare ('…very perillous for schippis be reason of the starknes of the stream'). The mainland was scarcely any safer. Readers turning to Camden's *Britannia* of 1586, and Joan Blaeu's atlas of 1654, found that northern Scotland was infertile due to the cold climate, which had also led to the region being devasted by wolves. Timothy Pont, whose sketch maps had been used by Blaeu for his atlas, had labelled the far north: 'Extreem Wildernes'. The description of Scotland in Mercator's famous *Atlas* was no more encouraging: 'Those who inhabit the western coast,' he wrote, 'are called *Hechtlandmen,* that is "higher" Scots and speak Hibernian, and are fierce enemies of the lowlanders who use the English language.' Through to the 1740s, perennially feuding clans, and the Jacobite uprising, successfully repelled most southerners. 'The Highlands,' observed Captain Edmund Burt, an English military engineer posted to Inverness in the late 1720s, 'are but little known even to the inhabitants of the low country of Scotland… But to the people of England, excepting some few, and those chiefly the soldiery, the Highlands are hardly known at all.' Burt's contemporary, Daniel Defoe, felt equally ill-informed: 'Our geographers,' he complained (meaning mapmakers), 'seem to be almost as much at a loss in the description of this north part of Scotland, as the Romans were to conquer it; and they are obliged to fill it up with hills and mountains, as they do the inner parts of Africa, with lions and elephants, for want of knowing what else to place there.' Nearly ten thousand years after Rum was first sighted by Mesolithic explorers, the Highlands and islands were still a mystery to southern Britons.

\* \* \*

Into the void stepped a Welsh ornithologist. Thomas Pennant had been born in the summer of 1726, the year after Daniel Defoe completed the book that would become *A Tour Through the Whole Island of Great Britain*. Although the two men shared a passion for the geography of Britain, they were utterly dissimilar in background and temperament. A gentleman of means, Pennant could trace his family's presence at their seat at Downing, on the coastal plain of north Wales, back to David Pennant ap Tudur ap Ithel, in the 1440s. Where Defoe matured into bankruptcy and the pillory, Pennant would be elected to Royal Societies and become High Sherrif of Flintshire. In his autobiography, Pennant recalled how a boyhood gift had set him on the road: 'A present of the ornithology of Francis Willughby, esq. made to me, when I was about the age of twelve,' he wrote, 'first gave me a taste for that study, and incidentally a love for that of natural history in general.'

First published in 1676, *The Ornithology of Francis Willughby* revolutionised ornithological taxonomy, and it woke young Pennant to the joys of fieldwork. Willughby and the naturalist John Ray had spent four years travelling through Britain and Europe observing 'all the birds hitherto known'. Instead of organising their findings according to the alphabetical order of their names – as was the accepted method – they had arranged their species by physical characteristics. The relationships between species were clear on every page. Illustrated with eighty exquisite engravings, Willughby and Ray's 441-page *Ornithology* was the world's first systematic classification of birds, and it marked the beginning of scientific ornithology as we know it today.

To the detriment of his education at Wrexham, Pennant was soon collecting and cataloguing flora and fauna. In 1746 or '47, he left Oxford University without graduating and took off to Cornwall, where – inspired by Dr. William Borlase, the vicar of Ludgvan and 'father of Cornish archaeology' – he developed 'a strong passion for minerals and fossils'. Then in his fifties, Borlase had amassed a vast collection of fossils, and his devotion to God had been accompanied by research into the natural history of Cornwall. In no apparent hurry to reveal himself as a serious investigator of natural history, Pennant spent the 1750s indulging his gentlemanly enthusiasms; in the summer of 1754, a boozy journey to Ireland failed to deliver any useful fieldwork, 'such was the conviviality of the country'. More productively, he opened a correspondence with the Swedish botanist, Carl Linnaeus, whose new system of classification had revolutionised botanical understanding. Finally, in 1761, Pennant began work on the book he would title *British Zoology*. Two years later, Pennant's world shook on its axis. In 1763, his father died, leaving him responsible for the Downing estate. And then, the following year, his wife of only five years, Elizabeth Falconer, also died.

A page from the book which set Pennant on the road to discovery: Francis Willughby's *Ornithologia*, published in 1676. Within twenty years of Willughby's book appearing, the flightless giant at the top of the page was extinct.

Two deaths and an inheritance must have played a part in Pennant's decision to depart in 1765 for the continent on a Grand Tour of influential thinkers. First, Paris, where he found himself 'happy in the company' of the celebrated naturalist Comte de Buffon, who was then nearing completion of his mammoth *Histoire Naturelle*. Then to the Alps, where he called on 'that wicked wit', Voltaire. Back on the North Sea coast, he enjoyed a 'momentous' meeting with the German naturalist Peter Pallas, who would soon leave the Low Countries to explore the Urals, Altai mountains and western Siberia.

To Pennant, it must have seemed that everyone he met was caught in a thrilling centrifuge of exploration and discovery. And then one of them came knocking at his door. On March 19, 1766 (a date meticulously recorded in his autobiography), a wealthy young botanist called Joseph Banks called at Pennant's lodgings and presented him with a valuable copy of William Turner's sixteenth-century work on ornithology – the first printed book entirely devoted to birds. Days later, Banks sailed for Newfoundland on a plant-collecting expedition, returning early in 1767 with no less than 340 specimens. In August, 1768, he sailed again, but this time with one Lieutenant James Cook, on a round-the-world expedition, equipped, at a cost of £10,000, by Banks himself.

While those about him explored distant shores, Pennant turned his eyes to his own isles. He had, at last, decided to mount his own, amateur expedition: 'This year,' he recalled of 1769, 'was a very active one with me; I had the hardiness to venture on a journey to the remotest part of North Britain, a country almost as little known to its southern brethren as Kamtschatka.' Thomas Pennant was going to explore Scotland.

\* \* \*

Pennant rode his horse across the border at the beginning of July, 1769. It was rather too late in the travelling season to embark upon such a journey, and Pennant later suggested that it had been a fairly impulsive decision, following the long-awaited publication of *The British Zoology*. Comparing himself to a traveller who discovers that, in order to see a country, it is 'preferable to travel by day than by night', Pennant declared:

> 'I cannot help making this applicable to myself, who after publishing three volumes of the Zoology of Great Britain, found out that to be able to speak with more precision of the subjects I treated of, it was more prudent to visit the whole than part of the country: struck therefore with the reflection of having never seen SCOTLAND, I instantly ordered my baggage to be got ready, and in reasonable time found myself on the banks of the Tweed.'

Scribbling as he travelled, he followed the least-difficult route northward, through Edinburgh and Aberdeen to Inverness, and then on to Caithness, With the exception of a diversion through the Grampians, he clung to the low-lying land of the east coast, recording everything from farming practices to local geology and the treasures of country houses. The return journey southward gave him the chance to ride General Wade's military road alongside Loch Ness, and to visit the awesome chasm of Glencoe.

*A Tour in Scotland* was published in 1771. To many, it was a groundbreaking book. Pennant's Scotland was a country of staggering physical diversity and huge natural resources. Edinburgh, he announced, was a city 'that posseses a boldness and grandeur of situation beyond any that I had seen.' Here, at last, raved *The Scots Magazine*, was a work which broke the political fashion 'to ridicule and vilify the Scots and Scotland in the keenest and grossest manner'. The 'more candid, the more gentleman-like' Pennant would, continued the reviewer, 'excite an earnest desire in his readers to make the same excursion … to the mutual advantage, perhaps, of both nations.' Thus did a Welshman find himself cast in the role of literary healer between the English and the Scots.

A romanticised view of Glencoe, from around 1695. The inclusion of Alpine rock walls in topographical guides to Scotland prolonged the impression of Highland inaccessibility.

But Pennant knew that the tour of 1769 was incomplete. Shortage of time, and the timidity of a first-time visitor, had restricted him to riding Scotland's safest routes. The various deficiencies of the journey filled him, he admitted, with 'that species of restlessness that infects many minds, on leaving any attempt unfinished'.

The remedy for that restlessness would be a return to the far north. But this time, it would be a full-blown expedition, with its own ship, and a systematic programme of research. Using horses, a sailing ship, rowing boats and his own two feet, he planned to push far beyond the reach of military roads, to explore the most remote region in Britain: the Hebridean islands, and the north-west coast of mainland Scotland.

Pennant's expedition was an ingenious hybrid. Travelling with a small team of hand-picked specialists, he would record observations, interview 'the natives', collect samples, take measurements, make sketches and so on. But he would also take advantage of the fact that the *The Scots Magazine* penetrated parts of the Highlands beyond the reach of convenient travel. Through the letters' page, Pennant attempted to recruit a dispersed team of voluntary researchers who would accumulate information in advance of his visit. He advertised his intentions in a letter dated January 27, 1772:

> 'It has now become fashionable among the English to make a tour into Scotland for some few weeks or months; and there is a moral certainty of this fashion increasing, as the foolish prejudices against the country and its inhabitants daily decrease. But it is to be regretted that an intelligent curious traveller from England has no proper helps to assist him; so that it often happens, that many return without having seen one third of what is most curious in the country…'

To this end, Pennant announced that the journey would result in the publication of 'a new tour … in two pocket volumes'. Prejudice would not be allowed to corrupt the findings: 'the greatest care should be taken to keep clear of all party-work, either in religion or politics, because such peculiarities will disgust some readers, and thereby effectually condemn the work.' A eulogy upon the beauty of the Highlands followed, and then the sting in the tail: a list of no less than ninety-seven 'Queries' addressed 'to Gentlemen in the several parts of Great Britain'. Covering fields as diverse as the materials used to construct the local church, road communication, the price of rabbits, the presence of barrows and tumulii, the methods of tillage and the number of fishing vessels, Pennant was requesting his gentleman-readers to furnish descriptions of their localities so thorough that Camden would look like a beginner.

Pennant's principal companion on this epic odyssey would be the Rev John Lightfoot, of Shalden in Hampshire, who would contribute botanical observations. Accompanying the pair as translator would be Gaelic expert, the Rev John Stuart, who would provide 'a variety of hints, relating to customs of the natives of the Highlands, and of the islands'. Recording the expedition with sketches, would be Pennant's servant, the 'able artist' Moses Griffiths. Bringing the total to eight men, would be two further servants, a fowler and a groom. In a letter written to the Scottish antiquary, George Paton, three weeks before he left home, Pennant referred excitedly to his team as 'my troop'. They were a tight-knit group, and appear to have enjoyed each others' company. The distance Pennant intended to travel was around two thousand miles.

\* \* \*

Pennant set off from Chester on Monday, May 18, 1772. Many months later, when he came to tackle the structure of his book, he portrayed his first day on the road as a sunlit prologue. Chester rises from the page as an exemplary British city, 'a city without parallel' for its neat and congenial layout; a model emporium then trading with Guinea and the Baltic. In keeping with Pennant's new role as a trans-national mediator, Chester

CHESTER BRIDGE CHESHIRE

Pennant's home town, Chester, which he celebrated for its location on the main thoroughfare between two kingdoms.

Beseiged twice during the Civil War, and then plundered for building stone, Halton Castle was a ruin by the time Thomas Pennant rode his horse up to its walls to gaze upon the celebrated view across the mouth of the River Mersey; the site chosen by a later generation for the Runcorn chemical works.

is 'a *place d'armes*, a great thoroughfare between two kingdoms, and the residence of a numerous and polished gentry.' The city is also an example of humanitarian munificence. Here, in Chester (with mortality rates to prove it), is the best poorhouse in the land. 'Might I be permitted to moralize,' warns Pennant, 'I should call this the reward of the benevolent and charitable disposition, that is the characteristic of this city.'

Beyond the city, he rides across the Cheshire Plain to Halton Castle, where the countryside appears as an eighteenth-century Garden of Eden: 'From the castle is the most beautiful view in Cheshire; a rich prospect of the meanders of the Mersey, through a fertile bottom; a pretty wooded peninsula jutting into it opposite Runcorn; the great country of Lancashire, filled with hedgerow trees; and beyond soar the hills of Yorkshire and Lancashire; and on the other side appears Cheshire, the still loftier Cambrian mountains.'

Pennant's day of inaugural wonders closed with Warrington, its 'long, narrow, ill-built' streets 'crowded with carts and passengers' engaged in the manufacture of a range of products, from pins to locks and hinges, to cast iron, glass and sugar. Nearly half of the navy's sail-cloth came from Warrington. Warehouses and cranes lining the wharves of Bank Quay, serviced 80-ton vessels bound for distant markets. The town had doubled in size in the past twenty years. Warrington even had its own publisher, W. Eyres, who would issue a new edition of *The Agricola*, to coincide with the publication of Pennant's

All roads led to Warrington: transport between Cheshire and Lancashire had to cross the Mersey here, and the same bridge also carried all traffic using the east coast route from London to Scotland. This view from 1772 shows Warrington from the north bank of the Mersey, just downstream of the town's wharves.

new book. That night, the travellers slept at the family seat of John Blackburne, whose collection of hardy exotics and hothouse plants was, claimed Pennant, 'at least equal to that at Kew.' Blackburne was celebrated for being 'the second in these kingdoms that cultivated the pineapple'. By the end of Day One, readers had been introduced to Pennant's model of benevolent, charitable civilisation. By the end of the journey. they would have visited a land of Swiftian horrors.

From Warrington, Pennant made his way through the Lake District and southern uplands of Scotland to Greenock, on the Clyde, where he boarded *Lady Frederic Campbell,* a ninety-ton sailing cutter skippered by Archibald Thompson. An outstanding sailor, Thompson would be taking his ship to one of the most treacherous coasts in Europe. Leaving Greenock, *Lady Frederic Campbell* was 'conveyed rather by the force of the tide than wind', southward down the Firth of Clyde. Unlike a journey on land, where itineraries could be planned with a degree of reliability, this would be a sea voyage, steered by the wind and tide. Pennant would soon get used to abandoning plans and modifying ambitions, for this would be a narrative written by meteorology and the moon.

The first few days on board set the tone for the expedition. Here, for example, is Pennant's account of their departure from East Loch Tarbet, on Loch Fyne:

'In the afternoon attempt to turn out, but am driven back by an adverse gale. Get out early in the morning… Most of the morning was passed in a dead calm: in the afternoon succeeded brisk gales, but from points not the most favourable, which occasioned frequent tacks in sight of port: in one broke our topsail yard.'

After successfully exploring the islands of Bute and Arran (where he measured a harpooned basking shark), and then Ailsa Craig (where the 'deafening chorus' of seabirds was amplified by a blistering hot, still day), the ship was once again becalmed as she attempted to round the Mull of Kintyre. Issuing Thompson with instructions

One of my most exciting moments, while following the wake of Pennant: at the wheel of *Spirit of Fairbridge,* steering a course for Canna. The 92-foot schooner is about the same size and tonnage as Pennant's *Lady Frederic Campbell.*

*Opposite:* On top of the Paps of Jura: the south ridge on Beinn an Òir, with the island of Islay in the distance. Pennant observed that 'the depth below was tremendous on every side'.

to round the Mull and wait by the island of Gigha, Pennant took to the ship's boat and rowed for seven miles to Campbeltown, where (according to local custom) he consulted the Oracle of the Bottle about his future voyage (he fails to pass on what the Bottle predicted). After exploring Gigha 'in a rotten, leaky boat', Pennant was back on board, preparing to sail for Islay: the 'capital' of the Hebrides: 'The weather extremely fine; but so calm that Mr Thompson is obliged to tow the vessel out of this little harbour.' A short while later: 'Attempt to steer for the island of Islay, but in vain…' About noon, a breeze sprang up, and the ship was

moving again, towards the island of Jura, which they collided with, lightly: 'About one o'clock on June 30, receive notice of getting into the harbour of the small isles of Jura, by the vessel's touching ground at the entrance.'

They had reached the Hebrides.

*Above:* The 'vast crag' of Ailsa Craig, 'appearing' wrote Pennant, 'like an inclined haycock'. Pennant found the island uninhabited but for vast colonies of seabirds. On the shoreline, he came across a ruined chapel, and the 'vestiges' of seasonal shelters used by cod fishermen each year between January and April.

\* \* \*

Unable to begin his Hebridean odyssey with Islay as he had planned, Pennant opens his account with Jura, 'the most rugged of the Hebrides'. Procuring local horses, Pennant and Lightfoot rode the island with their tick-list of 'Queries', recording Jura's physical characteristics, its produce, its wildlife (which included wildcats, otters, stoats and rats, and about one hundred stags), the health of its population, its superstitions (old women still preserved a stick of the wicken tree, or mountain ash, as a protection against elves), and its local diseases (a nasty flesh-worm curable only by a poultice of cheese and honey). They also came across a 'grotesque group' of shelters being used as a summer camp by the families that were tending cattle in the mountains. Jura would be Pennant's portal into unknown Scotland. But before he left the island, he had to climb a mountain: Beinn an Òir, the mountain of gold.

Beinn an Òir is the highest of Jura's 'Paps', the distinctive range of conical peaks which run down the spine of the island. They are a captivating sight, and as Pennant observes, 'perfectly mamillary'. From afar, their flanks appear smooth and symmetrical; up close, it becomes apparent that the Paps are sheathed with interminable screes composed of angular blocks. I've climbed to the 2,500-foot summit a couple of times, by different routes, and neither was particularly easy. On the last occasion, the 'mountain of gold' was smothered by a gale-force cloud. Streaming with freezing water, I felt as if I was trapped in a wind-tunnel full of fog. Gratifyingly, Pennant found the climb 'a task of much labour and difficulty'. Once on the summit, he plotted the landmarks:

*Opposite:* The screes of Beinn an Òir are 'composed of vast stones, slightly covered with mosses near the base, but all above bare, and unconnected with each other. The whole seems a cairn, the work of the sons of Saturn…' You're not kidding, Thomas.

> 'To the south appeared Ilay, extended like a map beneath us; and beyond that, the north of Ireland; to the west Gigha and Cara, Cantyre and Arran, and the Firth of Clyde, bounded by Airshire; an amazing tract of mountains to the north-east, as far as Ben Lomond; Skarba finished the northern view; and over the western ocean were scattered Colonsay and Oransay, Mull, Iona, and its neighbouring group of isles; and still further the long extents of Tirey and Col just apparent.'

The ascent of Beinn an Òir might have provided Pennant with an invaluable overview of uncharted waters, but it did not prepare him for the distressing sights for him waiting on Islay:

*Below:* One of the engravings derived from Moses Griffiths' expedition sketches, showing some of the 'grotesque' sheilings that Pennant came across on Jura. Inhabited by families tending cattle, they were 'constructed with branches of trees, covered with sods', and 'no other door than a faggot of birch twigs'. Inside were beds made from heather, 'placed on a bank of sods', covered with 'two blankets and a rug'.

> 'A set of people worn down with poverty: their habitations scenes of misery, made of loose stones; without chimneys, without doors, excepting the faggot opposed to the wind at one or other of the appertures, permitting the smoke to escape through the other, in order to prevent the pains of suffocation. The furniture perfectly corresponds: a pothook hangs from the middle of the roof, with a pot pendent over a grateless fire, filled with fare that may rather be called a permission to exist, than a support of vigorous life: the inmates, as may be expected, lean, withered, dusky and smoke-dried.'

Famine would have been inevitable, writes Pennant, 'but was prevented by the seasonal arrival of a mealship'. The contradiction was all too evident: despite the 'excellency of the land', people were starving. Pennant quickly found the reason. Cattle. Land grazed by cattle made more money for the laird than land under corn. Pennant discovered that Islay was exporting around 1,700 cattle each year, at a price of fifty shillings each. In fact, the island was so overstocked with cattle that 'numbers died in March for want of fodder'. To a man from the edge of the Cheshire Plain, it made no sense:

*Sheelins in JURA and a distant View of the Paps.*

'The country is blessed with fine manures: besides sea-wrack, coral, shell-sand, rock and pit-marl, it possesses a tract of thirty-six square miles of limestone. What treasures, if properly applied, to bring wealth and plenty to the island.' It would become a debilitating refrain. A staggering 7–8,000 people were living on the island. The population today is half that number.

From Islay, *Lady Frederic Campbell* sailed northwards, calling at the twin islands of Oronsay and Colonsay, then Iona, Canna, Rum and Skye. Each island was subjected to the same, methodical scrutiny. On Oronsay, Pennant found that 'good management', and a mix of pasture and arable, provided for the entire population. Two hundred yards across the water, Colonsay's greedy proprietor had reduced the population to starvation on an island with good soil, 'excellent' pasturage, plenty of limestone, sufficient peat, and a sea 'abounding in fish'. For the first time, Pennant allows anger to break across the page: 'How inadequate then is the produce of cattle, and how much more so is that of corn!'

On Canna, the plight of the islanders was heartbreaking. As *Lady Frederic Campbell* anchored in Canna's sheltered natural harbour, the shores 'appeared pleasing to humanity; verdant, and covered with hundreds of cattle…' But 'the natives soon dispelled this agreeable error'. Bread and meal had run out some time ago, and with their stock of fish hooks almost exhausted, the islanders' plight was now desperate. Pennant suddenly found himself utterly inadequate to the task: 'The ribbons, and other trifles I had brought would have been insults to people in distress. I lamented that my money had been so uselessly laid out; for a few dozen of fish-hooks, or a few pecks of meal, would have made them happy.' Why, he wondered, could not emergency 'magazines of meal' be established on the islands, just as the Turks provided 'caravansaras', and Alpine nations 'hospitia'.

VIEW IN CANNAY.

Griffiths' impression of Canna, looking across Coroghon Bay to the great rock known as the 'Prison'. Pennant landed in this bay, then climbed by 'a narrow and horrible path' to the top of the rock, where he found 'a little tower … so small as scarce able to contain half a dozen people'. The ruins of the tower still remain, balanced precariously above the bay.

Described in Martin Martin's ground-breaking guide of 1695, Compass Hill on Canna has a spot where the rock is so magnetic that it tugs a compass needle one quarter of the way around the dial. Like Pennant, I had a bit of what he calls 'broken' weather.

Despite the human misery, Pennant and Lightfoot gathered useful data on the island's natural resources and impoverished economy. Before leaving, they also investigated Martin Martin's bizarre claim that there was a 'high hill in the north end' of the island, where the compass needle 'instead of settling towards the north, as usual … settled here due east.' By the 1700s, this hill had acquired the name 'Compass Hill', and testing their own compass, Pennant found that the needle did indeed 'vary a whole quarter'. After an hour or so traversing the gale-swept cliff-tops, I did find the exact spot: a patch of sodden turf and rock just a few metres square, where the compass needle suddenly lurched a full ninety degrees off magnetic north. As Pennant had concluded, the cause is an area of rock so rich in iron that it overrides the earth's magnetic field.

Sailing on northward, each island produced a wealth of material. On Rum, Pennant listened to tales of second sight, and learned of a woman called Molly MacLeane who could forsee the future 'through a well-scraped blade-bone of mutton'. Unlike Gerald of Wales, who wrote six hundred years earlier of Flemings in Dyfed who could perform the same trick with the shoulder blades of rams, Pennant was sceptical. Skye, however, produced some real science.

'Visit a high hill, called Briis-mhawl, about a mile south of Talyskir, having in front a fine series of genuine basaltic columns, resembling the Giant's Causeway…' Pennant appears to have been the first to record the Talisker site in print.

Earlier in the voyage, Pennant had been disappointed when bad weather had prevented him from landing on Staffa and examining the basalt columns. But on Skye, he had the good fortune to be directed to a mountain he calls 'Briis-mhawl'. Pennant's mountain can be found just south of Talisker. Here, indeed, he discovered 'a fine series of genuine basaltic columns, resembling the Giant's Causeway'. The entire western side of the mountain is lined with faceted columns, which are so geometrically precise that they defy the normally chaotic rule of mountain-building. To Pennant, 'these were the ruins of creation: those of Rome, the work of human art, seem to them but the ruins of yesterday.'

On local horses, Pennant rode to the northernmost tip of Skye, where he found *Lady Frederic Campbell* anchored in Duntulm Bay. He had now reached the furthest extent of the Inner Hebrides. His plan had been to cross The Minch to the Outer Hebrides, but stories had been circulating on Skye of a 'putrid fever' that was raging 'with great violence' on the Hebridean island of Lewis.

As the cutter rode at anchor off Skye, Pennant made a decision which would alter the course of his expedition. Later in the book, he reveals what he had in mind: 'It was our design,' he writes, 'to have penetrated by land, as far as the extremity of the island.' It was an audacious, difficult, and undoubtedly hazardous twist to the itinerary. Pennant planned to sail *Lady Frederic Campbell* to the mainland, and then to ride horses overland to the north coast of Scotland, possibly even to Cape Wrath itself. He knew well that the risk and effort would be rewarded with recognition. No published account existed of the overland, western route to the 'top' of Scotland. This was, after all, the region Timothy Pont had labelled on his map as 'Extreem Wildernes'. And Pont was rare among mapmakers for having actually visited the north of Scotland. If Pennant succeeded, and returned to tell the tale, he would be applauded for his scientific endeavour.

Hauling the anchor at two in the afternoon, on July 24, *Lady Frederic Campbell* was wafted on an 'easy breeze' into The Minch on a course for Loch Broom. They sailed all night, and when Pennant climbed on deck at daybreak, he found the ship taking endless 'teasing tacks' through the Summer Islands towards Loch Kanaird. The anchorage, in the lee of Isle Martin, is a fiercely intimidating spot. Looming over the far side of the bay are the southern cliffs of Ben Mor Coigach, which appear to fall straight to the sea from a two-thousand foot summit. The reader can almost sense Pennant shivering with apprehension as he describes the 'vast and barren mountains' which blocked the view northward. The heights were, he noted, 'patched with snow' – a spectacle which seems extraordinary in this era of July heatwaves.

The explorers had effectively landed on another island, for the whole north-west corner of mainland Scotland was cut off from eastern Scotland by belts of mountains. It was easier to travel by sea than by land. Ominously, the weather had broken: 'Still on board,' notes Pennant tersely. 'The weather very bad.' Waiting on his creaking

'This is the most northern basalt I am acquainted with; the last of four in the British meridian: the Giant's Causeway appears first; Staffa succeeds; the rock Humbla about twenty leagues further, and finally the column of Briis-mhawl; the depth of the ocean in all probability conceals the lost links of this chain.'

cutter, Pennant had all too much time to brood upon the challenge he had set himself. Everything Pennant had read, or heard, had prepared him for what he knew would be the greatest physical – and navigational – challenge of his life. James Dorret's map of 1761 described a region strewn with formidable obstacles. Between Loch Kanaird and the north coast lay numerous mountains and four long seawater inlets, each fed by sizeable rivers. Not one road was marked between the Kyle of Localsh, opposite Skye, and Cape Wrath. To Camden, this was the most impoverished, remote region in mainland Britain, crippled by infertility due to the harsh climate, and plagued by 'very rapacious wolves'. Of Eddrachillis, the parish Pennant would have to cross on his way north, Blaeu had warned of it being 'impassable because of deserted cliffs'. But there was a prize for the taking: Pennant knew that if he could push northward to the Kyle of Durness, the sea loch adjacent to Cape Wrath, he would have pioneered a route which connected the west coast of the Highlands with the east coast.

The weather eventually eased, and Thompson was able to put his expeditioners ashore. In Strath Canaird, Pennant managed to procure some horses. They were diminuitive beasts, unshod, but sure of hoof. The climb from the valley began encouragingly: 'Kindreds and hospitality possess the people of these parts. We scarce passed a farm but the good woman, long before our approach, sallied out and stood on the roadside, holding out to us a bowl of milk or whey.'

To a man who had ridden, sailed and walked all the way from the Welsh border, 'the extremity of the island' must have seemed enticingly close: no more than sixty miles on horseback. But the climb from Strath Canaird went on for five miles, and rose to almost one thousand feet above sea level; it would have been the longest climb Pennant had ridden on his entire journey. 'Ascend a very high mountain,' he notes, 'and pass through a birch wood, over a pretty little loch…'; this was presumably Loch Cul Dromannan, whose magical waters still reflect the ridges of Coigach.

The 'road' was abysmal: 'a variety of bog and hazardous rock, that nothing but our shoeless little steeds could have carried us over.' Today, the crest of the pass is marked by a loop of abandoned single-track road, curving in a forgotten arc through the bog. Look west from this point and the prospect is truly intimidating. A peaty track (similar, probably to the one Pennant was attempting to follow) meanders off towards the dark bulk of Cul Beag, while the foreground is puddled with random

James Dorret's 'accurate Map of Scotland drawn from all the particular surveys hitherto published with many additional improvements'. Published in 1761, this was the most accurate, commercially-available map of Scotland on the market when Pennant left Chester, and may well have encouraged him to undertake his doomed overland expedition towards Cape Wrath: Dorret marks a road running all the way up the east coast of Scotland, to John O'Groats, and another road running west along the Pentland Firth, to Durness, the last settlement before Cape Wrath.

lochans. In low cloud and slashing rain, this is a grey and frightful place, with no shelter and a sense of utter isolation. Somewhere among the heathery mounds and sucking mosses, there is a parting of the waters, for one side of this vast bog drains southward towards Strath Canaird, while the other side dribbles northward into the vast parish of Assynt. For Pennant, it would be a watershed too far.

As the riders began the long and difficult descent on the far side of the pass, they had to creep beneath a sheer cliff whose footings were strewn with fallen rock: 'Pass under some great precipices of limestone,' noted Pennant (correctly identifying the rock of Knockan cliff), 'mixed with marble.' To his left, he could see 'a most tremendous view of mountains of stupendous height'. Nowhere else in Britain do mountains present themselves in such singular magnificence. Cul Beag, Stac Pollaidh, Cul Mor, Suilven and Canisp appear as a series of sheer-sided peaks, each separated from its neighbour by U-shaped gulfs which seem to plummet to sea-level. There was little in this view to comfort Pennant and his companions. 'I never saw,' gasps the explorer, 'a country that seemed to have been so torn and convulsed: the shock, whenever it happened, shook off all that vegetates.' At the foot of the peaks, observed Pennant, 'the blackness of the moors by no means assisted to cheer our ideas.'

The riders descended into a desperate land. Assynt, a vast, bleak, parish of some 1,700 unhappy souls, blocked the route that led to the north coast. As the sodden track picked its way through a dejected landscape, an anguished howl is released onto the page:

> 'This tract seems the residence of sloth; the people almost torpid with idleness, and most wretched: their hovels most miserable, made of poles, wattled and covered with thin sods. There is not corn raised sufficient to supply half the wants of the inhabitants: climate conspires with indolence to make matters worse; yet there is much improveable land here in a state of nature: but till famine pinches they will not bestir themselves: they are content with little at present, and are thoughtless of futurity; perhaps on the motive of Turkish vassals, who are oppressed in proportion to their improvements. Dispirited and driven to despair by bad management, crowds were now passing, emaciated with hunger, to the eastern coast, on the report of a ship being there loaden

Assynt and its monumental peaks, seen from the west. Pennant was eventually defeated by the terrain, and it would be another hundred years before a road was pushed north through Sutherland to Durness on the north coast. An intriguing entry in the 1722 edition of Camden's *Britannia* provides a possible motive for Pennant's interest in reaching Durness. 'The Shire,' records Camden of Sutherland, 'affords plenty of Iron-ore, and some Pearls. They have Coal, Freestone, Limestone, and good Sclate, in abundance: it is said also that they find some Silver; and it is supposed that there is Gold in Durinesse [Durness].' In Pennant's library in Wales were no less than five editions of Camden's *Britannia*.

with meal. Numbers of the miserables of this country were now migrating: they wandered in the state of desperation; to poor to pay, they madly sell themselves for their passage, preferring a temporary bondage in a strange land, to starving for life in their native soil.'

As evening drew in, the small troop of horsemen made their way over the mosses of the Ledmore valley, and then turned left to follow a tributary up towards the next watershed. A short way up this tributary, they came to a small, dishevelled township perched on the exposed ramp of moorland. The township was called Ledbeg – 'small slope'.

Pennant's Ledbeg has disappeared, except for a white-painted house on the far side of a tumbling river. Thought to be the oldest inhabited house in Assynt, it was built in around 1740 by a tacksman farmer, Alexander Mackenzie of Ardloch. Pennant makes no mention of what he found here, but the survey carried out in the summer of 1774, two years after Pennant's visit, still exists. Charged with assessing the Sutherland estate, John Home recorded that there were seven families, consisting of thirty-five people, living at Ledbeg, and that among them were 'Ardloch & Lady & 9 Serts' [servants]'.

Pennant's bleak note, that they 'obtained quarters, and rough hospitality' at Ledbeg, suggests that Mackenzie of Ardloch hardly made them welcome. This cannot have been a happy encounter, for Mackenzie was presumably one of those lairds whose 'bad management' had driven the local population to despair and emigration. Overnight, Pennant's plans unravelled. Perhaps the misery of his circumstances had sapped his spirit. Perhaps – after nearly three months of travel – he was tiring. On most arduous journeys, there comes a point when the sum of imagined difficulties launches a surprise-attack on the will to continue. It takes a doughty spirit to ride it out; to push on when all appears impossible. Pennant provides no insight into his own state of mind. He merely states that they 'were informed' that the route to the north coast 'was impassable for horses'. The explorers seem to have considered continuing on foot, but this too was deemed too difficult, for they were also advised 'that even a Highland foot-messenger must avoid part of the hills by crossing an arm of the sea' – a reference perhaps to the long tentacle of Loch a' Chàirn Bhàin, which reaches far inland from Eddrachillis Bay, to join with Lochs Glendhu and Glencoul, all of them hemmed-in by formidable mountains.

The most northerly point Pennant reached. This is Ledbeg's last surviving house, reputed to be the oldest in Assynt. It was in this building, or in one of the adjacent (demolished) crofts, that Pennant was finally persuaded that his plan to push on to the north coast would be too difficult and dangerous.

Until a concrete bridge was opened in 1984, all west coast traffic had to cross by ferry from a slipway at Kylesku.

Finally defeated, Pennant and his companions retraced their route through bog and rock, and over the appalling pass to Strath Canaird. 'At length,' notes Pennant with relief, 'we arrive safely on board the ship:

> 'A wond'rous token
> Of heaven's kind care, with necks
> unbroken.'

* * *

*Lady Frederic Campbell* probably left Isle Martin on the last day of July. With his failure to reach the north coast, the expedition was now homeward bound. 'Weigh anchor,' Pennant wrote, 'and sail with a favourable breeze towards the mouth of the bay, with a design on returning south…'

But as the cutter sailed clear of the Summer Isles that evening, the wind changed and they were struck by 'cold weather and hard adverse gales'. With the crew at the ropes, Thompson was forced to change course and tack into the mouth of Little Loch Broom, unaware that he had sailed into the jaws of a trap.

*Lady Frederic Campbell* sought shelter in the lee of a gigantic mountain which Pennant calls 'Tallochessie'. It 'may vie,' he writes, 'with the highest I have seen.' 'Tallochessie' can only be mighty An Teallach, 'the forge' – a name thought by many to derive from the smokey mists which often writhe from its tortured summit ridge. An Teallach is one of the largest, and most spectacular peaks in the Scottish Highlands, a massif of enormous spurs rising to a bristling spine of pinnacles. Protected from the worst of the wind, the explorers diverted themselves for a couple of hours by fishing with hand-lines. Little Loch Broom quickly yielded plentiful cod, some dogfish, 'and a curious ray'.

With darkness falling, Thompson decided to remain at anchor. For those who knew its confined waters (and Thompson clearly did not), Little Loch Broom was – and still is – prey to its own, extraordinary weather system. The sheer bulk of An Teallach, rising straight from the waters of the loch, had the nasty habit of converting easterly or southerly winds into chaotic downdraughts which could blast a ship onto it beam.

During the night, the wind picked up again, and as the gusts increased, Thompson began to fear that the cutter would drag its anchors and fetch onto the rocky foreshore, or worse, onto an unseen reef. Unsurprisingly, all on board now seem to

An Teallach, a giant among giants. Pennant's overland trek from Dundonnell to Loch Maree took him through the wild back-country southward from this mountain.

have been awake. Rather than drag the anchors, Thompson now considered cutting his cables. Better to risk the ship in the open sea, than to be driven ashore and wrecked. Neither option was particulary attractive, and Pennant remarks with amusing detachment that 'the circumstances of a black night, a furious storm, and rocky narrows, did not contribute to the repose of freshwater seamen'. The situation, he concludes, 'was disagreeable.'

As it happened, the storm seemed to subside, and by the time Thompson decided to weigh anchor, the wind was merely 'moderate', and Pennant was sufficiently in command of his observational faculties to note that the anchor chain reappeared from the waters of the loch clustered with 'several very uncommon asteriae'. It was, however, a deceptive moment of calm, for as soon as the anchor was lashed to the gunwhale, they were struck again by the curse of Little Loch Broom:

'No sooner was our anchor on board,' writes Pennant, 'but a furious squall arises, and blows in blasts like a hurricane, driving us before it at a vast rate.' Unable to regain the open sea, the cutter was hurled into the throat of the loch, a narrow constriction no more than one thousand metres wide. Beyond the constriction, the loch widened slightly to run inland between rocky shores for over seven miles. On the northern side of the loch, the mountains rose to 1,500 feet; on the southern shore, An Teallach topped 3,000. *Lady Frederic Campbell* was trapped. With little room to manoeuvre, Thompson struggled in vain to sail his way out of trouble. The further the ship was driven inland, the closer the mountains loomed, and the greater the downdraughts. Careering out of control, the ship 'arrived within a mile of the bottom of the loch'. Thompson realised that they were about to run aground. Pennant's own words more than adequately describe the cutter's struggle for survival:

'Drop anchor, but without effect; are obliged to weigh again, while the furious gale engages an attention to the sails, and flings us into a double perplexity in this narrow strait, where for an hour our tacks were almost perpetual, and the vessel frequently in no small danger. The blasts from the mountains were tremendous, not only raising a vast sea, but catching up the waves in eddies, and raising them up in the air to a surprising height.'

The 'waterspouts' Pennant describes are well-known on the loch, and it was a miracle that the cutter did not run into the rocks.

'At length,' he writes, 'we were relieved from our distress by a successful anchorage, under a high and finely wooded hill, in eight fathoms water, but within a small distance of eighty.' The wooded hill was probably Torr Garbh – 'rough mound'. With *Lady Frederic Campbell* riding securely at anchor, the travellers were rowed ashore. Yet again, Pennant's expedition was about to take an unexpected turn.

The narrow entrance to Little Loch Broom. Once the storm had driven *Lady Frederic Campbell* into the loch, she was trapped. The huge massif rising from the loch's southern shore is An Teallach. After the ship had narrowly avoided being wrecked at the head of the loch, Pennant landed on the southern shore and trekked overland to Loch Maree, which meant riding and walking from left to right through the mountains in this photograph. Strath na Sealga, which he crossed, can be seen as a deep trough, parallel to Little Loch Broom, behind An Teallach.

\* \* \*

The tempest could not have cast Pennant ashore at a more propitious spot. No sooner were they safely on dry land, than horses were provided for them 'by favour of Kenneth Mackenzie, Esq., of Dundonnel'. Mackenzie was both the local landowner, and a man whose reputation and influence carried far beyond the shores of Little Loch Broom. For over forty years, he had been developing and enlarging his father's land-holding around the loch.

Riding along the side of the hill towards the head of the loch, Pennant came to a broad, flat-bottomed valley, '…a small but fertile plain, winding amongst the vast mountains, and adorned with a pretty river and woods of alder.' After the storm, and the horrors of Assynt, the travellers could scarcely believe their eyes. For the first time in weeks, they were gazing upon enclosed fields: 'Here,' continues Pennant, 'we rejoiced with the sight of enclosures long strangers to us: the hay was good, the bere and oats excellent…'

The sudden view into the head of Strath na Sealga. Ahead, is the narrowing valley rising southward towards Loch an Nid, and Bealach na Croise. Pennant makes no mention of local inhabitants in Strath na Sealga, despite the fact that between thirty and forty families were living in the glen at the time. During the Highland Clearances, they were evicted, in spite of George Mackenzie's reluctance.

This was all the work of Mackenzie's tenants. Three miles from the head of the loch, Pennant came to Mackenzie's house. Built only five years earlier, it was an imposing, two-storey building, five windows wide, rising beside the river in the sheltered neck of the strath. In such fearsome surroundings, it is still a sublimely-calm haven. 'We found ourelves,' writes Pennant, 'seated in a spot equalised by few in picturesque and magnificent scenery. The banks of the river that rushes by the house is fringed with trees; and the course often interupted by cascades.'

Pennant had much to share with Kenneth Mackenzie, who had devoted considerable effort to improving the returns from his estates. Mackenzie recognised that the land and waters of the western Highlands could only be made productive through investment. Besides his commercial cattle interests, he had also tried to turn the herring into an income, hiring a cooper to make barrels, and commissioning a skipper to ship the fish to market. In 1758, he had applied to the Forfeited Estates Commissioners for financial assistance to construct a road to Loch Broom, and he had also paid to repair the local church. He was described by one who knew him well as 'a man of real worth', as prominent 'among his Neighbours as the full moon among the stars in a frosty night'.

Like Pennant, Mackenzie had high expectations and would proudly boast that of his seven sons, one was in Virginia, one in Holland, one in London, one in Edinburgh, one at home and two at school. However, his concern that there was 'neither Chief or Leader in this Country, particularly in our Name, to take any Concern with the growing generation' proved to be well founded. Although his son, George, was to be a very able custodian of the estate, the Mackenzie dynasty ran out of luck in 1813, when George's son Kenneth took over. Kenneth, who did not do well at school, developed a passion for the supernatural, and for hens. The estate was sold in 1834, for £22,000. By the 1990s, Dundonnell House and its enormous holdings were owned by lyricist Sir Tim Rice, whose extensive musical credits include the song 'No Chicken'.

Pennant's unplanned call at Dundonnell opened the door to a second attempt to explore the mainland. 'Determined,' he writes, 'to go by land to visit Loch Maree, a great lake to the south: and direct Mr Thompson to sail, and wait for us at Gairloch.'

Given his experiences in Assynt, this was a courageous – and perhaps foolhardy – idea. But he may have deemed it less unpleasant than another encounter with Little Loch Broom. To reach Gairloch overland, he would have to trek for twenty miles through the mountains and then find a boat to carry him the length of Loch Maree. Pennant left Dundonnel early in the morning with Mackenzie, one of the laird's sons, 'and another gentleman of the name' – perhaps another son. Of Pennant's team, only Lightfoot seems to have participated in the adventure.

On a day of buffeting wind and horizontal rain, I followed Pennant's mountain traverse. In any weather, this is an absolutely stunning hike. Coming down the zig-zag track into the head of Strath na Sealga, sunlight suddenly touched every fleck of water in the glen. Streaming slabs dazzled, and the river looked for a few moments like a serpent of molten metal. Throughout the trek, the various features Pennant describes can all be picked out. The 'vale with birch trees thinly scattered' is clearly Strath na Sealga; 'Loch Nanniun, or 'the lake of birds' is the Ordnance Survey's Loch an Nid, the 'loch of the nest'; the 'amazing mountain' whose flanks 'appear like an enormous sheet of ice' is Mullach Coire Mhic Fhearchair, whose wet, tilted slabs do indeed look like ice sheets. If you look in the bed of the stream beyond the slabs, you can even find chunks of the 'red and white marble' Pennant came across.

Shortly after this, Pennant's party reached Bealach na Croise, 'the pass of the trouble'. In mist, this is a notorious spot for getting lost; the correct route from the pass cuts slightly upward, across a vast, slanted peat bog. Scrambling up and down the peat hags, soaked and covered in black slime, I found it impossible to comprehend how Pennant managed to negotiate the slope with a horse. As if this section of the route could not be more tricky, the map leads you straight to the brink of a gorge into which are funnelled all the waters collected in the mighty corrie on the south side of Mullach

Coire Mhic Fhearchair. The only safe way to cross is to follow the lip of the ravine downstream, descend to the bed, hop across the boulders and then return up the far side to regain the compass bearing across the the peat bog. Pennant did at least concede that the going wasn't easy… 'The way horrible,' he notes, 'broken, steep and slippery.' He too, had trouble with the ravine: 'but our cautious steeds tried every step before they would venture to proceed.'

Bealach na Croise, 1,391 feet, one of the most remote spots in Britain. In Pennant's day, this was the standard overland route between Little Loch Broom and Loch Maree. Shortly after passing this cairn, hikers heading south must negotiate a peat bog and a ravine. In mist, it is navigationally challenging.

He must have been as glad as I was to see Loch Meallan an Fhudair sitting like an inky puddle in the peat below the crags of Sithean Biorach; there are few sights more pleasurable than a recognisable landmark on a misty mountain. Above the lochan is a slight levelling on the mountainside. At around 1,600 feet, it is the highest point on the trek. Far below, Lochan Fada's wrinkly shores run along beneath the massive bulk of Slioch. Mountains fill every horizon. It is a liberating, wild place, and about as far from a road as it is possible to be on mainland Britain.

A natural ramp of stone leads down the mountainside rather like a pavement. From the foot of this descent, there are no more navigational hazards. 'Dine on the side of a rill at the bottom,' notes Pennant, 'on plentiful fare provided by our kind host.' Kenneth Mackenzie bade farewell and set off back towards Dundonnell, leaving the two younger Mackenzies to guide Pennant and Lightfoot 'to the next stage'. Another seven miles of rough track led the travellers down to the 'meadowy plain' of Kinlochewe, where Pennant was set on procuring a boat, and pressing on down Loch Maree. But the weather turned 'wet, and tempestuous', and they decided to defer the voyage and take shelter in a 'whisky house'. For a man who professed to disapprove of such distillations, Pennant seems to have enjoyed this odd billet:

> 'Mr Mackenzie complimented Mr Lightfoot and me with the bedstead, well covered with a warm litter of heath: we lay in our clothes, wrapped ourselves in plaids; and enjoyed a good repose.'

Before dropping off to sleep, Pennant was amazed to observe the manner in which the two Scotsmen prepared their bed:

Lochan Fada, with the lower slopes of Slioch on the left. The route from Bealach na Croise descends the slope on the right, to join the footpath. It must have been close to this spot that Pennant dined 'on the side of a rill … on plentiful fare' provided by his guides, the MacKenzies.

'Our friends did not lose their sleep; but great was our surprise to see them form their bed of wet hay, or rather grass collected from the fields; they flung a plaid over it, undressed, and lay most comfortably, without injury, in what, in a little time, must have become an errant hotbed: so blest with hardy constitution are even the gentlemen of this country!'

By seven the next morning, Pennant and Lightfoot were climbing into a six-oared rowing boat. It wasn't until they had rowed some distance down the loch that Pennant's attention was drawn to 'a young man of good appearance', who was running along the shore 'hailing the boat in Erse language'. Thinking that he was trying to hitch a lift in the fully-loaded boat, Pennant ignored him. It was only after the young man had raced after them for two miles, 'through every difficulty', shouting dire threats as he did so, that one of the rowers informed Pennant that he was actually the owner of the boat, and merely wanted the honour of taking the place of one of the rowers. An apologetic Pennant mused that, 'Instead of insulting us with abuse, as a Charon of South Britain would have done, he instantly composed himself, and told us through an interpreter that he felt great pride in finding that his conduct gained any degree of approbation.'

Hugging the north shore, where the looming cliffs of Slioch leap straight up from the water for three thousand feet, the rowing boat inched westward. It wasn't until I rowed a heavy wooden boat into the centre of Loch Maree that I sensed its disquieting power. A vast body of water (the fourth largest freshwater loch in Scotland), pinched by sombre peaks, it can make a small boat seem microscopic. Like Little Loch Broom, the surface of Loch Maree can be stirred by violent squalls to a howling fury of white-capped waves. On a grey, gusty day with ice in the air, it is difficult not to row with a certain urgency.

In equivalent distance, Pennant and his crew were attempting to row nearly two-thirds of the way across the English Channel. Two hours of hard pulling would have placed Pennant's boat in sight of the waterfall which tumbles down the crags of Letterewe. Above the boat's bow he would have seen Loch Maree's archipelago of thirty or so islands, scattered as if a giant had snatched a chunk of Slioch and hurled its shards at the loch. Yet in the detail of the islands, in their pebbled coves and stands of pine, he might have sensed a still, and almost shocking, beauty.

'Land on that called Inchmaree, the favoured isle of the saint,' begins Pennant, 'the patron of all the coast from Applecross to Loch Broom.' It was of course this stretch of coast which had come so close to wrecking *Lady Frederic Campbell*. Inchmaree is the only island which has a clear line of sight to both ends of the loch. It is a sacred place. Barely two hundred metres across, it looks from an approaching boat like a verdant fragment of Amazonia. At the western end is a tiny shingle beach. Pennant and Lightfoot leapt ashore and picked their way through 'a beautiful grove of oak, ash willow, wicken, birch, fir, hazel and enormous hollies'. In the midst of the island, the explorers found 'a circular dike of stones, with a regular narrow entrance'. It is still there. And so are the medieval cross slabs, side-by-side among the fallen leaves, said to mark the burial places of a Norwegian prince and his wife. Pennant conjectures that Saint Maree had practised Pagan rites here 'as the readiest method of making a conquest over the minds of the inhabitants'. (Bulls were still being sacrificed on the island as late as the 1670s.) To Pennant, the 'curiosity of the place' was the well of Saint Maree, whose waters were known for their 'power unspeakable in cases of lunacy'. Pilgrims finding the well full could expect their onward journey to be propitious, but if it was empty, they could expect to proceed with 'fears and doubts'. Pennant fails to record the water level. Today, it is permanently dry.

Five miles beyond the end of the loch, Pennant and Lightfoot found *Lady Frederic Campbell* riding at anchor on the south side of Gairloch's bay. Blessed by 'a good breeze', the ship sailed away from the troublesome northern coast of Scotland.

*Lady Frederic Campbell* would take ten days to sail southward from Gairloch to Ardmaddie, where Pennant's Hebridean expedition would end. With the ship headed towards safer, more familiar waters, the tension on board lifted, and Pennant produced some of his best work. Two days after leaving Gairloch, the cutter anchored off Skye, and Pennant took the ship's boat ashore to gather information on the parish of Glenelg, and to examine two brochs which had been described fifty years earlier by

Loch Maree… Having trekked twenty miles from Dundonnell, over two mountain passes, bogs, rivers and a ravine Pennant borrowed a rowing boat at the southern end of the loch and set off on a thirteen-mile voyage.

Alexander Gordon. A few miles south of Glenelg, the ship dropped anchor in Loch Hourn, and Pennant took the ship's boat eight miles up the loch, where he chanced upon a fleet of one hundred herring boats, and a shore station constructed from 'multitudes of little occasional hovels and tents'. For Pennant, Loch Hourn was a happy epiphany:

> 'So unexpected a prospect of the busy haunt of men and ships in this wild and romantic tract, afforded this agreeable reflection: that there is no part of our dominion so remote, so inhospitable, and so unprofitable, as to deny employ and livelihood to thousands; and that there are no parts so polished, so improved, and so fertile, but which must stoop to receive advantage from those dreary spots they so affectedly despise.'

In Pennant's new utopia, cities and wilderness 'must be obliged to acknowledge the mutual dependency of part on part, howsoever remotely placed, and howsoever different in modes or manner of living'.

Six days later, *Lady Frederic Campbell* passed into the Sound of Jura, and after an excursion to see the great whirlpool of Corryvrekan, Pennant landed on the eastern shore of Seil Sound, beneath the 'small, but elegant' house of Ardmaddie. Here, he took leave of his skipper, Archibald Thompson, acknowledging his 'attention' to the expedition's aims, his 'obliging conduct throughout and skill in his profession'. At Ardmaddie, Pennant found his groom and horses waiting, ready for the onward journey through mainland Scotland, and eventually back to Chester. 'Thus ended,' he mused, 'this voyage of amusement, successful and satisfactory in every part, unless where embittered with reflections on the sufferings of my fellow-creatures.'

That night, at Ardmaddie, Pennant writes that he had a dream; 'a waking of the soul'. In this dream, the explorer is confronted by a clan chieftain from two centuries earlier. Armed with a targe and huge claymore, the grizzled warrior explains to Pennant how the 'mighty chieftains' were transfomed into 'rapacious landlords', exchanging the 'warm affections of their people for sordid trash'. The misery and idleness which now fill the glens can only be addressed if the 'famished clans' are instructed in 'the science of rural economy', in fishing and weaving, and given the opportunity to serve in Briatin's army and navy. In the dream, the chieftain tells Pennant that he must inform the world of the poverty he has witnessed.

The book which Thomas Pennant came to write is all the more remarkable for its triple role, as the first thorough guide to the natural history of Scotland, as the literary 'key' which would unlock the mysteries of Scotland to outsiders, and as a humanitarian plea to address the suffering of those closest to home.

'Our geographers,' complained Daniel Defoe, 'seem to be almost as much at a loss in the description of this north part of Scotland, as the Romans were to conquer it.' Fifty years later, Thomas Pennant had opened the door to the Highlands and islands.

# William Cobbett *1822-6*

## *Champion of the countryside*

When William Cobbett set out on horseback in the early 1820s, Britain was reeling from war, threatened by revolution, and struggling to adjust to runaway industrialisation and a population explosion. The countryside appeared traumatised by sudden change. Riding the back-country of south-east England, summer and winter for four years, this incendiary, witty journalist brought the rural crisis to the doors of Westminster. Scribbled in inns and farmhouses, the account he kept of his tours to the agricultural front-line is an exhilarating mix of invective and rustic vignettes. *Rural Rides* is a snapshot of the countryside in mid-revolution, and the last glimpse we have of England as a truly rural land.

* * *

'This morning I set off, in rather drizzling rain, from Kensington, on horse-back, accompanied by my son James…' It was Wednesday, September 25, 1822. Aged fifty-nine, William Cobbett was leaving home on the first of his 'Rural Rides'. On the saddle of each horse was a thin leather roll containing spare clothing. They carried no map, but knew where they were going. Heading west along Kensington Road, the two riders passed through the turnpike gate, then turned left onto a rutted lane which kinked gently downhill through fields and smallholdings to Earl's Court and Walham Green. Passing several muddy junctions, they picked up another lane, lined with cottages, which led to Fulham and the bridge over the Thames.

For the next five days, father and son wove a zig-zag course through Middlesex, Surrey and Hampshire, to the little village of Hurstbourne Tarrant, where an old friend of Cobbett's kept a farm. As Cobbett observes, he could have covered the sixty-six miles from Kensington in about eight hours. But that wasn't the point. His object was 'not to see inns and turnpike-roads, but to see the *country*; to see the farmers at *home*, and to see the labourers *in the fields*'. On back-roads and field paths, the two Cobbetts could explore a Britain invisible from the turnpike.

Riding along at walking pace, there was little that Cobbett could miss. With every mile, he noted the state of the countryside, the mood of the labourers, the soils and the crops. This autumn the rain had come, he decided, just in time for the wheat-sowing season. The turnips looked good, if a little '*backward* in some places'. And the fine summer had brought 'excellent' fruit: grapes were 'as good as those raised under glass', and apples 'much richer than in ordinary years'. The hop harvest had been 'not only large, but good in quality'. In fields and inns, he chatted with all classes of countryman, from destitute hop-pickers to 'opulent yeomen'. Throughout the ride, there is a spirit of discovery; of travelling with a stranger's eye. At Chertsey, he'd come

*Previous pages:*
Netheravon, Wiltshire,
from the tower of All
Saints Church.

across a livestock fair and investigated the prices being paid for horses and cattle. In mid-Surrey, he found a bridleway which led down to a 'narrow and exquisitely beautiful vale', a vertiginous Garden of Eden, with fine soils, ample woodland and corn-fields 'nearly as steep as the roof of a tiled house'. A necklace of small lakes lined with meadows and hop-gardens completed the picture. In this vale of plenty, there were coppices for hop-poles and charcoal for the powder-mills.

On this introductory ride, Cobbett took James back to his roots. Avoiding the 'level road to Guildford', they turned onto the open grassland of the North Downs and climbed to the crest of a whaleback ridge. Behind and in front of them was a seemingly-infinite pattern of heath, field and woodland. For one hundred miles, between his birthplace in Farnham and the white cliffs of Dover, the high, green wave of downland undulated across southern England like the time-worn wall of a lost generation of giants. Geology is seldom so emblematic. Chalk is the youngest of England's rocks, and there is nothing else in the geological record which has such a telling relationship with landscape and farming. It's given us billowing downs for sheep, and watered vales for cattle. Cobbett was born on chalk, and most at home on chalk. Midway between the city and the sea, these downs were known as 'the Surrey Hills', for this section of the North Downs neatly bisected the county. 'This county of Surrey,' mused Cobbett, 'presents to the eye of the traveller a greater contrast than any other county in England. It has some of the very best and some of the very worst lands, not only in England, but in the world.'

Two days later, on the county's western border, Cobbett walked his horse beneath a towering oak on a village green. He remembered the oak from his childhood, when it was 'but a very little tree, comparatively'. Now, he tells his son, it is 'by far the finest

The prospect south and east from the Surrey Hills. The crest of the downs is only twenty miles from central London, but 'Green Belt' planning restrictions have meant that the view has changed little since Cobbett's day.

tree that I ever saw in my life.' With James pacing and counting, the oak was subjected to a full survey. Reckoning it be 'full *thirty feet round*' its trunk, with 'fifteen or sixteen limbs, and many of them from five to ten feet round', Cobbett assessed its circumference at 'about three hundred feet'. The oak appeared to be free of decay, and it had 'made great shoots in all parts of it this last summer and spring', and there were 'no appearances of white upon the trunk, such as are regarded as the symptoms of full growth'. By the time he had finished, the Tilford Oak had been elevated to the status of a national monument.

On they rode, over the river and across sandy heathland to a deep, narrow valley known as 'the Bourne', an old Viking name given to places by springs and young streams. The soil here was too poor to attract landowners, and the valley was scattered with the cottages and pigsties of families who'd acquired the skills to live well from infertile ground. They were known locally as 'Bourners'. 'We went to this Bourne,' explained Cobbett, 'in order that I might show my son the spot where I received the rudiments of my education.'

Standing before the stream, Cobbett recalled those days:

> 'There is a little hop-garden in which I used to work when from eight to ten years old; from which I have scores of times run to follow the hounds, leaving the hoe to do the best that it could to destroy the weeds; but the most interesting thing was a *sand-hill*, which goes from a part of the heath down to the rivulet. As a due mixture of pleasure with toil, I, with two brothers, used occasionally to *desport* ourselves, as the lawyers call it, at this sand-hill. Our diversion was this: we used to go to the top of the hill, which was steeper than the roof of a house; one used to draw his arms out of the sleeves of his smock-frock, and lay himself down with his arms by his sides; and then the others, one at head and other at feet, sent him rolling down the hill like a barrel or a log of wood. By the time he got to the bottom, his hair, eyes, ears, nose and mouth, were all full of this loose sand; then the others took their turn, and at every roll, there was a monstrous spell of laughter.'

Cobbett's birthplace, the Jolly Farmer in Farnham. It's still there in Bridge Square, re-named the William Cobbett. His grave is a couple of minutes away, in the churchyard of St Andrew's.

Only a mile away, in the centre of Farnham, stood the Jolly Farmer Inn. Cobbett's father, George, had been the landlord, and a farmer. William had grown up under an open sky and here in the Bourne, he recognised the origins of his own nature:

> 'I am perfectly satisfied that if I had not received such an education, or something very much like it; that, if I had been brought up a milksop, with a nursery-maid everlastingly at my heels, I should have been at

THE BIRTH PLACE OF
WILLIAM COBBETT
Farnham,
SURREY.

this day as great a fool, as inefficient a mortal, as any of those frivolous idiots that are turned out from Winchester and Westminster School or from any of those dens of dunces called Colleges and Universities. It is impossible to say how much I owe to that sand-hill; and I went to return it my thanks for the ability which it probably gave me to be one of the greatest terrors, to one of the greatest and most powerful bodies of knaves and fools, that ever were permitted to afflict this or any other country.'

Cobbett's county has changed a little. The Jolly Farmer has been renamed the 'William Cobbett'. The Bourne has become a manicured suburb puddled with swimming pools, and Surrey's tranquil byways are now an automotive Hades. Tilford's oak is still on the green, though, a treasured stump which breaks into leaf each spring.

\* \* \*

There are two young Cobbetts. The William (or 'Bill') known to his brothers and sister was a mischevious, rebellious boy who revealed few signs of 'uncommon intelligence'. There was, apparently, 'nothing about him of the prodigy', although older brother Tom did remember William enjoying his father reading aloud from his newspaper. Parliamentary speeches were a favourite, and Cobbett later told his daughter that he used to wander on the common 'making speeches to the furze bushes'. Misdemeanours reported by his siblings included cutting from his father's map the head of a crocodile because it looked ugly, and absconding from pig-keeping because there was 'some business that better suited his taste'. To Tom, his younger brother was 'an ungovernable rather than a tractable youth'; a shirker of steady work, with 'an obstinate resolution for what he was bent on'. Biographer Richard Ingrams takes the view that Cobbett was, from the beginnning, exceptionally 'self-centred and self-sufficient'.

For his own readership, however, Cobbett created a diligent boy of the soil who began working the land when he was so young that he 'was hardly able to climb the gates and stiles'. William raced through a rustic syllabus from bird-scaring and weeding to harrowing barley. After learning to hoe peas, he wrote, 'I arrived at the honour of joining the reapers in harvest, driving the team and holding the plough.' His principal ambition was, he recalled, 'surpassing my brothers in the different labours of the field.' His education was heath and furrow: 'No teachers of any sort,' he would later claim. 'Nobody to shelter me from the consequences of bad, and no one to counsel me to good behaviour.'

An etching from Cobbett's autobiography, showing the young William in the yard of the Jolly Farmer. 'A pig in almost every cottage sty; and that is the infallible mark of a happy people.'

At least twice during the Farnham years, Cobbett walked away from farming. At the age of eleven, having learned of the botanic gardens at Kew, he set off on foot across the heaths, with thirteen and a half pence in his pocket. Passsing through Richmond, he spotted in a shop-window a book called *Tale of a Tub*. Intrigued by the title, he bought it for three pence. In Cobbett's version of events, Swift's satirical assault on the church led to a conversion on the road to Kew. The book remained with him until it was lost overboard in the Atlantic. A second breakout from Farnham, at the age of nineteen, saw Cobbett heading for Portsmouth and his first sight of the sea. From a long, high down called Portsdown, he gazed down stubbled fields to the naval dockyards and a silvery passage separating the mainland from the Isle of Wight. Like many a young labourer before and since, his impulse was to join a ship. He was ejected from the first vessel he boarded, and when he applied more formerly through the Port Admiral, he was again rejected.

The Portsmouth episode opened his eyes to further shores. 'I sighed for a sight of the world;' he recalled, 'the little island of Britain seemed too small a compass for me. The things in which I had taken the most delight were neglected; the singing of the birds grew insipid, and even the heart-cheering cry of the hounds … was heard with the most torpid indifference.' The final break came on May 6, 1783: 'I, like Don Quixote,' began the farm boy from Farnham, 'sallied forth to seek adventures. I was dressed in my holiday clothes…' Aged nineteen years and two months (although he actually throught he was seventeen at the time, since he mistakenly believed that he'd been born in 1766), he took the London turnpike and found a job with a Gray's Inn lawyer. Trained to draft documents in a brisk, copperplate hand, this was a tedious if invaluable apprenticeship for a man who would ultimately write something like thirty million words for publication.

Portsdown Hill, circa 1814–25, by Willam Daniell. The hill was a famous vantage point, visited over a century earlier by Celia Fiennes, who praised it as 'a very fine down … very pleasant for Sports Hawking and Hunting'. It always held a special place in Cobbett's heart, for it was from here that he first saw the sea, and the ships which would tempt him into leaving home. The hill's south facing slopes were celebrated later by Cobbett for having the earliest corn in the country. Most of the Down is now covered with housing.

Two of Gillray's etchings from Cobbett's autobiography.
*Left:* The farm-boy from Farnham enlisting in the 54th (West Norfolk) Regiment, and, *right*, the regiment's officers, hard at work.

The making of Cobbett, the Rural Rider, took another forty years, a couple of continents, and several reversals of fortune, ranging from imprisonment to bankruptcy. He hadn't lasted at Grays Inn, and after a few months, he enlisted with the recently-formed 54th (West Norfolk) Regiment of Foot, and sailed – as Corporal Cobbett – to adventure. The regiment landed in Nova Scotia in 1785 and then moved on to the wilderness of New Brunswick, where Cobbett made the most of 'skaiting, fishing, shooting, and all the other sports of the country', including canoeing. While there, he was reading everything to hand, from Shakespeare and Milton, to more of Swift. Already an incorrigible improver, he compiled a handbook on mathematics and geometry for his fellow infantrymen. But the intemperate forests were also nurturing a rebel, and when Cobbett reached the rank of sergeant major, he collided with 'the epaulet gentry', most of whom, so it seemed, neglected their regimental duties so that they could 'swagger about and get roaring drunk'. Back in England, when Cobbett attempted to get four of his superior officers court martialled for profiteering from his mens' food rations, he found himself stitched-up by the accused, and in March, 1792, he was forced to flee to revolutionary France, and then to recently-independent America. 'The Thing', as Cobbett would come to call the establishment, had created a contemptuous patriot. Settled with his new wife in Philadelphia, America's political nerve-centre, Cobbett found work teaching English, but soon began writing political pamphlets attacking American republicans, and their frenzied enthusiasm for all things French and revolutionary. He was so successful, that in June, 1800, a volley of libel suits forced him to flee back to England.

History is ill-equipped to record the privately-held fears of nations, but there is every reason to suppose that these were extraordinarily anxious times. Revolution gripped the western world. The American Revolution had been followed in 1789 by the French Revolution. In Britain, radicals raised the spectre of a *coup d'état*. Absent for the best part of sixteen years, Cobbett returned to a country in crisis. Harvests had failed and food prices had soared. Britain was in the midst of the greatest, most expensive war it had ever fought, and Pitt had been forced to introduce a new tax – income tax – to pay for munitions and equipment. War weary and fearful of invasion by revolutionary France, the country was wide open to home-grown insurrection. The Navy had mutinied, twice. Food riots were hitting cities and market towns; in the countryside, ricks were burning. Common land was being enclosed by a new breed of acquisitive farmers and landlords, and rents were spiralling. On average, land rents rose by 80 per cent between 1790 and 1813. Back in Farnham, Cobbett found two of his brothers struggling for survival on their small farms. Labourers across the Home Counties had lost their livelihood:

> 'The *clock* was gone; the *brass kettle* was gone; the *pewter dishes* were gone; the *warming pan* was gone… All was gone! How miserable, how deplorable, how changed that Labourer's dwelling, which I, only twenty years before, had seen so neat and happy!'

In Cobbett's youth, farm labourers lived with the farmer – a practice he maintained at his own farm in Botley. One of the few farmhouses to survive from this era is Emley, on the northern slopes of Hindhead, in Surrey. Now owned by the National Trust, it has its own interior well, large fireplace and upstairs rooms which would have been shared by labourers.

Cobbett went back to the land, using money he'd earned in America, to buy a house and eighty acres of land in Hampshire, on the sunny side of the South Downs. The soil was nothing special, 'a deep and stiff clay', Cobbett said, but it was good for oaks and for wheat. Here, he experimented with species imported from America and planted over twenty thousand trees – mainly oaks, elms and ashes. He kept Botley for twelve years, while his political life resumed its reckless trajectory. Having attacked prime ministers Addington and then Pitt for making peace with Napoleon, he launched his vitriolic periodical, the *Political Register*, which briskly matured from a Tory organ to the mouthpiece of radical reform. The aim was not revolution, but 'a pretty complete change of men' at the top, and a roots-up reform which would allow the free election of politicians, and the means of making 'change in the management of affairs'. The price to pay for radical journalism was a two-year spell in Newgate Prison, and then a second flight to America. When he came back to England two years later, the reform movement was in disarray, infiltrated by government spies, and shocked by the massacre in Manchester of eleven reformers, and the wounding of four hundred. The government blamed the Press, and new measures crippled the circulation of Cobbett's *Register*. Bankrupted, he had to sell his beloved Botley and move to London.

By the beginning of 1821, Cobbett and his family had been back in England for just over a year. In April, they moved into a small cottage in Kensington, then a fashionable suburb draped over a hill just to the west of Hyde Park. Gazing down from the heights was Kensington Palace. On the north side of the village, the area known as 'Gravel Pits' gave way to open country which ran down to Notting Dale and Notting Barn, but the soul of the village lay to the south. Here was London's most lively suburban strip. For a few hundred yards along each side of the turnpike, a busy, transitory community jostled for space amid workshops, houses and over a dozen inns. The Cobbetts had managed to get hold of an undeveloped, four-acre plot on the south side of the turnpike, between Tucker's candle factory and the Scarsdale House Boarding School (a site now occupied by Kensington High Street Underground Station). The walled smallholding already contained a pigeon house, and Cobbett quickly imported three cows, and laid plans to breed turkeys and establish a seed farm and nursery garden.

For most people, a four-acre research station would have been an adequate challenge. But Cobbett was also busy on a series of instructional guides to rural self-sufficiency, 'containing information relative to the brewing of beer, making of bread, keeping of cows, pigs, bees, ewes, goats, poultry, etc.' Writing the introduction to *Cottage Economy* in July, 1821, he launched his campaign to fight rural poverty and to create '*abundant living* amongst the people at large'. Three months later, with winter

The turnpike gate on Kensington Road – now Kensington High Street. The print dates from 1820, the year before Cobbett and his son, James, rode down the turnpike at the start of the first Rural Ride.

drawing in, he rode out from Kensington to Hampshire on a mission to gather information from the agricultural front line. His report appeared in the *Political Register*: 'The farmers here, as everywhere else, complain most bitterly,' he wrote, ' but they hang on, like sailors to the masts or hull of a wreck.' In only eight years, between 1814 and 1822, the wages of agricultural workers plummetted by one third.

Over the next ten years, Cobbett undertook many more rides, but the ones which he eventually packaged in 1830 as the 'Rural Rides', took place in a four year period, between September 25, 1822, and October 26, 1826.

* * *

A map describing Cobbett's *Rural Rides* would look like a tangle of noodles. Never has an documentary author created such an unchartable itinerary. His strenuous aversion to turnpikes, and the obscure locations he wanted to reach, meant that many a journey got from A to B by way of Z. In general, he roamed in an area which extended from Kent in the east, to Wiltshire in the west, and as far north as Gloucestershire. More often than not, he headed west from London, through Surrey and Hampshire.

No matter how far Cobbett rode from Kensington, the capital maintained its presence. But this was not the London celebrated by Defoe a hundred years earlier for its ability to permeate the provinces with trading wealth. To Cobbett, London is the 'Great Wen', the wart, the revolting sebaceous cyst on the face of Britain. And it wasn't just London. The industrial revolution was creating a multitide of mini-Wens, 'other Hell-Holes', as Cobbett put it, 'of 84 degrees of heat'. The problem was not the nature of cities themselves, but the people who ran them: 'the monopolizers and the tax-eaters and their purveyors and lackeys and harlots'. Cities waged war and bred corruptions like paper money and speculation. They harboured 'The Thing', and they were growing at a frightening rate. London's population in 1820 was just over one million. Only one century earlier, the population had been 300,000. And two centuries before *that*, when John Leland was walking to school in the yard of St Paul's, London had been – by modern standards – a small town of forty thousand.

By Cobbett's day, London was perceived as two zones. The inner, metropolitan zone was a tightly packed urban mesh of nine thousand streets and 180,000 houses crammed into an area measuring about four by seven miles. Outside this built-up zone was a broad suburban swathe of villages and market towns whose character could be seen as more urban than rural. When John Cary published his exquisite one-inch-to-the-mile pocket atlas of the metropolis in 1817, he extended his survey to 'the country fifteen miles round London.' Thomas Moule's map, 'The environs of London', understood the suburban radius to extend for about eight miles.

Cobbett loathed the suburbs. 'All Middlesex is *ugly*,' he memorably pronounced, after repeated journeys through the county. London's satellite communites were fair game for abuse. The Middlesex villages of Twickenham, Hampton, Sunbury and Shepperton, wrote Cobbett, 'consist generally of tax-eaters' showy tea-garden-like boxes, and of shabby dwellings of labouring people, who, in this part of the country, look to be about half *Saint Giles's*: dirty, and have every appearance of drinking gin.'

Expanding London, and its suburban sprawl, from Cary's *Actual Survey of Middlesex*, 1786.

When Cobbett has to return to London at the end of 'a most beautiful ride through the Weald', he ascends the steep flank of the North Downs to suffer a collapse of spirit: 'When you get to Beckenham, which is the last parish in Kent,' he sighs, 'the country begins to assume a cockney-like appearance; all is artificial, and you know longer feel any interest in it.'

For Cobbett, rural England began where Middlesex ended, on Chertsey Bridge. His methods for engaging with the countryside were almost as stringent as William Gilpin's 'Picturesque rules'. Turnpikes and carriages were 'out'; field paths and horses were 'in': To see the country properly, he wrote, 'you must go either on foot or on horse-back. With a *gig* you cannot get about amongst *bye-lanes* and *across fields*, through bridle-ways and hunting-gates; and to *tramp it* is too *slow*, leaving the *labour* out of the question, and that is not a trifle.' Public transport was out of the question, too: 'In any sort of *carriage*,' he pronounced, 'you cannot get into the *real country places*.' Cobbett's countryside was open and accessible. He wasn't limited to 'public footpaths' and 'public bridleways';

The bridge over the Thames at Chertsey. The river here marked the county boundary between Middlesex and Surrey. For Cobbett, this was the threshold of rural England; the moment he left the 'Great Wen' behind.

he doesn't come across barbed-wire blockades or 'Keep Out' signs. Flexibility was essential, for bad weather could close roads, or make progress too difficult. His rides were often wonderfully spontaneous, changeable affairs: 'On Monday,' he writes while overnighting in Dover, 'I was balancing in my own mind whether I should go to France or not. To-day I have decided in the negative, and shall set off this evening for the Isle of Thanet; that spot so famous for corn.'

Although Cobbett's routes appear whimsical and convoluted, some of them at least may have been quite carefully planned; on one occasion, he mentions that he 'must adhere to a certain *route* as strictly as a regiment on the march', as he had to 'get to London by a certain day'. To this end, he had '*written* the route' in advance. Earlier, when setting off to explore Kent, a county he knew little, he writes that he 'got a list of places from a friend in Sussex, whom I asked to give me *a route to Dover*, and to send me through those parts of Kent which he thought would be interesting to me.' In the same passage, he admits that he 'had not looked at a map of Kent for years, and, perhaps, never.' Given that the great age of British mapping was in full swing, it's a fairly astonishing confession. The first Ordnance Survey map had just been published, in 1801, and it covered Kent. By the 1820s, the OS and various private publishers had printed maps of southern England in unprecedented detail and accuracy. During a ride in the far west, another new territory for Cobbett, he had made a tracing from a 'fine map' belonging to Sir Thomas Winnington, of Stanford Park in Worcestershire, to help him find his way home through the unfamilar back-country of the Cotswolds.

Cobbett's map of Hampshire, from his *Geographical Dictionary of England and Wales.* For an insight into his spatial awareness, compare the outline of this map, with that on the following page.

The result was infuriating: 'A *route*, when it lies through *villages*, is one thing on a *map*,' complained Cobbett, 'and quite another thing on the ground.' He wasn't the first to discover that a map could be a misleading simplification: 'Our line of villages, from Cheltenham to Fairford was very nearly straight upon the map; but, upon the ground, it took us round about a great many miles, besides now and then a *little going back*, to get into the right road; and, which was a great inconvenience, not a public-house was there on our road, until we got within eight miles of Fairford.' The suspicion that Cobbett could not read a map is supported by his own attempts at cartography. A couple of years after *Rural Rides* was published, he produced his hefty *Geographical Dictionary of England and Wales*, which included the most deformed county maps published in the nineteenth century.

In this age of GPS and market-induced phobias about 'getting lost' and 'losing time', there is something enormously liberating about Cobbett's attitude to navigation. He senses his way forward, using a combination of topographical nous, memory and local advice. Luckily for his readers, it doesn't always work. In Kent, he suddenly finds himself 'upon the sea-beach', apparently unaware that he had ridden all the way to the English Channel. 'Never,' he muses, 'was I so much surprised as when I saw a sail.' In deepest Surrey, having been warned not to try the direct route between the villages of Chiddingfold and Thursley because of thick woodland, Cobbett goes ahead anyway ('the great thing was to see the interior of these woods; see the stems of the trees, as well as the tops of them'). Inevitably, he gets lost, but the occupant of an isolated cottage agrees to act as a guide, and Cobbett is led through a sylvan paradise into an ash coppice, which produces an impassioned diatribe upon the economic and social benefits of planting the heaths of southern England with locust trees. A fast-growing deciduous hardwood now regarded as a weed, the locust was ideal, argued Cobbett, for 'small fencing, hedge stakes, hurdle stakes, fold-shores', and furniture. Not only that, but the stump of each locust could produce two eighteen-inch locust pins for ship-building, at 'twenty-two thousand locust pins to the acre, probably enough for the building of a seventy-four gun ship'. Locust trees 'would be a prodigous creation of real and solid wealth' (unlike paper money, 'which only takes the dinner from one man and gives it to another'). The locust tree, 'being of the very first importance to the whole kingdom', would put Britain back on its feet. At the time, Cobbett's own locust plantation in Kensington was doing well, although some trees he'd sold the previous year to a 'gentleman' had all died. Eaten by hares, concluded Cobbett.

Mud-spattered and curious, Cobbett had the knack of disarming those he met on the road. Rural England was his heart, soul and manner, and Cobbett had that travellers' gift of humility. In an age of metropolitan ostentation, he could pass for a ploughman: 'Never,' observed the journalist James Grant, 'were the looks of any man more completely at variance with his character. There was something so dull and heavy about his whole appearance, that any one who did not know him, would at once have set him down for some country clodpole … who … had never read a book, or had a single idea in his head.' Cobbett, however, was confidently in his element. To a man who had honed his survival skills in the forests and rapids behind the ragged shores of the Gulf of St Lawrence, southern England was unthreatening. The days of highwaymen on Hounslow Heath, and of August snowstorms, were gone. He could ride through England's softest shires as if they were a vast market garden. He was entirely at ease in the countryside.

\* \* \*

Although there was no such thing as a typical day in the saddle for Cobbett, the style of his travelling invited the kinds of incidents and insights that made a man feel glad to be alive. He had one of his most fruitful days on the road late in November, 1822. It was a Sunday, and he had set himself the goal of riding from Hambledon, a village in the South Downs not far from Portsmouth, to the village of Thursley, about five miles south-west of Godalming. Unusually, he had a map. Unfortunately, the map described Hampshire, and Thursley was in Surrey. Undeterred, he simply plotted a straight line towards a village called Headley, on the edge of his map. From there, he reckoned it was 'about five

John Harrison's county map of Hampshire, published in 1788. The turnpike Cobbett was so desperate to avoid can be seen heading up from Portsmouth through Petersfield towards Hindhead, on the Surrey/Sussex border. The scale is about six miles to the inch, which provides nothing like the detail required to undertake an off-road journey.

miles' to his destination. This would have been a perfectly logical method of navigating at sea, but on land, it set Cobbett on a collision course with a precipice and a swamp. Relishing the prospect, he set out 'in spite of all the remonstrances of friends, who represented to me the danger of breaking my neck at *Hawkley* and of getting buried in the bogs of *Woolmer Forest*.'

It takes an intense engagement with the landscape to turn a one-day ride through Hampshire and Surrey into an epic which reads like a surveying expedition in the heart of a new continent. There was, of course, an easier route between Hambledon and Thursley. A mere twenty-seven miles, it involved following the London turnpike over the top of Hindhead. But Hindhead was a problem. The 800-foot hill was one of Cobbett's most loathed locations. Not only was it covered in barren heathland, but it had been disfigured by one of the government's Semaphore stations, and it lay within the 'sink-hole' borough of Haslemere. It was also said to be haunted. Hindhead had to be avoided at any effort.

It all started well enough. The opening miles from Hambledon are bathed in an expectant glow, as Cobbett and his servant ride north over the shoulder of Old Winchester Hill and onto the long, downland ramp descending to the Meon Valley: 'If I had not seen any thing further to-day,' sighed Cobbett, 'I should have dwelt long on the beauties of this place. Here is a very fine valley, in nearly an elliptical form, sheltered by high hills sloping gradually from it; and, not far from the middle of this valley there is a hill nearly in the form of a goblet-glass with the foot and stem broken off and turned upside down. And this is clapped down upon the level of the valley, just as you would put such goblet upon a table. The hill is lofty, partly covered with wood, and it gives an air of great singularity to the scene.'

What follows is characteristic of Cobbett's carrot-and-stick journalism. No sooner have we fallen for East Meon, than he beats us soundly with the truth: 'I am sure,' he continues without breaking-out a new paragraph, 'that East Meon has been a large place.'

Near Old Winchester Hill. Cobbett came this way early in the morning of November 24, 1822 – a day which he later claimed was the most interesting he had passed in his life. Cobbett would not be able to undertake his ride today without frequent trespassing.

A 'large place'. Readers of the *Political Register* knew this to be the opening rumble of the Depopulation Rant. Here was yet another village that had suffered the flight of its labourers: 'The church has a Saxon Tower pretty near equal, as far as I recollect, to that of the Cathedral at Winchester … and it shows that the church (which is still large) must, at first, have been a very large building.' And there was more amiss in East Meon. On the ride over from Hambledon, Cobbett had observed 'many square miles of downs near this village, *all bearing the marks of the plough*, and all out of tillage for many many years'. Regulars of Cobbett flinch at this point, for once he's spotted a brutalised landscape, he starts thwacking. There is 'not one single inch', he begins, of these Hampshire downs 'but what is vastly superior in quality to any of those great "improvements" on the miserable heaths of Hounslow, Bagshot, and Windsor Forest. It is the destructive, the murderous paper-system, that has transferred the fruit of labour, and the people along with it, from the different parts of the country to the neighbourhood of the all-devouring *Wen*.' And off he goes, accusing the government of inventing Census returns which show Britain's population to have increased by four million over the last twenty years. The rant is followed by an open letter to one of Cobbett's enemies in the 'Pitt-system', George Canning, in which he asks the head of Foreign Affairs 'what *sort of apology*' is going to be offered to the nation for allowing the 'French Bourbons' to intervene on behalf of the royalists in the Spanish Civil War. Within the space of a few lines, pretty East Meon has become a war zone. But then the carrot is proffered again, and Cobbett leads his readers away from the Meon and across the Petersfield turnpike into a disquisition upon soil-types and the benefits of spreading chalk on fields of difficult clay.

At a friend's house near the turnpike, Cobbett asked for advice about the hazards ahead. 'I got instructions to go to *Hawkley*,' relates Cobbett, 'but accompanied with most earnest advice *not to go that way*, for that it was *impossible to get along*.' The words 'not' and 'impossible' being terms of encouragement to Cobbett, he set off towards Hawkley, receiving further inducement from a woman in a wayside cottage who warned: 'Sir: you can't *ride* down: will your horses go *alone*?' Cobbett was most in his element when there was new land to explore: 'On we trotted up this pretty green lane; and indeed, we had been coming gently and generally *up hill* for a good while. The lane was between highish banks and … out we came, all in a moment, at the very *edge of the hanger*! And, never, in all my life, was I so surprised and so delighted! I pulled up my horse, and sat and looked; and it was like looking from the top of a castle down into the sea.'

Although his horse was standing no more than ten miles from the sandy valley he'd rolled down as a boy, Cobbett – despite being England's off-road authority – realised that he was gazing upon a landscape that was utterly foreign: 'Those who had so strenuously dwelt on the dirt and dangers of this route, had said not a word about the beauties, the matchless beauties of the scenery. These hangers,' he explained, 'are *woods* on the sides of *very steep hills*. The trees and underwood *hang*, in some sort, to the ground, instead of *standing on* it. Hence these places are called *Hangers*.' Deciphering the folds in the slopes, Cobbett saw that he was on the edge of a convoluted, wooded cliff which had protruding spurs, 'like *piers* into the sea'. The ends of two of these promontories are, he writes 'nearly perpendicular, and their tops so high in the air, that you cannot look at the village below without something like a feeling of apprehension.' Despite the bare, winter trees, 'the spot,' he concluded, 'is beautiful beyond description, even now.' In the distance, the two riders could make out the vast heaths of southern Surrey and the looming bulk of Hindhead: 'Men, however, are not to have such beautiful views as this without some *trouble*. We had the view, but we had to *go down the hanger*.'

Cobbet, a few months from his sixtieth birthday, stepped gingerly over the edge:

> 'The horses took the lead, and crept down partly upon their feet and partly upon their *hocks*. It was extremely slippery too; for the soil is a sort of *marle*, or, as they call it here, *maume*, or *mame*, which is, when wet, very much like *grey soap*. In such a case it was likely that I should keep in the *rear*, which I did, and I descended by taking hold of the branches of the underwood, and so *letting myself down*.'

Having survived the descent, and remounted, they crossed a field, then a farmyard, forded a river and then joined one of the strangest roads Cobbett had ever seen. Ahead of them was a deep, gleaming trench: 'The banks were quarries of *white stone*, like Portland-stone, and the bed of the road was of the *same stone*; and, the rains having been heavy for a day or two before, the whole was as clean and as white as the steps of a fund-holder or dead-weight door-way in one of the Squares of the *Wen*.' It was, Cobbett realised, bedrock: 'How many ages it must have taken the horses' feet, the wheels, and the water, to wear down this stone, so as to form a *hollow way*!' He was wrong about the Portland limestone, though. This was chalk.

Dropping off the edge of the hanger which cuts across Hampshire to the south-west of Hawkley. Several public footpaths and bridleways wriggle down the face of this beautiful inland cliff.

Reaching the village of Hawkley, they asked a farmer for the way to Thursley. Again, Cobbett was advised to abandon his projected route through the 'low countries' and to head instead for the turnpike over Hindhead. Again he declined, but as he approached the bogs of Woolmer Forest, yet another passer-by warned him off his route. 'These people,' he complained, 'seemed to be posted at all these stages to turn me aside from my purpose.' A short while later, a more helpful local pointed out the little-used track they should follow through the dreaded mires. Following hoof prints in the spongy soil, Cobbett instructs his servant: 'Keep you *close to my heels*, and do not attempt to go aside, not even for a foot.' With some relief, they entered Headley: 'This road was not,' he admits, 'if we had been benighted, without its dangers, the forest being full of *quags* and *quick-sands*.'

Woolmer had reminded Cobbett that Crown lands were being wasted with plantations of fir. Why fir, Cobbett wanted to know, 'seeing that the country is already over-stocked with that rubbish?' There should be an investigation, he demanded: 'Is there a man in Parliament that will call for it? *Not one*.' And, he continues, there never will be, 'until there be *reform*'.

Cobbett and his servant reached Headley at dusk, just as it began to rain. They must have been riding for the best part of eight hours. In the warmth of the Holly Bush ('a nice little public house') they sat down to cold bacon, bread and milk, and Cobbett began to feel uncomfortable: 'I at first intended to stay the night,' he recallled, 'an intention that I afterwards very indiscreetly gave up. I had *laid my plan*, which

Taking its name from 'Wolf Mere', Woolmer Forest, on the eastern border of Hampshire, was one of the region's accident blackspots. Notorious for its quagmires and pools, it lay right in the gap between the chalk downs, on the route from Portsmouth to London. Largely due to the Ministry of Defence, fragments of Woolmer have been preserved today.

included getting to Thursley that night… I began to feel ashamed of stopping short of my *plan*, especially after having so heroically persevered in the "stern path", and so disdainfully scorned to go over Hindhead.'

The servant, by now, has disappeared from the tale: 'There was a *moon*, but there was also a *hazy rain*. I had heaths to go over, and I might go into quags. Wishing to execute my plans, however, I, at last, brought myself to quit a very comfortable turf-fire, and to set off in the rain, having bargained to give a man three shillings to guide me out to the Northern *foot of Hindhead*.' There, he would find the village of Thursley, and the house of his friends, the Knowles's.

Well, to cut a very long story short, the man led Cobbett through darkness and driving rain for six miles in the wrong direction. Various misadventures ensued, which culminated in the sodden pair emerging from the trees onto the turnpike close to the summit of Hindhead; 'that very Hindhead,' cursed Cobbett, 'on which I had so repeatedly vowed I would not go!' Maddeningly, they then had 'the whole of *three miles of hill to come down at not much better than a foot pace*, with a good pelting rain at our backs.' The guide was denied his three shillings for luring Cobbett onto the Hindhead turnpike after claiming that he knew the back-road to Thursley. With 'skin soaking' and 'teeth chattering', an exhausted, elated Cobbett changed into dry clothes and warmed up before his friend's fire: 'Thus ended,' he mused, 'the most interesting day, as far as I know, that I ever passed in all my life.'

\* \* \*

Hindhead, described by Cobbett as 'the most villainous spot that God ever made', had a dark past which he never mentioned. The summit of the hill had been the spot where criminals were hanged, and their tarred bodies left to rot in irons. As recently as 1787, three murderers had been left swinging on Hindhead. The gibbet appears in Turner's sketch of 1807, and the upright was still standing while Cobbett was taking his Rural Rides. The hill was held in so much dread by travellers, who particularly feared being caught there at night, that in 1827, a granite cross was erected on the site of the gibbet. The engraving of 1811 on the left is by Robert Dunkerton, after Turner.

It wasn't until I drifted across Hampshire in the basket of a hot air balloon, that I began to understand how the physical patterns of rural England had been reinvented during Cobbett's life. From five hundred feet, all you see is a vast plain of evenly-coloured crops ruled occasionally by fine, pencilled lines of tarmac. There are few hedgerows, and no humans. It's a landscape born of the revolution which obliterated the traditional 'open field' pattern of agriculture. Ever since they had been introduced to the landscape in the great farming revolution which had swept the island in the late Saxon/early medieval era, open fields had been as much a part of rural England as elms and fords. Most villages with tillable land were surrounded by hundreds of long, narrow strips of cultivation, which were rotated between crops and pasture, and managed communally. Any one farmer might cultivate several strips. Catch sight of an open field today, and it would be an extraordinary sight: a multi-textured, many-coloured blaze of stripes arranged in a chaotic patchwork of blocks, rather as if a child had practised hachures with every pen in the house. And at various times of the year, those stripes would have been covered with people, hoeing and ploughing, weeding and planting. At the peak of the open-field system, around the time of the Black Death, something like one-third or one-quarter of England was farmed in strips. The abandonment of open-field farming began gradually, with farmers exchanging strips to create continuous blocks of land which they demarcated with hedges. In this piecemeal fashion, the process of

Flying to Nutley, over the enclosed fields of Hampshire.

'enclosure' had been slowly altering the form of the English landscape for at least five hundred years before Cobbett rode over the horizon. But from the 1720s through to the 1840s, a tidal wave of enclosure by private act of parliament swept the land. Within a year or two of an act being passed, a parish could see its multitude of strips being entirely replaced by a few large, enclosed fields, owned or managed by the few. In all, something like three thousand English parishes were affected, and 4.5 million acres of open field wiped out by parliamentray enclosures. Around two million acres of heaths, commons, mountains, moors and 'barren' land were enclosed, too.

Peering over the edge of the balloon basket, with a copy of an open-field map from 1653 to hand, I watched as the village of Nutley slid towards us. The three-hundred year old map showed the village at the hub of an intensely-detailed pattern of strip cultivation. On the outskirts of the village, I was able to match a block of seventeenth-century open fields against the modern hedges and fences. In one place (later I found that it was called 'Burnham Field') no less than ninety-nine strips had been amalgamated into a single, modern field. Parliamentary enclosures had a disproportinate impact on chalk uplands.

In principle, Cobbett was not against a rationalisation of land-use, but Acts of Enclosure all too frequently drove labourers from the land and destroyed existing stands of valuable timber and common grazing. His comments on the transformation to Waltham Chase, an area of open country and woodland close to his old farm at Botley, in southern Hampshire, is typical. Hearing of a new Act to enclose the Chase, and knowing it as 'very green and fine', and populated by a great many famiilies, Cobbett was appalled: 'Therefore, besides the sweeping away of two or three hundred cottages; besides the plunging into ruin and misery all these numerous families, here is one of the finest timber-lands in the whole kingdom, going to be cut up into miserable clay fields, for no earthly purpose but that of gratifying the stupid greediness of those who think that they must gain, if they add to the breadth of their private fields.' The Chase was enclosed.

Two estate maps of Nutley. On the left, a map of 1653, showing the open fields which surrounded the village; on the right, a map from 1823, after Nutley's fields had been enclosed. Burnham Field can be seen in the centre of the map.

Cobbett was convinced that the emptied villages he kept coming across had been sucked dry by parliamentray enclosure. *Rural Rides* is scattered with references to churches – such as All Saints at East Meon – which seem too large for the local population. On a ride in the summer of 1826 across Salisbury Plain, he borrowed from a friend 'a *very old* map of Wiltshire', from which he traced the location of every church, manor house and mansion in the Avon valley. Astonishingly, there were no less than thirty churches in as many miles. When he rode down the Avon, which had been described to him 'as one of the finest pieces of land in all England', he found a ghost valley. Cobbett assessed the agricultural output of the valley and weighed it against the existing population of 9,116 persons. There should have been, he concluded, an enormous food surplus, but the people and the produce of the Avon were going 'from this valley towards the WEN.'

What Cobbett could see from his saddle, didn't accord with Government figures:

> 'I do not believe one word of what is said of the *increase* of the population. All *observation* and all *reason* is against the fact; and, as to the *parliamentary returns,* what need we more than this: that *they* assert, that the population of Great Britain has *increased* from *ten* to *fourteen* millions in the last *twenty years*! That is enough! A man that can suck that in will believe, literally believe, that the *moon is made of green cheese.*'

The Avon Valley in Wiltshire, where Cobbett conducted a horseback survey intended to show that the area had been subject to massive depopulation.

But it was Cobbett who believed in celestial dairy produce. Britain's population was exploding. By the first official census in 1801, Britain's population had increased by about 25 per cent since 1750, which was about 50 per cent above the European norm. Between the 1801 and the 1821 census – the twenty years Cobbett was referring to – the returns did indeed show a surge of four million Britons. In concert with the political cataclysms Cobbett had lived through, he was also in the grip of a demographic revolution.

For many at the time, Cobbett included, the figures were too incredible to believe. And in the underfilled churches, abandoned plough-land and relic villages, he genuinely believed that he could see the evidence of a tax-eaters' hoax to justify low wages and further enclosure. The very rural 'improvements' Cobbett despised had converted Britain into the most efficient food producer in Europe. Enclosures, turnpikes and canals had already helped to make English agriculture 2.5 times more productive than the continent's leading farmer, France. Along with improved hygiene, it was the staggering productivity of British farmland that was fuelling the population increase. While Cobbett's *Cottage Economy* was trying to woo labourers back to smallholdings, the number of Britons working in agriculture was in freefall, from 75 per cent in 1750, to a mere 21 per cent by 1851. Cobbett's eyes were not deceiving him. There were fewer people working on the land, and those who had survived, were often living in poverty, in a rural culture which had acclimatised to sudden dispossession. But he was wrong about population growth: in the fifty years leading up to the publication of *Rural Rides* in 1830, Britain's population doubled in size. Lingering in England's agrarian past, and locked to his rural itineraries, Cobbett refused to accept that ports, towns and cities had replaced the cottage as the labourer's habitat. As for the enormous churches, their scale reflected the ambition and prosperity of their medieval builders. Building big moved you closer to God.

A contemporary print showing a family abandoning their cottage and smallholding following an Act of Enclosure.

\* \* \*

It is at the outer limits of Cobbett's rides that he discovers the extremes of injury to man and landscape. A distant sixty miles from the Great Wen, the Cotswold Hills, the Channel coast and the New Forest extracted from Cobbett some of his most impassioned diatribes. The further from London he rides, so it seems, the less pleasing he finds the land. And the more evidence he uncovers of squandered taxes and rural injustice.

In the far west, where the Cotswolds peer across the Vale of Severn to Wales, the problem was partly geology. Cobbett just didn't like limestone: 'ugly country', he called it, with thin soils of '*stone brash*', no trees and fields divided by walls – an alien sight in chalk country. Without a surface 'smooth and green like the downs,' Cobbett wrote, 'this is a sort of country, having less to please the eye than any other that I have ever seen, always save and except the *heaths* like those of Bagshot and Hindhead.'

The limestone had another unfortunate characteristic. Unlike chalk, it's a good building stone. Where the clay-lump and timber cottages of the south-east crumbled and rotted once they'd lost their roofs, abandoned limestone buildings remained as eerie shells: 'But how melancholy is the sight of these decayed and still decaying villages in the dells of the Cotswold,' sighed Cobbett, 'the ruins do not *totally disappear* for ages!' Withington, deep in the hills, displays '*all* the indubitable marks of most melancholy decay': a complex of intersecting lanes which he thinks were once streets; a large, open space where markets or fairs might have been held; a church 'like a small cathedral'; and two large, old houses with stone upping-blocks against their walls. These, he decides, 'were manifestly considerable *inns*'. A man he finds in a barn confirms that Withington once had three public houses. Here, concludes Cobbett, is yet another village whose fields had been grabbed by 'some tax-eater' or 'wicked loan-mongering robber'. Today, Withington's honey-coloured cottages and hideous acres of stone brash lie at the heart of an Area of Outstanding Natural Beauty.

Withington, in the Cotswolds. When Cobbett rode up this lane, the place had been virtually abandoned.

Cobbett's horror at the permanence of stone is a bizarre reversal – in just a century – of the wonder expressed by Celia Fiennes and Daniel Defoe, for whom stone was the material of the future. But they had travelled in an age when industry was still a novelty, and when the countryside teemed toiling folk who sold their surplus produce at thriving market towns. Cobbett's Britain was the laboratory of irreversible change; of revolutions in industry and agriculture; of explosions in population and

Cobbett reserved one of his most spectacular outbursts for Cheltenham. 'It is,' he exploded, 'situated in a nasty, flat, stupid, spot, without any thing pleasant near it.' The illustration depicts some of Cobbett's '*spa-people*' exhibiting their taste on Montpelier Promenade, c.1835.

urbanisation; of experiments in political reform. He was right to be fearful. And when we look at the foot of the infamous J-curve which measures concentrations of carbon dioxide in the atmosphere, guess when it started to rise? The early 1800s.

There was little in runaway capitalism to console Cobbett. Paper money and stock-jobbing was eroding self-reliance and turning Britain into a nation of spineless hypochondriacs. And nowhere was there a more repellent exhibition of urban excess than in the Cotswold town of Cheltenham, a 'watering place,' spluttered Cobbett, 'that is to say, a place, to which East India plunderers, West India floggers, English tax-gorgers, together with gluttons, drunkards, and debauchees of all descriptions, *female* as well as male, resort, at the suggestion of silently laughing quacks, in the hope of getting rid of the bodily consequences of their manifold sins and iniquities.' It's fair to say that you wouldn't have caught Cobbett in a jacuzzi: 'When I enter a place like this,' he finished, 'I always feel disposed to squeeze up my nose with my fingers.'

Just as far from London, in the opposite direction, Kent hid even more horrors than Gloucestershire. In the south-east corner of England, where the chalk ran right to the sea, Cobbett found outstanding soils, yet poverty and waste. There was much to his liking in the orchards and hop-gardens, the stands of timber and the corn. But when he eventually reached the coast, he found a military front line littered with extravagant relics. Hythe, he thunders, 'is half *barracks*; the hills are covered with barracks; and barracks most expensive, most squandering, fill up the side of the hill.' Nearby, he comes across an enormously costly, thirty-mile canal which had been constructed as an invasion barrier. And then he works himself into a whirlwind about Martello towers: 'I think I have counted along here upwards of thirty of these ridiculous things, which, I dare say, cost *five*, perhaps *ten*, thousand pounds each; and one of which was, I am told, *sold* on the coast of Sussex, the other day, for TWO HUNDRED POUNDS!' (Nowadays they sell for half a million quid.)

Here on the margins of Kent, he discovered where the taxes had gone; the taxes that had crippled rural labourers: 'All along the coast there are works of some sort or other; incessant sinks of money; walls of immense dimensions; masses of stone brought and put into piles… The whole thing, all taken together, looks as if a spell had been, all of a sudden, set upon the workmen; or, in the words of the Scripture, here is the "*desolation of abomination, standing in high places*".'

One military edifice symbolised more than any other the futility and bungling which lay at the core of Britain's costliest war. Dover, 'ancient, most interesting, and beautiful', is chewed and gouged by caverns, tunnels and trenches. 'This is, perhaps,' writes Cobbett, 'the only set of fortifications in the world ever framed for mere *hiding*. There is no appearance of any intention to annoy an enemy. It is a parcel of holes

The Martello towers Cobbett came across had been constructed at speed between 1804 and 1812 to defend southern England against invasion from Napoleonic France. Together with the Royal Military Canal, they formed a line of defence which plugged the forty-mile gap on the south coast, between the terminal cliffs of the North and South Downs. To Cobbett, they were yet another example of squandered taxes.

made in a hill, to hide Englishmen from Frenchmen.' All the French had to do, explained the ex-sergeant-major, was to land on the adjacent, flat beaches of Romney Marsh or Pevensey Levels, and bypass Dover's 'honeycomb' defences: 'And for a purpose like this; for a purpose so stupid, so senseless, so mad as this, and withal, so scandalously disgraceful, more brick and stone have been buried in this hill than would go to build a neat new cottage for every labouring man in the counties of Kent and of Sussex!' Pitt's real fear, believed Cobbett, was not French beach-landings, but an invasion of ideas; Cobbett once referred to the titanic struggle with Napoleon, as 'the late wars against the liberties of the French people'. In dumping the old order, the 'spirited and sensible' French, reasoned Cobbett, had rid themselves of the burden 'of which our farmers so bitterly complain'.

Nowhere was the cause of that misery clearer than here in Kent, on the fertile Isle of Thanet. Alongside the vast barns, the huge crops of wheat and the enormous ricks, Cobbett found labourers' houses 'beggarly in the extreme', and the people 'dirty, poor-looking; ragged'. Compared to the impoverished gravels and sands of heathland further west, Thanet's level, chalky soils were 'a garden indeed'. But the people were in a wretched state: 'Invariably have I observed,' wrote Cobbett, 'that the richer the soil, and the more destitute of woods; that is to say, the more purely a corn country, the more miserable the labourers... In this beautiful island every inch of land is appropriated by the rich. No hedges, no ditches, no commons, no grassy lanes: a country divided into great farms.' In some counties, the number of small owner-occupiers fell by as much as 40 per cent between 1770 and 1825. This was the future of farming. For ordinary folk, Thanet was uninhabitable: 'All the rest is bare of trees; and the wretched labourer has not a stick of wood, and has no place for a pig or a cow

The 'famous Isle of Thanet ... a garden indeed'. Here on the fertile chalk lowlands at England's extremity was some of the best corn country in the kingdom. Cobbett was amazed by the size of the barns and huge ricks, and appalled by the extreme poverty of the labourers and their families. Stopping at a pub for breakfast, he could get no bacon for himself, and no corn for his horse. 'It is impossible,' he raged, 'to have an idea of any thing more miserable than the state of the labourers in this part off the country.' Kent would be one of the flash-points of the imminent rural revolt.

BLIND MANS BUFF _ with the poor

Pray open your eyes

I can't See you

have pity on us

THERE IS NONE SO BLIND AS HIM WHO WILL NOT SEE

A cartoon mocking the indifference of the Establishment to England's starving underclass. 'For my own part,' wrote Cobbett, I really am ashamed to ride a fat horse, to have a full belly, and to have a clean shirt upon my back, while I look at these wretched countrymen of mine; while I actually see them reeling with weakness; when I see their poor faces present me nothing but skin and bone, while they are toiling to get the wheat and the meat ready to be carried away and devoured by the tax-eaters.'

to graze, or even to lie down upon. The rabbit countries are the countries for labouring men. There the ground is not so valuable.' England's threatened tribes of countrymen would have to look to the woods for survival.

Cobbett saw trees as the last resource of the cottage economy. Thousands of miles in the saddle had convinced him 'that people in woodland countries are best off, and that it is absolutely impossible to reduce them to that state of starvation in which they are in the corn-growing part of this kingdom. Here is that great blessing, abundance of fuel at all times of the year, and particularly in the winter.' Cobbett's enormous tree nurseries, and his endless column inches in the *Register* promoting their sale and distribution, was rooted in his belief that woodland would be the salvation of the cottager.

Cobbett delayed visiting the largest, best known forest in southern England until the end of his final Rural Ride. When he eventually took the long road south-west, late in October, 1826, he mentions that his purpose was to investigate how much progress had been made in establishing locust-tree plantations, but it turned into an extended field trip which produced more words than any equivalent-sized tract of land in *Rural Rides*. Three days of zig-zagging, getting lost, and chance encounters, produced the material he needed to conclude his four-year quest.

In a sense, it did all have to come to an end in the New Forest. Here, were the worst soils he had ever seen; soils so spectacularly bad 'that a poorer spot than this New Forest, there is not in all England; nor, I believe, in the whole world.' It was even 'more barren and miserable,' he decided, 'than Bagshot Heath.'

In theory, such an 'intolerable heath' was, of course, ideal for subsistence families, who would find in the forest everything they needed: timber for building and fuel;

common grazing for cattle and sheep; plentiful game to hunt, and beech cover for pigs. Cobbett claimed to have seen in the forest, 'many, many thousands' of pigs in just one day. On one occasion, he counted 140 hogs and pigs within sixty yards of his horse. With elaborate calculations and historical research, Cobbett argued that the Forest had once supported a huge human population. So why not again? There was, as always, a problem. The New Forest was a Crown Estate and not available for colonies of labourers' cottages. Or for growing plantations of locust trees. Firing a closing broadside at 'the Thing', Cobbett demanded that the Forest be handed back to the nation.

Cobbett wrote up his three-day exploration of the New Forest at Weston Grove, a grand house elegantly located on a promontory between the mouth of the River Itchen, and Southampton Water. The views, he said, were 'the most beautiful that can be imagined.' Like a conjuror pulling his best-kept trick out of his hat at the end of the show, Cobbett produced the owner of Weston Grove, Mr William Chamberlayne, MP for Southampton and beacon of political virtue. Chamberlayne, an old friend of Cobbett's from his Botley days, owned all the land between the Itchen and the Hamble, and was so generous to his day-labouring men that he had held their wages at thirteen shillings a week for twenty years, despite the national collapse in incomes. Here, at last, was the model land-owner:

Much of the New Forest is unchanged since Cobbett spent three days exploring its lowland heaths and woodland in the autumn of 1828. The infertile, acidic soils have never appealed to farmers, and although the eastern fringes of the Forest have been encroached upon by urban developments, oil refineries and an industrial complex, the remainder was enclosed within a National Park in 2004.

'I know how much good he must do; and there is a great satisfaction in reflecting on the great happiness that he must feel, when, in laying his head upon his pillow of a cold and dreary winter night, he reflects that there are scores, aye, *scores upon scores*, of his country-people, of his poor neighbours, of those whom the Scripture denominates his brethren, who have been enabled, *through him*, to retire to a warm bed after spending a cheerful evening and taking a full meal by the side of their own fire. People may talk what they will about happiness; but I can figure to myself no *happiness* surpassing that of this man who falls to sleep with reflections like these on his mind.'

* * *

For years, Cobbett was predicting that the crisis in the countryside would come to a head in the early winter of 1830. Right on time, Kent and Sussex went up in flames, and then Hampshire, Berkshire and the western counties. Labourers turned on farmers, smashed threshing machines and demanded higher wages. Two thousand were arrested, and special commissions condemned to death nineteen rioters, imprisoned six hundred, and transported to Australia and Tasmania a further five hundred. In the months that followed, pressure for parliamentary reform intensified until – in 1832 – the Reform Act was passed 'to prevent', in the words of its chief architect, Earl Grey, 'the necessity for revolution'. Cobbett, an MP at last, spent his final years in a rented farm at the foot of the Hog's Back, the long, high ridge of chalk which provided the opening prospect of *Rural Rides*.

Can there be a bridleway, or field path, or green lane, in the softer shires of England that hasn't measured the prints of Willam Cobbett's horse?

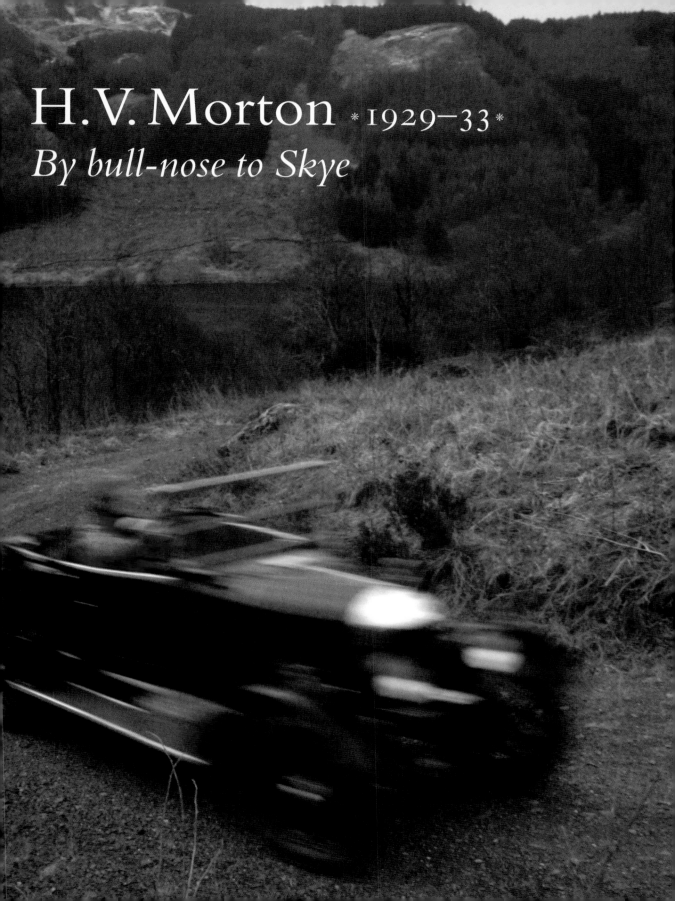

# H.V. Morton *1929–33*

*By bull-nose to Skye*

John O'Groats
Tongue
Wick
Lairg
Bonar Bridge
Skye
Dingwall
Elgin
Portree
Inverness
Aviemore
Aberdeen
Black Cuillins
Fort Augustus
Corrieyairick Pass
Lairig Ghru Pass
Braemar
Mallaig
Blair Atholl
Montrose
Fort William
Ben Nevis 4406'
Pitlochry
Blairgowrie
Tobermory
Dundee
Mull
Crianlarich
Perth
Oban
St Andrews
Stirling
Edinburgh
Dunbar
Linlithgow
Glasgow
Berwick-upon-Tweed
Arran
Kilmarnock
Galashiels
Kelso
Ayr
Selkirk
Jedburgh
Goat Fell 2808'
Merrick 2784'
Newton Stewart
Dumfries
Carlisle
Mull of Galloway

N
S

# H. V. MORTON IN SCOTLAND

1929 – 33

**W**HEN mass-produced motor-cars began rolling off production lines in Cowley and Longbridge in the 1920s, the man who led the charge into the countryside was a journalist in a Bullnose Morris. The evangelist of recreational motoring would have been appalled by his success; the number of cars on British roads has exploded from a few hundred when Morton was a child, to 31 million today. But, to a generation seared by war and then the Great Depression, H.V. Morton's motoring odysseys promised romance, adventure and an archipelago of delights. *In Search of England* was published in 1927, and it was quickly followed by *In Search of Scotland* (1929), *In Search of Ireland* (1931) and *In Search of Wales* (1932). With forty books to his name, Morton became the most successful travel-writer of his generation.

\* \* \*

The car Morton drove had three gears, a top speed of around forty and looked a bit like a highly-polished bathtub bolted to pram wheels. He called it 'Maud'. Approach a Bullnose Morris today, and it is immediately apparent why motoring was so adventurous in the 1920s. There are no seat belts and no roof (although some kind of canvas contraption can be stored in a cavity at the back). Entering the driver's seat is a bit like clambering into the cockpit of a biplane, stepping off the running board and then lifting and twisting each leg over the nickel-plated broom handle used for dipping the headlights. All the instruments and controls are at odds with a modern car. The pedal which influences the speed of the contraption nestles between the clutch and the brake, placed so that a moment of inattention from a modern driver will cause the car to accelerate into double-bends and garages. Where you would expect to find a speedometer, there is a large ticking clock. Should you ever suspect the vehicle of going fast, a pair of binoculars will be required to read a distantly-located dial above the passenger's left knee. A quaint glass tube running up the centre of the dashboard turns out to be the petrol gauge. You can't actually *see* the petrol inside it, so the only way of finding out whether you're almost empty is by lowering a dipstick into the tank. And each time you park, you must remember to turn off the petrol using the big brass plumbing tap beneath the dashboard. Just in case she catches fire as you walk away.

Henry Canova Vollam Morton was born in Ashton-under-Lyne in the summer of 1892. His mother was a lowland Scot and his father a newspaperman. The Mortons were disposed to mobility. Joseph Morton had been born in India, studied medicine in Edinburgh and then switched to journalism just as newspapers became the medium

*Previous pages:*
Glen Trool, Galloway
Forest Park.

for the masses. Circulations were soaring, new titles were being launched, and old titles amalgamated. In the space of just seven years at the turn of the century, the *Daily Mail*, the *Daily Express*, the *Times Literary Supplement* and the *Daily Mirror* all appeared on newstands. The *Mail's* circulation catapulted from zero to over a million in its first three years. Newspapers were glamorous and risky, and the workaholic editor of the *Ashton-under-Lyne Herald* had ambitions beyond Lancashire. Chasing up the editorial ladder, Joseph moved the family to Manchester and then Birmingham. Henry saw more of his mother, who brought him up on tales from her homeland. 'Some stray old wind from Culloden blew,' remembered Morton, 'into my nursery when I was a child, for almost the first stories I heard were stories of Skye and of a brown-eyed prince hiding in a cave. Bred on the folk heroics of Bonnie Prince Charlie, Rob Roy and William Wallace, Morton's Britain was a land of light and shade; of teeming metropolis and mythological wilderness.

This was also a Britain waking to hypermobility. The expanding rail network already stretched to over twenty thousand miles, and roads were becoming busier by the year with all manner of vehicular inventions, many of them forged in the workshops of Birmingham and its industrial satellites. A new type of vehicle – the motor car – could occasionally be spotted, but the device which gave flight to 'Harry' Morton was the 'safety bicycle'. Multiplying cavalcades of pedal-propelled machines had been tearing along England's byways since the 1860s, and by the time Harry's parents moved to Birmingham (home, as it happened, of Britain's largest cycle manufacturer, Starley Brothers), cycling had become an Olympic sport, and John Foster Fraser and his two companions had cycled around the world in 774 days. Bicycles were exciting, simple, convenient and cheap. Railways had created a culture of efficient, mass-transportation, but bicycles offered a return to the long-distance freedoms that were once enjoyed by lone horsemen. Anyone with a few pounds to spare could buy a bicycle and take to the shires in the spirit of Fiennes and Defoe. In 1897, the Scottish Mountaineering Club could report that its members were using bicycles to reach peaks way beyond railheads. By then, there were around one million active cyclists in Britain, and H. G. Wells had given English fiction its first cycling hero, the gravitationally-challenged Mr Hoopdriver in *The Wheels of Chance*.

Harry Morton, an H. G. Wells fan, got the bug in around 1909, escaping from Birmingham into the lanes of Warwickshire and pedalling as far as

Harry's birth had coincided with the greatest breakthrough in the history self-propelled human transport. 'The art of walking is obsolete,' chortled *Scientific American* in 1869. By the mid 1890s, there were around one million active cyclists in Britain. Anybody with taste and a sense of adventure had to own a bicycle, including writer Thomas Hardy, seen left.

Coventry, Warwick and Stratford-upon-Avon, where he could indulge in his passion for the theatre and girls. 'It is not easy to explain to the young the layer of tranquility that appeared to be spread over England in 1909,' he would recall, 'and a modern generation would find it difficult to believe that one could cycle for miles along roads and lanes meeting only a farmer in his trap, a shepherd with his sheep, cows moving across from one pasture to another, and loaded wagons drawn by two or more huge shire horses. The roads of England were a cyclist's paradise; never again will there be anything to match it.'

Those last, long summers before the outbreak of the Great War imprinted upon Morton's memory the England he would later come back to find. 'I have come to the conclusion,' he would write, 'that the only completely magic age in life is between the ages of ten and fourteen, a time when the senses are vividly aware of beauty yet unawakened to evil.' In April, 1909, three months

Emptying the tomb of Tutankhamun in February, 1923. Morton was on the spot, and managed to talk his way into the Royal antechamber, where he stared in astonishment at treasures that had been hidden for thirty centuries. 'Nothing stranger,' he wrote, 'would ever happen to me.' Events which followed led him to 'go home in search of England'.

before his seventeenth birthday, he left school and took a short-term teaching job before joining his father's paper, the *Birmingham Gazette and Press*, as a junior reporter. He stayed with the *Gazette* for four years, and then, in 1913, he left his rustic playground for the capital. Packing three crates of books, he set off for London. He was twenty-one.

Morton's eventual return to the shires to search for the essence of England may not have occurred if his arrival in Fleet Street hadn't coincided with the most catastrophic war to strike the planet. Having cut his teeth on the *Evening Standard*, the young provincial had graduated to Northcliffe's mighty *Daily Mail*, early in 1915, just as world affairs intervened. Morton's war was peculiarly uneventful: he found himself serving as a cavalry officer in Essex, trained as he put it, as if he was 'going to fight Napoleon'. On being demobbed, he surprised himself by recovering an enthusiasm for journalism, but he had lost his pre-war momentum. He found himself back on the *Standard*, and it wasn't until he joined Beaverbook's *Daily Express* at the end of 1921 that he won his day of fame on the front page. A year after joining the paper, he was despatched to Luxor to cover the opening of Tutankhamun's tomb. His story made the front page headline.

In Morton's romanticised version of events, the emergence of Egypt's fabulous king from his lost vault in the Middle Eastern desert was also the moment which defined his own calling. After the tomb had been covered again, Morton decided to extend his Middle Eastern tour so that he could visit Jerusalem. Aptly, it was here that he had a revelation. Writing later, behind the guise of the amusingly-feeble narrator he had created for his travel books, Morton relates that he had been feeling unwell. 'In the black depths of misery', he had climbed a hill overlooking the Holy City, and there he had succumbed – in the absence of a woman to convince him otherwise – to the conviction that the pain in his neck was 'the first sign of spinal meningitis'. What actually happened in 'the cold, unhappy mountains of Palestine' was known only to Morton, but it was unquestionably a clever place to suffer a personal crisis. Four years later, he was able to begin the book that would re-launch his career with the words: 'I believed that I was dying in Palestine'.

Jerusalem turned him towards a green and pleasant land: 'I took a vow,' wrote Morton, 'that if my pain in the neck did not end for ever on the windy hills of Palestine I would go home in search of England, I would go through the lanes of England and the little thatched villages of England, and I would lean over English bridges and lie on English grass, watching an English sky.' Thus did 'H.V. Morton' begin his progress from homesick hypochondriac to national treasure.

It took Harry Morton four years of Fleet Street graft to navigate his way through the dispiriting labyrinth separating journalism from authorship. It wasn't until the spring of 1925 that he got the break he needed, when the chairman of Methuen invited him to collate into a book a series of newspaper articles he'd written on London. *The Heart of London* was an immediate success, and in an incredible spate of productivity, Methuen published a further four of Morton's books about London by the end of 1926.

In the midst of this frenzy, Morton rekindled the fevered vision he'd had on a hill above Jerusalem. He would take to the lanes of England again. Armed like Leland with a commission, he would strike out from London, as the *Express* announced, 'at random into England and discover people and places.' His conveyance would be 'a two-seater motor-car'. In post-war Britain, this was a fantastically liberating image.

The ex-cyclist and cavalryman in Morton saw the motor-car as the key to unlocking England's identity. At heart, Morton despised mass transportation. The train carriage and the motor-coach were an assault on a traveller's right to stray from the beaten track; in his books, the image of the 'charabanc' crammed with pitiable trippers

A photograph taken a couple of years before Morton experienced a revelation on the hill overlooking the Old City of Jerusalem, that he should return to England and become the best-selling travel writer of his generation.

lurches onto the page whenever Morton feels the need to reassert his vehicular supremacy. And he knew he was backing a winner: by the time Morton took to the road for his new *Express* series, the railways had lost their monopoly. The number of passenger journeys being taken by rail had been stagnant since before the War, but the number of cars on the roads raced from 77,000 in 1918 to 981,000 by 1929. The bicycle, celebrated for a few short decades as the 'King of the Road', had been usurped. The car promised all the independence of bicycle travel, at three times the speed and none of the effort. 'More people than in any previous generation are seeing the real country for the first time,' enthused Morton. 'The roads of England, eclipsed for a century by the railway, have come to life again; the King's highway is once more a place for adventures and explorations.'

The vehicle which Morton adopted for his newsprint tours was not a racy Bentley Speed Six Tourer but a £300 Morris Oxford. The 'Bullnose' was the kind of motor-car likely to be driven by district nurses and travelling salesmen; a people's car. With the wind in his hair, Morton set off to rediscover pre-War England: 'For the first time in history,' he wrote, 'these panting and efficient little machines were beginning to take individuals and families all over England, inaugurating a new age of discovery, called, in the typically deceptive English way, "motoring". Probably nothing like it had occurred since the days of medieval pilgrimage.'

The *Express* ran the pieces through the spring and summer of 1926. By June, 1927, Morton had converted them into a book called *In Search of England*. In a skilful cut-and-paste job, he had assembled his motoring excursions into a single, geographically-coherent journey in a clockwise direction around England, from London to Land's End, then up the western side of the country to the Scottish border, then back down the east. Maud was removed from the story, which gave

On Planet Morton, the motor car put the romance back into travel. Between 1923, and 1929, the price of motor cars dropped by a third, and the Bullnose Morris became the top selling car, accounting for 45 per cent of the British market. Roads which had evolved over centuries for the passage of horses and pedestrians, were taken over by motorists who could suddenly penetrate the furthest reaches of rural Britain. Four hundred years before this Bullnose turned its wheels over the River Exe in Exford, John Leland had ridden past the same spot.

Harry's narrator more room to manoeuvre. The 'H. V. Morton' who sets off in search of 'people and places' is driven by nostalgia rather than an internal combustion engine. He is obliged to record his impressions of 'New England; an England of crowded towns, of tall chimneys, of mills and canals of slow, black water; an England of coal and chemicals; of cotton, glass and iron.' But the England of his *quest* is 'the beautiful Old England that I love', an England crossed with pilgrims' ways and dotted with musty pubs; an England populated by Chaucerian packmen, and calloused flint-knappers. Even the traffic jams are cultural adventures: 'In front of me was a heavy forty-five horse-power touring car containing a rigid old man in a young Stetson; in front of him was a dashing two-seater driven by a woman; in front of her was a closed limousine full of American tourists; in front of them was a family in a Ford; in front of that was a Rolls Royce, and leading the procession was a hatless young obstructionist lying full length in a fifteen horse-power scarlet bath with aluminium fittings and an exhaust pipe like a stove-pipe.'

Methuen had to reprint *In Search of England* twice in its first six months. 'I have made a name for myself,' Morton wrote in his diary, 'and I am 36.' Two years later, Morton exported his quest to Scotland.

\* \* \*

*In Search of Scotland* took motoring to the end of the road, and beyond. At one level, it was a loose memoir of a petrolhead's adventures in the Highlands and Lowlands.

At another, it was a deeply personalised quest for a lost cultural ideal. The book appeared in 1929 and was followed in 1933 by a sequel, *In Scotland Again*. Both books had an edge to them which had been absent in Morton's English jaunt. The middle-class Londoner was at his most displaced in the wind-blown mountains, and in the interval between the two Scottish books, Britain had been devastated by economic recession. Just three months after the publication of *In Search of Scotland*, the Wall Street stock market had crashed and triggered the Great Depression. Overseas demand for British products collapsed and, by the end of 1930, unemployment had more than doubled to 2.5 million.

Morton has changed, too. The traveller who heads for the glens in 1929 is a lot more adventurous than the motorist who managed to traverse the Lake District two years earlier without getting out of his car. In Scotland, he leaves the road to climb mountains, hike over misty bealachs and visit remote islands. On one occasion he even takes to the sea on board a working trawler. The car is less visible. Indeed, some of the episodes he writes about in Scotland – such as the visit to Skye and his treks in the Grampians – may not have involved the use of a motor-car at all. 'It hurt me,' he writes of the misted Don one autumn morning, 'to go over roads so quickly in a machine when I would have been walking with wet boots on grass and through the browning bracken of the woods. I stopped…'

His Scottish excursions are also populated by a different species of hero and heroine. Up here, Morton can draw on the cast of his mother's land. Bonnie Prince Charlie strides the heather of Culloden and the shores of Skye, Rob Roy lurks in the Trossachs, and Robert the Bruce stalks the hills of Galloway. Covenanters, Jacobites and dispossessed crofters drift into chapters like armies of wraiths. As Morton's England subsided into the Great Depression, and national socialism began to exert its grip on listless Europeans, the clans were upheld by many of Morton's ilk as the last thread connecting Britons with a more ordered, feudal past – 'a genuine link', as Morton put it, 'with the Golden Age.' Highlanders were 'the lineal descendants of the Homeric heroes'. Up here, too, Morton can associate himself with the last generation of British travellers who could legitimately call themselves 'explorers'. 'Most Englishmen,' avers Morton, 'who know little about the history of Scotland and nothing at all about that of Ireland, do not realize that, with the exception of the North and South Poles, the Highlands of Scotland were the last portion of the earth's surface to be explored. This sounds inconceivable, but it is true!'

Among the doughty trailblazers Morton turns to are heroes like Thomas Pennant, and more dubious characters like Sir John Carr, whose *Caledonian Sketches* of 1807 were lapped-up by travellers who'd turned to the Highlands because war prohibited continental tours; *The Quarterly Review* was unsympathetic to Sir John, panning his book as derivative, and recommending that its author be punished by 'tight flagellation'. Although he'd read widely on Scotland, and been brought up by a Scot, Morton gives the impression that he is setting off into the great unknown: 'There is,' he suggests in his introduction, 'something to be said for books written by an explorer who admits frankly, as I do, that he knew nothing about Scotland when he set out, because then commonplace knowledge comes freshly with an air of discovery…'

Scotland was even better suited to exploration by car than England. There were far fewer rail lines north of the border, and in Morton's view, the 'easy and comfortable escape' offered by rail travel had created a generation of idlers who'd left 'no record of a circuit of Scotland since the day of the horse and coach'. Now, announced Morton, 'with the motor-car we have returned to road travel, so that once more books will be written from the standpoint of Pennant, Boswell and Carr, by men able to move freely about the country in touch with the inhabitants.' There was only one snag: Morton wasn't facing storms at sea in sailing ships or riding a locally-procured horse over unmapped terrain, but tearing along tarmac in a modern motor-car. His trials were more humdrum: the losing of underwear in hotel rooms, the occasional blister. And rain. Somewhere between the era of horse and car, adversity had been replaced by absurdity.

I wondered, before I set off in Morton's tracks, which maps he had used. Only once does he give any real clues. Right at the start of *In Search of Scotland*, as he leaves England on the long road north, he stops his car in the Cheviot Hills, picks up his map, and strikes off over a field to a heathery summit so that he can take his bearings: 'What names men have given to these hills! How snugly they fit! To my left is Corby Pike and Windy Crag, Dour Hill and Hungry Law; six miles away is Bloodybush Edge and Beefstand Hill. Six names as right and racy as a ballad! On my right looms the bulk of Blackman's Law and beyond it the height of Oh Me Edge. It is almost too good to be true!'

In the British Library, I found each of these place-names on *"The Times" Contour Motoring Map of Scotland in 6 Sheets*, published in 1921 by Geographia in Fleet Street, just a few doors from the *Express* office. The maps had been carefully engraved at a scale of three miles to the inch, under the direction of Alexander Gross, a Fellow of the Royal Geographical Society. Three categories of motorable road were marked, together with distances, steep hills and golf courses. A rich palette of greens and browns gave an immediate sense of the lie of the land, and every square inch was crammed with minutely-italicised place-names, of villages and streams, hills and peaks, forts and churches. Major footpaths, such as the Lairig Ghru through the heart of the Cairngorms, were shown. The motorists using these maps were expected to leave their machines and strike out for the hills.

*Opposite:* It wasn't all smooth driving. 'I have had a frightful time with "Maud",' Morton once confessed to his *Express* readers. 'She indulged in two entirely temperamental punctures the first day and developed a hysterical engine yesterday… An expert, however, has done things to her interior.'

*Below:* Skye, and the Black Cuillins, on *"The Times" Contour Motoring Map of Scotland*. Maps unlocked the open road. And in their detail and colouring, they informed Twenties motorists of the topography that lay beyond the verges.

Following Morton through the Southern Uplands, I felt mildly embarrassed that I'd ignored such a wonderful region for so long. Glen Trool, with its secret loch, is like a less-trodden version of the English Lake District. By Loch Trool, where Robert the Bruce had bloodied the English in a warm-up for Bannockburn, Morton had paused by the memorial and re-enacted the fourteenth-century independence campaign across several pages. 'Bruce in Galloway and Prince Charlie in the Highlands,' he sighs, 'the two most romantic men in the history of Scotland.' Above the loch, he climbed Merrick, the highest peak in southern Scotland. The view was sensational. To the west, he could see the island of Ailsa Craig, and eastwards, a chain of lochs lying in 'utter solitude'. I'm ashamed to say that I still haven't climbed Merrick, or met anyone who has. 'Here,' concluded Morton, 'far south of Glasgow, is a wilderness deeper than that of the better known Highlands.'

*Above:* **Morton's pursuit of romance re-drafted the Scottish tourist trail. One of many natural wonders he put on the map was Glen Trool, where Robert the Bruce routed a greater English force by hurling rocks on them from the heights of Muldonach.**

I did, however, follow Morton up Goat Fell, the highest mountain on the island of Arran. It's a thrilling hill to climb, though a little less Himalayan than Morton implies. It was up here that he revealed doubts about the suitability of his chosen transport: 'Give me sunlight,' he sighs, 'a blue sea, the dry smell of heather, and the hill streams brown with peat, and you can have all the motor-cars in the world.'

Leaving Arran, Morton was confronted by some rather inconvenient geography. The ferry which had transported him back to the mainland, put him ashore at Ardrossan. From here,

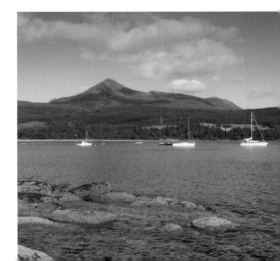

the spirit of enquiry should have led him northward, along the coast and then up the Clyde to Glasgow. But on the pretext of having run out of socks, he took a more direct route to the 'black city', thus avoiding the Clyde altogether. Morton had his reasons for dodging Scotland's greatest river. The Scottish economy had been in a bad way long before the crash of 1929, but by the time Morton came north for his second Scottish book, three years into the Great Depression, the situation in Scotland's manufacturing belt was absolutely desperate. At the height of the depression in 1932, nearly one third of the Scottish workforce was out of a job. Unemployment among shipworkers on the Clyde was running at over 50 per cent, and newspapers were carrying stories about Glaswegian razor gangs. None of this was particularly suitable material for a feel-good travelogue. Later in the chapter, Morton does insert a brief, sepulchral description of a visit that he made to the offices of a Clyde shipyard – 'a solid, polished mahogany room from

*Above:* **Work on 'Cunard hull No 534'** was suspended in December, 1931, due to the Great Depression, resuming in April, 1934. She was launched that September as *Queen Mary*. Morton's vignette of the Clyde shipyards was published in October, 1933, and occupied just one page of *In Scotland Again*.

*Opposite:* Morton considered 'the view from Goatfell on a clear day finer than that from Ben Nevis. From the Ben you look over miles of mountain-tops; from Goatfell you see land and water.'

which all knowledge of world chaos had been carefully concealed'. It's a bleak passage, in which he recalls the 'bright prosperity of the Edwardian Age … the age before the War', when men in silk hats and frock coats took orders for ocean liners and Britannia's warships. On a great polished table surrounded by gigantic padded chairs, stand pots 'that hold about half a pint of ink'. When Morton's friend shows up, he takes him by the arm and leads him out 'into the silent place where the empty slipways go down to the Clyde, in order that the magnificent room might hear nothing of our troubles, and go on dreaming of the old ships and the old times and – the old cheques.'

The Mortonian palliative for economic distress is romance. Myths and heroes give body to a nation's self belief, and each 'Great Age' reminds us that more will follow. But behind Morton's mask of authorship, there was a troubled man who knew that the Britain he described was a lie. His 'word pictures' were as selective as Gilpin's picturesque views. Behind the chummy, middle-class mixer known as 'H.V. Morton' was a man who wondered in his diaries whether Britain wouldn't be better off with Adolf Hitler; behind the family man whose pages are decorated with pretty girls in frocks was a serial philanderer who treated his numerous mistresses like so many motorway service stations. He did however come to address the poverty he'd shied from on the Clyde. Shortly after the publication of *In Scotland Again*, the Labour Party published a 48-page booklet by Morton, called *What I Saw in the Slums*.

\* \* \*

Morton's lowlands are a prelude to his Highlands. Then, as now, the most striking gateway to the Highlands was the water-filled, glacial trough which slices south from the Grampians to the Clyde. To Victorian tourists, there were four Scottish lochs worthy of appreciation; Loch Katrine in the Trossachs was admired for its delicate colouring; Loch Coruisk on Skye for its 'wild grandeur', Loch Maree for its 'dignity'. But Loch Lomond had them all: 'a greater variety', as Baddeley put it in his guide of 1895, 'of the elements which we admire in lake scenery than any other Scottish loch.' Above all else, Lomond was 'the most beautifully "islanded" lake of the kingdom'. In Baddeley's day the loch and its surroundings were largely unspoiled; tourists heading out of Glasgow would take the steam train to Balloch, at the southern foot of the loch, and then transfer to a steamer for the 25-mile voyage into the mountains at the northern end of the loch. Adventurous passengers could disembark at Ardlui and join the new West Highland railway which would take them on to Fort William. Then came H. V. Morton, puttering along the western shore in his personalised transportation. Travelling at his own speed past crag and promontory, he was able to gaze upon the mists 'stealing from the hills', and on the loch-side rowans and rowing-boats. He could stop and take a photograph. From the stitched leather seat of his open-top tourer he could smell the woodsmoke as he motored through Luss. To accommodate the millions of Mortons who followed him, the A82 has now been widened, straightened, and supplied with motoring amenities – from car-parks and lay-bys to lavatories and viewpoints. It is a hellish coupling between tarmac and the picturesque; between the realised worlds of Morton and Gilpin.

Less distressing is the road over Rannoch Moor. This was one of the sections of Morton's itinerary that I was able to repeat in a Bullnose, and it was up here at dusk that I sensed for a moment the spirit of twenties motoring. For eight miles the road snakes through a dun tundra of lochans, rocks and bog. It was a clear evening, at the end of winter, and the mountains beyond the moor were creamed with snow. The slipstream was freezing, and every time I nudged the old beast into third, the revs faded until I could hear the wind rushing over the ornamented bodywork of the eighty-year-old

*Above:* 'When I am old I hope I shall be sufficiently placid to sit back contentedly and remember the many early morning journeys I have made in my life… And so it was when the sun rose in the hush of the morning, and I took the road that runs into the Highlands along the west bank of Loch Lomond.' Unfortunately, millions of motorists now think the same, and Loch Lomond's western shore has become the howling verge of the A82.

*Opposite:* 'Had I more time, I would buy a Scout's outfit … for the only way to enjoy this country is to climb away from the crowds and seek solitude in the bosky silence of woods or on the craggy heights of fells'. *In Search of England,* 1927.

Morris. Eventually the road tipped into the throat of Glencoe and there was the prow of Buachaille Etive Mor, and the crest of Aonach Eagach. Grinning on the car's open-air bench seat, I felt as if I was viewing my favourite peaks from a slow-moving sofa.

The indolent Mr Toad who searched for England in the *Express* is a distant memory by the time the Grampians fill H.V. Morton's windscreen. 'I decided to walk the Larig Ghru,' he announces. Nowadays, this would be a bit like waking up and saying 'I think I'll climb Everest'. To remind his readers that he was undertaking the most extreme trek in Britain, Morton called on his guidebooks:

> 'There is no pass to compare with it in all Scotland,' says Mr. Seton Gordon. 'One of the wildest and grandest passes of the lofty Cairngorm Range,' says Mr. Muirhead, who adds, 'There is no inn or house of shelter on the route.' 'This is about the longest day's march in the Highlands,' says Mr. Baddeley. Forty miles! It was a rash and impetuous adventure for one who had 'done no walking since the War.'

Morton's 'War' had been spent in Essex, rather than Flanders, and in truth he'd done quite a bit of walking since 1918. In the pages of *In Scotland Again*, he'd already climbed two mountains (Merrick and Goat Fell), and had hiked the length of the Corrieyairick Pass. So he wasn't quite as catatonic as he implies. And it seems that his Cairngorm epic was not as solitary as he suggests. Morton seems to have been in company; his biographer Michael Bartholomew has uncovered diary entries recording that Morton drove with two companions from Edinburgh to Aviemore on September 12, 1929, then walked through the Lairig Ghru the following day. Not

Crossing Rannoch Moor in a Bullnose: 'The thin mist changed to rain and I could see the vast blue shapes of the mountains and, far away to the northward, a blackness in the sky where the storm lay. I put on speed and slid on over the mountain road. I dislike a motor-car most of all in a storm.'

only was he not apparently alone, but the Lairig Ghru episode had not been part of the single, continuous journey described in the book.

But Lairig Ghru would be good for sales. Among those who had popularised Britain's ultimate pedestrian adventure was Baddeley, who'd opened his guide with a first-hand account of a narrow escape he'd had when trying to walk over the Cairngorms from Braemar to Aviemore, in April, 1876. On the way, Baddeley and his friend had planned to climb Ben Macdui, the 3,900-foot mountain which dominates the mid-section of the Lairig Ghru. Equipped with sandwiches and 'a fair quantity of whiskey', the pair had set off up the wrong glen, climbed the mountain in Arctic conditions, failed to descend into Lairig Ghru due to sheer ice and snow, then got lost for the night in Rothiemurchus Forest. After twenty-one hours, they found the road to Aviemore.

So this was the nature of the challenge that Morton had set himself. It didn't help that Baddeley's misadventure had been thrilling readers of the *Thorough Guide* for more than thirty years. Morton's account of his own traverse of Lairig Ghru is correspondingly melodramatic: 'In certain lights,' he begins, 'the Larig Ghru, seen from Aviemore, looks like an early Italian painter's idea of hell. It is seven and a half miles away: a great cleft in the Cairngorms: steep, dark, cruel, with something about it that suggests to you that there, if anywhere, a man might find the last dragon.'

Sensibly, Morton and his friends approach Lairig Ghru from the north, so that they would avoid blundering for hours through Rothiemurchus Forest at the end of the day. Instead, they tackled the trees first thing in the morning. Morton's Cairngorm experience could not measure up to Baddeley's, but he managed to make it sound tough enough. After six miles, his pack 'felt like a piece of granite' and it rained incessantly. As he climbs into the cleft of the pass, with water squirting through the eyelet holes of his boots and 'every unused muscle' aching, he confesses that he'd seldom been happier in his life.

Climbing through Lairig Ghru today, it's possible to tick off the various features Morton mentioned: in clear weather, the 'few white dots which were houses', six miles away over the forest in Strathspey, are clearly visible as the suburban sprawl of Aviemore; the 'gaunt mouth' of the pass is just that, for the path curves around the

Passing the last pine in Rothiemurchus Forest, on the way to the Lairig Ghru pass.

'The stiffest part of the Larig is a crazy wilderness of red granite boulders. Here the track ends and you have to climb and slide over the rocks. They lead down to a reward: the lovely Pools of Dee…' Like most stony, mountain routes, the 'track' over the summit of Larig Ghru is more apparent from a distance, than when it's under your feet.

mountain side just above the tree line, and is suddenly swallowed by an ominous defile. The 'avalanches of stones' can be identified as vast heaps of glacial rubble, and when he writes of there being 'no more melancholy sight than the Larig', it's easy to understand how depressing it must have been in the rain and mist. The crest of the pass, the 'crazy wilderness of red granite boulders', is all too recognisable. 'Here,' writes Morton, 'the track ends and you have to climb and slide over the rocks.' The Pools of Dee, 'three tarns of icy water', still sit like glacial puddles at the southern exit of the pass. Down by the cataract known as the Linn of Dee, a 'small white building' continues to gaze at Victoria Bridge. Unable to use the bridge because the Royal Family were at Balmoral, Morton had waded the river, then staggered up to the cottage in a state of advanced exhaustion. Inside, he had succumbed to 'the joyful warmth of a peat fire'.

Morton's description of his Cairngorm traverse rings true at every step. He suffered for his words. But he was treading a very old path. This shortcut through the mountains must have been in use since the Mezolithic Age, when hunter-gatherers would have favoured it as the fastest, least dangerous route through the heart of the Cairngorms. The pass was known to cattle thieves in the 1700s, and just sixty years before Morton undertook his 'solo' trek, Lairig Ghru had been a droving route for cattle heading from the Spey to Braemar and the south. Apparently it was used as a cattle route until about 1873. Men from Speyside were sent up into the Lairig Ghru every spring, to clear the track of boulders which had tumbled down during winter frosts.

\* \* \*

A little bit of jeopardy can go a long way in a travel book. But motoring is not the most exciting activity in the world, and Morton didn't make it easier for himself by skipping both the Outer Hebrides and the fjords of the west coast. Only once did his itinerary give him the chance to take on Pennant.

'I came to a mighty resolution…' he announced in Inverness. 'I decided to go north and see what John O'Groats is like.' Nowadays, a three-hour spin up the A9 is not going to make a bestseller (unless you're Bill Bryson). But in 1933, the road to John O'Groats was quite a drive. The distance was around 150 miles, with a tight coil of hairpins above the tiny coastal village of Berriedale. As Morton cues his adventure, one can detect echoes of Camden and Pont: long-gone geographers warning of wolves and wilderness in the land of Calgacus. Morton had a decent map, but this would be the furthest he had ever strayed from London in his motor-car. (Having cycled to John O'Groats – from Land's End, naturally – I'd sooner tackle the Braes of Berriedale by bicycle than Bullnose.) This, then, was as courageous as British motoring could get, and Morton makes the most of the geography:

> 'The three most northerly counties – Ross and Cromarty, Caithness, and Sutherland – are the least known in all Scotland. If you look at a railway map you will see that, with the exception of one line running along the east coast from Inverness to Wick and Thurso, these enormous counties are without the railway… So here in the extreme north of Scotland is an area of nearly

Morton was disappointed that John O'Groats hadn't 'the finality' of Land's End or Scotland's southern tip, the Mull of Galloway, so he hiked the two miles to Duncansby Head for a view he would 'never forget': the Stacks of Duncansby, looking north across 'the deep blue firth' towards the Pentland Skerries.

6,000 square miles which is right off the main line of communication. If any part of Scotland can in these days be called "unknown", when one of the most efficient systems of motor coaches explores the Highlands, I think these three northern counties deserve the name.'

So off he went, into the unknown. And true to his predecessors, he wrote about wolves and wild country. Morton seems to have driven from Inverness to John O'Groats in a single day. He was, he wrote, 'dreadfully weary' as he left Wick for the final 'seventeen long, awful miles' to John O'Groats, 'miles at that time of night and after such a long day, when each mile seems like ten.' He was nodding off at the wheel: 'Every shadow on the road became a grotesque flying demon and the blanched walls seemed to beckon me to destruction.' From John O'Groats he headed east towards Cape Wrath, and like Pennant, he found himself drawn inexorably towards a bleak confrontation with his own frailty. Initially, the road was stupendously exciting: 'In no part of Britain,' he gasped, 'is the cliff scenery so consistently fine.'

Then, as his car chugged around the mountainside beyond the crofts of Coldbackie, he suddenly saw the Kyle of Tongue and found himself 'in another world: the world of loch and yellow weed, of high, impregnable hill and dark gorge, of brown moor and wild forest.' Down at the waterside, there was, he relates, a little ferry which conveyed foot passengers across the mouth of the sea loch to rejoin the coast road on the far side. But motorists had to take the long route, a twelve mile

From the old road along the west side of the Kyle of Tongue: 'I thought,' gasped Morton as he approached Ben Loyal, 'that he was one of the most fearsome mountains I have ever seen. His sides are scored by fearful ravines and dark gullies, and the eye moves over his grim and awful bulk, noting secret blue recesses, high up, where the splintered rock has fallen apart, making caverns and ledges, a fit playground for devils or a cradle for the Valkyrie.'

drive all the way around the shore of the loch. For Morton, this was one of the most memorable roads in Scotland. At first, the road twists and turns through a patchwork of hard-won fields, heading all the while towards the castellated peaks of Ben Loyal; 'the Coolin of Sutherland,' thrills Morton, 'rising in a series of precipices to a height of 2,505 feet … a hill on which Norse gods might have sharpened their swords.' At the head of the loch, the narrow, single track road turns tightly and follows the western shore back towards the coast. The views are wonderful: a foreground of tidal shallows set against stands of birch and the luminescent slopes of Ben Loyal. 'What a wilderness it is,' writes Morton, 'this northern coast of Sutherland! I felt, as I invaded it, more remote from civilisation than when I crossed the Sierra Nevada… Every mile plunged me more deeply into the wilds. It is the very workshop of God.'

Today, motorists career across the mouth of the Kyle on a modern concrete causeway, but the old road is still there, tempting the inquisitive into a by-passed paradise. Morton was right: a motor-car is an invasion of this place, and the only ways to absorb its beauty are to leave the village of Tongue wearing boots or riding a bike.

Beyond the Kyle of Tongue, it all went horribly wrong for Morton. The road ascends a bleak, heathery moor, then plummets to the grey waters of Loch Eriboll. 'And as it grew dark,' he recalls, 'and the long northern twilight fell over Loch Eriboll, all sense of adventure deserted me. I wanted to hear some one speak. I wanted to see a fire. I wanted to get away from the threat of the hills and their implication that I, and all men, were intruders on the surface of the earth.' In Durness, he could find nowhere to stay, and ended up in a fisherman's hotel down on the shore of the nearby Kyle. In the morning, he bolted for Inverness. His escape route, down the road that has become the A838, was dramatic.

Leaving Durness, Morton found himself hemmed in by 'another Glencoe, and with Glencoe's air of dark brooding'. To his left loomed the crags of Beinn Spionnaidh and Cranstackie; to his right, the ramps of moorland rising to Ghlas-bheinn and Farrmheall. Behind these two hills lay one hundred square miles of wild country, terminating in Cape Wrath. This was the district Timothy Pont had labelled 'Extreem Wilderness' during his sixteenth-century reconnaissance of Scotland, identifying between his little pictogram of Farrmheall and Cape Wrath, a mountain pass called 'Bhellach maddy or Woolfs way'. Thomas Pennant had been

Morton's first sight of Loch Eriboll, and the strange little 'non-island' of Ard Neckie. Until the 1890s, the only way to continue west from here to Durness, was by way of a ferry from Ard Neckie to Portcanon on the far shore. The ferry ceased to operate when the road around the shore of the loch was completed. It was while Morton was following this road, that 'all sense of adventure' finally deserted him.

heading here in 1772, when he was defeated by the terrain at Ledbeg. Since then, a surveyor called Peter Lawson had tamed the wilderness by connecting Durness to Ledbeg. On the roadside beneath Farrmheall, Morton came across a memorial erected by Lawson as 'a mark of gratitude and respect to the inhabitants of Durness and Eddrachillis for their hospitality while projecting this road'. The memorial is still there, cast in iron, painted yellow and set behind a drinking trough of fresh water. I've paused here several times, always in mist. It's dated 1883, when horses and feet were the only means of reaching the most remote corner of Britain by land.

* * *

Cars reconfigured Britain's landscapes with devastating speed. In ten years following the publication of *In Search of Scotland*, the number of cars on British roads nearly doubled, from 981,000 to just under two million. Today, the total is 31 million. And rising. The race to make wider, straighter, faster roads has left Scotland littered with single-track relics. If you know where to look, you can find them scattered across Ordnance Survey maps, where they survive as wriggles of faint, pecked lines bypassed by clean, blood-red slashes. Some of the relics are just a few hundred metres long; others run for miles. East of Skye, the road Morton drove so excitedly 'over the roof of the Highlands' has been superseded by the A87. 'If you wish to penetrate,' begins Morton, 'a country as wild and desolate as anything in the British Isles, take the road from Fort Augustus that branches right at Invergarry…' Follow this road today, and it disappears into the waters of a vast reservoir which has flooded Glen Loyne. Amazingly, eight glorious miles of this broken, pot-holed road can still be traced from the north, clawing upward to 1,400 feet above sea-level. The views are as rewarding as they were in Morton's day. Even better, the road is closed to traffic.

Bridges have had a far greater impact than the piecemeal removal of old roads. Throughout the Highlands, from Ballachulish to Tongue, Dornoch to Kessock,

Tomdoun Sporting Lodge, on the old road over 'the roof of the Highlands'. Built in 1895, the former hunting lodge is one of the few Scottish hotels Morton would still recognise. There are no televisions and telephones in the bedrooms, and in winter, an open fire crackles in the bar. The remains of the road to Glen Loyne can still be found on the mountainside above the hotel.

serpentine loops of loch-side roads have been restored to tranquility by brief spans of concrete and steel. But the bridge over Kyle Akin is different. Of all the modern structures in Scotland, the one most likely to make Morton spin like a broken camshaft in his grave, is the Skye Bridge.

'I feel,' Morton had thought as he approached Mallaig and the ferry to Skye, 'that I am on the way to wreck a dream.' The readers of the *Daily Express* wouldn't have liked wrecked dreams over breakfast, and so Morton's Skye doesn't let him down. The small ship which is to convey him up the Sound of Sleat to Kyle of Localsh is satisfactorily horrendous: 'drenched' in the smell of 'pea soup, fat mutton, batter pudding', and packed with a carnival of sheep dogs, a black horse and shaggy islanders in plus fours and unpolished boots. Typically, there is also 'a beautiful, long-legged girl in Harris tweed … perhaps, the daughter of some clan chieftain going home to a castle on a rock'.

At Kyle of Localsh, Morton transfers to the Skye boat, a paddle steamer which will take three hours to sail west past the island of Scalpay and Raasay, to the capital of Skye, Portree. In choosing to leave the mainland at Mallaig, Morton had created a sea voyage which would consume an entire day; sufficient to provide four pages of material, and to create the illusion that Skye was a remote, Atlantic outpost.

Skye was uniquely lit in the English imagination, set-dressed in literature and art to create a wildly romantic ,fantasy island. The sketchy sixteenth-century printed descriptions of the island by Donald Monro and Camden (who had copied Munro), had been overtaken by the more methodical

Somewhere beneath the rowing boat is the old stone bridge Morton crossed as he drove across Glen Loyne on the way to Glen Shiel.

One more bridge; one less island: Skye.

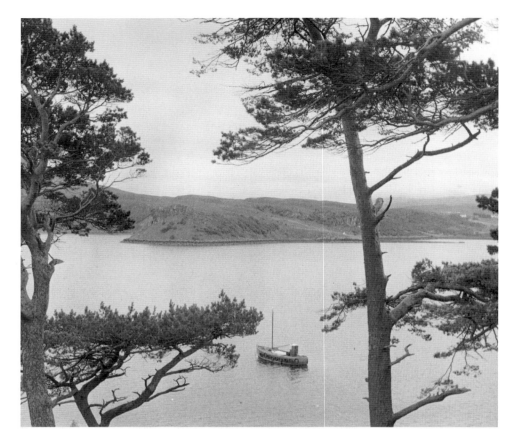

Since the turn of the century, 'the romantic Isle of the Mist' had been the essential ingredient of Highland tours. A three-day circuit with the Highland Railway Company from Inverness railway station would take in the east coast of Skye by way of Kyle of Localsh and Portree.

enquiries of visitors such as Martin Martin and Pennant. But with the arrival of Johnson and Boswell the year after Pennant, the process of mythologising began. It is on Skye that Pennant is dismissed by Dr Johnson ('the dog is a Whig'), while the canny Boswell pulls off the Scottish scoop of the century by tracking-down and interviewing the woman who had famously aided the escape of Bonnie Prince Charlie, 'the celebrated Miss Flora Macdonald'. Skye forms the core of Johnson and Boswell's convivial excursion of 1773, providing them with a wonderful catalogue of encounters, and a wealth of information on Hebridean culture and economics. Once embedded in Sir Walter Scott's *Lord of the Isles*, Skye became an essential way-station for poets, painters and then mountaineers. Turner came here, and so did Robert Louis Stevenson, George Fennel Robson, Horatio MacCulloch, Alfred Williams and John MacWhirter. By the 1830s, the first climbers were pushing into the deeper recesses of the Cuillins.

Four centuries of media attention preceded Morton's voyage 'over the sea to Skye'. There was a huge back catalogue of books and articles describing the island. Much of this popularity was due to the fact that it was relatively accessible; ever since the opening of the 'Skye Railway' to Kyle of Localsh in 1870 (and then to Kyle of Localsh in 1897), and the opening of the West Highland Railway to Mallaig in 1901, city-dwellers could take a train all the way to the ferry slip. Baddeley's description was typical: 'The scenery of the Island of Skye differs more than any other in Britain from that which mankind are familiar in the ordinary walks of life, and for this reason it is popularly called "savage".'

'Skye...' muses Morton as the ferry approaches the island. 'To me it is pure romance ... I cannot hope that anyone who has not felt the shadow of Skye for the first time will understand it. It would not have surprised me to see a galley put out from the dark shores and to come face to face with Ulysses or Jason...'

Morton's search for Highland Scotland is concluded on Skye. Here, he provides his readers with the quintessential mountain, castle and town. He heads first to Sligachan in the centre of the island. This is the most important road junction on Skye; the point at which travellers head east and south, or north or west. Beside the junction is the Sligachan Inn, warmly recommended by Baddeley for being 'a capital house' on the grounds that it enjoyed 'less of the "la-di-da" flavour than the majority of such places in Scotland'. The present inn was built in about 1830, and it is still the island's Base Camp for the many-hued pilgrims who wash to Skye's shores. 'Here,' observes Morton, 'are salmon-fishers, deer-slayers, artists in oil and water-colour, mountaineers, and the clipped voice of that which was once the English ruling class.'

Morton arrived in the dark, so it wasn't until morning, when he stepped outside, that he first saw the Cuillins close up. Initially 'mesmerised' by the Vesuvian cone of Glamaig ('He looks as though he might at any moment give a terrible explosion and belch flame'), he takes a few steps forward, clears the boundary wall of the inn, and instantly becomes aware of 'something tremendous' to his right. The sight, he recalls 'of the "Black" Coolins hits you like a blow in the face!'

'Skye, for me, has always been shrouded in the splendour of a lost cause. The sound of it is like a sword going home to its scabbard... It cannot be compared with anything. I thought that possibly it might fall into line with Aran off the west coast of Ireland, another Gaelic island of strange beauty, where life is different. But Skye stands alone, one of Nature's supreme experiments in atmosphere.' *In Search of Scotland*, 1929.

'I have spent nights in the Sinai Desert, I have slept in the Valley of the Dead in Egypt, I have seen the sun rise from the summit of the Silvrettahorn in Switzerland, I have stood all night on a ship in a great storm off the coast of Crete, I have been impressed by a number of other experiences, but I have never in all my life seen anything like the "Black" Coolins standing, grape-blue and still, in morning sunshine.'

Many have stood on that spot and gaped. Stretching skyward is a fang of riven stone, and what appears to be the beginnings of an impossibly sheer ridge. The fang is Sgurr nan Gillean, the 'peak of the young men', first climbed by a forester and a scientist, back in 1836.

'I gasped,' continues Morton, 'I lost my breath…' And so he goes on, asking his readers to imagine Wagner's *Ride of the Valkyries* 'frozen in stone and hung up like a colossal screen in the sky.' This is where the Highland section of *In Search of Scotland* reaches its literal highpoint.

'I sling a haversack full of rations over my shoulders,' he announces, 'make sure I have plenty of matches, take a map, a strong ash-stick and strike off over the hummocky moorland into the Valhalla of Glen Sligachan.' Morton planned to hike

The Black Cuillins, from Druim Hain.

the four miles or so up the glen and then climb the pass which opened the way to Loch Coruisk, on the southern side of Skye. It was a well-tramped route, used for the best part of a century by mountaineers, and described in some detail by Baddeley. In his day (thirty years or so before Morton's visit), a pony and guide could be hired at Sligachan for the round trip to Loch Coruisk, for the sum of eleven shillings. It doesn't seem entirely improbable that Morton availed himself of a similar service, but decided that a 'solo hike' might appear more adventurous for the book.

Morton never reached Loch Coruisk. There was no need. He was searching for the perfect view, and Baddeley had told him precisely where to find it. Having tramped down the glen and climbed up to the col, he turned right and followed the ridge of Druim Hain a little way north-westwards. Here, Baddeley had promised, he would find a 'fine view' into Harta Corrie, 'the wildest recess among the Coolins'. Behind the corrie, continued Baddeley, Morton could expect to see the 'the deep-scored precipices and jagged pinnacles' of the entire Black Cuillin range.

Until Morton led me to this spot, I wouldn't have believed such a view existed in Britain. I have been there twice now, and will go back. It was Baddeley who pointed out that 'the most truly beautiful views of British scenery are obtained from minor elevations, of from 500 to 1,500 feet above the valleys from which they rise'. He is right. Drum Hain stands at about one thousand feet above sea level, about three miles from the ridge, and forms a rocky viewing gallery at a mid-point in the arc of the Black Cuillins. Facing you is a single ridge almost six-miles long. Only here, on Druim Hain, is it possible to absorb the ridge in its entirety. It is a spectacle of unrelenting ferocity. 'This,' announced Morton, 'is surely the grandest and most gloomy view in the British Isles.'

From the Cuillins, Morton headed northward to Dunvegan Castle. No other castle in Britain can compete with the seat of Macleod of Macleod: 'Everything you have read about enchanted castles, captured princesses, wizards distilling the Water of Life, victims dying of thirst in dungeons, mermaids swimming up in moonlight to lure a man to his death, men beaten back to a whistle of swords and a hail of arrows, comes true as you see the turrets of Dunvegan lifted in the dusk above the trees on a spur of rock that leans over an arm of the sea in Skye.'

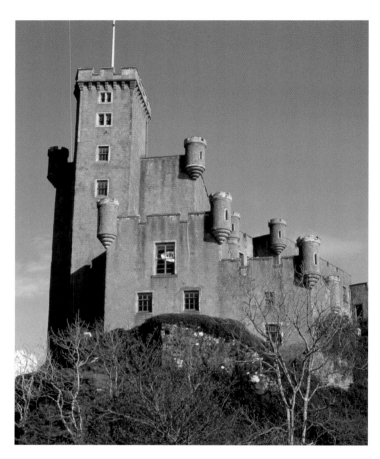

Enchanted Dunvegan, described in detail by Pennant in 1772, and then by Johnson and Boswell, and then by Morton.

Morton knew that he had no chance of outclassing Johnson and Boswell, whose long stay at Dunvegan Castle a century and a half earlier is an unsurpassed insight into the life, views and domestic style of an eighteenth-century clan chieftain. By the time Morton reached Dunvegan, the castle was being opened twice a week to tourists. Morton found Dunvegan occupied by middle-aged Englishwoman who acted as a guide and caretaker for the twenty-third clan chief, who was now over eighty and living – according to Morton – in England. In a glass case, Morton was shown the famous Fairy Flag, 'a tissue-frail bundle of fabric, brown with age, which looks like a yard of tussore silk'. According to Macleod lore, the flag could be waved to save the clan from disaster, but only three times. Waved for a trivial reason, it would invite catastrophe. The first occasion it had been waved, it helped the Macleods defeat the Macdonalds in battle. The second time, it brought a cattle plague to an end. But the third time, it had been waved by Macleod's factor, a man called Buchanan, who had decided in 1799 to test the curse. A series of terrible disasters befall the clan.

Morton's final call on Skye was the island's capital, Portree, where he sat 'in candlelight in the inn … waiting for a ghost'. That ghost was, of course, his boyhood hero, Prince Charles Edward Stuart. 'The rain beats up in sudden fury against the window. It is just such a night as that, many years ago, on which Prince Charlie said good-bye to Flora MacDonald in this room…' And off Morton goes, into the tale of brave Flora and the prince in disguise. 'Is there a more operatic farewell in history?' wonders Morton. 'Think of him standing there in the candle-light, hunted, beaten, bedraggled, in borrowed clothes, £30,000 on his head and all England after him…' In the event, it isn't Bonnie Prince Charlie who appears for Morton, but 'a vision of my own making: Flora MacDonald standing there, holding the miniature, still warm from his hands…'

Portree itself is the perfect haven for a wistful Englishman: 'A handful of houses stands among trees above the bay. Below is the wooden jetty to which the paddle steamer ties up each night with a ruby-red lamp on her masthead – our only reminder of the world. Life is quieter than in any capital I have known. The sound of Portree is not the roar of wheels, but the blowing of kine in the morning and the bleating of sheep at night. There are about nine hundred inhabitants, a few lamps which are lit on the coming of winter-time; one street of those satisfying shops full of sweets, aniseed balls, humbugs, boots, groceries, post-cards, jumpers, tobacco, and everything you can possibly want in this life; a tremendous square with its war memorial; a police force consisting of an inspector, a sergeant, a constable; and a jail which would certainly collapse if they found a prisoner for it!'

The next morning at dawn, Morton walks down to the quayside. 'I hate to leave Skye,' he mourns. 'I place it with Lindisfarne, Tintagel, and Connemara among the magic regions of this world.'

The paddle steamer fills up with sheep, shepherds and dogs. A soldier in the Cameron Highlanders gets a boisterous send-off. Down the coast at Broadford they berth to take on the mail and bulging sacks of whelks labelled for London. As the steamer approaches the mainland, Morton spots the smoke of a railway train: 'We are indeed,' he writes, 'back in the world.'

'All the wildness of vast mountains that lies piled up at Sligachan fades nine miles to the north in the gentleness of Portree – which might be the sister of Polperro.' On the quayside beyond the houses, Morton boarded a paddle-steamer called *Glencoe*, and sailed back to the mainland.

# Afterword

Is it still possible to make a great British journey? Well, I certainly feel as if I have just completed one. In the course of following eight extraordinary travellers across the length and breadth of Britain, this island has become a much bigger, more exciting place. Repeatedly, I've been led beyond the edges of my own mental map. My octuplet of explorers have led me into unfamilar territory, and taken me back to parts of the country that I mistakenly thought I knew.

Many times, I found myself gazing at landscapes which appeared not to have changed a jot over the centuries. Searching the western lip of Exmoor for Leland's 'hillokkes of yerth', I had little expectation of finding them, but there they were, aligned along the county boundary, just as he'd described, five hundred years ago. Much of Pennant's Scotland is immediately recognisable. Land on Canna, or Jura or Skye, and the mountains and caves – even some of the buildings – will fall into place. On Islay, a local farmer led me to one of the subterranean hide-outs that Pennant had seen over two hundred years ago. It was far too small to be shown on a map, and yet it was still there, roofed with stone slabs (and ankle-deep in slime). Paddle down the Wye with Gilpin's book in your hand, and it seems as if he described it yesterday. Walk the tunnelled bridleways of the Surrey Hills, and you might expect Cobbett to spring from the oaks with a diatribe against potatoes or Martello towers.

We may no longer be able to wander at will across unfenced, medieval open field systems and enormous, unenclosed commons and heaths, but we do still have 140,000 miles of public paths in England and Wales, and thousands of square miles of open country in Scotland. With a bit of ingenuity and an Ordnance Survey map, there is a bygone, slow-speed world out there, waiting to be rediscovered.

Some of the most astonishing discoveries I've enjoyed were those pointed out by guides who'd been dead for hundreds of years. It was Henry VIII's topographer, John Leland, who lured me onto the spectacular South West Coast path in search of a mysterious castle and sea-girt rock, which turned out to be Logan Rock. He also told me to skip Land's End and head for Cape Cornwall. Sound guidance. Celia Fiennes introduced me to potted char and the pleasures of mineral spas.

The spirit of adventure is recoverable, too. We don't have to worry ourselves about quicksands on trunk routes, as did Gerald of Wales, or highwaymen, as faced by Celia Fiennes. Cobbett's fearsome 'quags' are a thing of the past. But there is plenty of scope for challenging journeys. It was the book's token petrolhead, H. V. Morton, who inspired me to fulfil two lifelong dreams: to hike the Larig Ghru, and to track down (at last) what is, without any doubt, the most amazing mountain view in Britain. On another occasion, I borrowed a large horse, to find out whether I could ford the River Esk from England to Scotland. It was an interesting experiment, in which I discovered that I could not possibly have survived a single day with Fiennes on her 2,000-mile ride.

Eight travellers. Eight landscapes, layered one on the other since 1188. Over those eight hundred years, British landscapes have evolved in a series of catalsysmic leaps. The enclosure movement, the Highland Clearances, the Industrial Revolution and the Suburban Boom swept aside ancient patterns of rural settlement and land-use. The countryside has been shrinking since the Mezolithic. Now we're on the brink of the greatest landscape trauma since the Ice Age. If the scientists are right, and Britain is facing a future of extreme weather, rising sea-levels, and the steepest temperature increases for over ten thousand years, in a hundred years our congenial habitat may exist only in books.

NICHOLAS CRANE
London, July, 2007

# Further reading

**Gerald of Wales**

*Gerald of Wales, The Journey Through Wales and The Description of Wales*, translated with an introduction by Lewis Thorpe, Penguin Classics, 2004

*A History of Wales*, John Davies, London, 1994

*The Matter of Wales*, Jan Morris, London, 1986

**John Leland**

*John Leland's Itinerary: Travels in Tudor England*, John Chandler, Gloucestershire, 1998

*The Itinerary of John Leland in or about the years 1535–1543*, Lucy Toulmin-Smith (Ed.), foreword by Thomas Kendrick, London, 1964 (5 vols)

*Maps in Tudor England*, P.D.A. Harvey, London, 1993

**Celia Fiennes**

*The Illustrated Journeys of Celia Fiennes*, Christopher Morris (Ed.), Gloucestershire

*Through England on a Side Saddle In the Time of William and Mary, Being the Diary of Celia Fiennes*, introduction by The Hon Mrs Griffiths, London, 1888

*England's Thousand Best Houses*, Simon Jenkins, London, 2003

**Daniel Defoe**

*Daniel Defoe, A Tour Through the Whole Island of Great Britain*, abridged and edited with introduction and notes by Pat Rogers, London, 1986

*The Storm*, Daniel Defoe, London, 2003

*The Life of Daniel Defoe*, John Richetti, Oxford, 2006

**William Gilpin**

*Observations on the River Wye*, William Gilpin, London, 2005

*The Romantics and the British Landscape*, Stephen Hebron, London, 2006

*This Other Eden, Seven Great Gardens and 300 Years of English History*, Andrea Wulf and Emma Gieben-Gamal, London, 2005

**Thomas Pennant**

*A Tour in Scotland and Voyage to the Hebrides, 1772, Thomas Pennant*, Andrew Simmons (Ed.), introduction by Charles W.J. Withers, Edinburgh, 1998

*Peoples and Settlement in North-West Ross*, John R. Baldwin (Ed.), Edinburgh, 1994

*The Highland Clearances*, Eric Richards, Edinburgh, 2002

**William Cobbett**

*William Cobbett, Rural Rides*, introduction and notes by Ian Dyck (Ed.), London, 2001

*The Life and Adventures of William Cobbett*, Richard Ingrams, London, 2006

*The History of the Countryside*, Oliver Rackham, London, 1995

**H.V. Morton**

*In Search of Scotland*, H.V. Morton, London, 2000

*In Scotland Again*, H.V. Morton, London, 1933

*In Search of H.V. Morton*, Michael Bartholomew, London, 2006

**General Reading: The Past**

*The Discovery of Britain, The English Tourists, 1540–1840*, Esther Moir, London, 1964

*The Englishman's England: Taste, travel and the rise of tourism*, Ian Ousby, Cambridge, 1990

*Geography, Science and National Identity, Scotland since 1520*, Charles W.J. Withers, Cambridge, 2001

*The Little Ice Age: How Climate Made History 1300–1850*, Brian Fagan, 2002

**General Reading: The Future**

*Sea Change, Britain's Coastal Catastrophe*, Richard Girling, London, 2007

*Six Degrees: Our Future on a Hotter Planet*, Mark Lynas, London, 2007

*The Final Call: In Search of the True Cost of Our Holidays*, Leo Hickman, London, 2007

Intergovernmental Panel on Climate Change: www.ipcc.ch

# Acknowledgments

Great British Journeys has been a rucksack of joy: this book, eight one-hour films for the BBC, a DVD and various related articles and speaking events. Many people have been involved in what for me has been a wonderful couple of years.

The first I would like to thank is Annabel, for more patience and understanding than I deserve, and our children for putting up with the absenteeism.

At AP Watt, Derek Johns, Rob Kraitt and Yasmine McDonald put (and kept) the show on the road, and at Weidenfeld and Nicolson, Robin Douglas-Withers, Michael Dover, David Rowley, Justin Hunt, Tony Chung, Elizabeth Allen and Mark Rusher were responsible for producing this glorious book and getting it on to the shelves. The eight films were produced by Tern TV's outstanding team in Glasgow: Will Aspinall, Ian Ballantyne, Harry Bell, Emily Brunt, Jamie Gillespie, Ishbel Hall, Dan Lyth, Julie Maclaren, Neil Mackay, Helen Margerison, Angela Smith, David Strachan, Ian Stroud, Michael Waterhouse and Paul Wilson. At the BBC, I'd like to thank Neil McDonald, Richard Klein and Roly Keating. And finally, I would like to thank the crew who - along with Michael, Will, Ishbel, Emily and Helen - shared months of storms, snows and blistering heat to turn these stories into films. They are: Steve Robinson, Peter Eason, Mike Robinson, Barney Carmichael, Edmund Wright, Mark Littlewood and Lyndon Bruce.

# Picture credits

All photography by Peter Eason with the exception of the images listed below:

akg-images: 16c, 33a; /British Library: 84; Alamy: 18, 30, 32, 36, 37, 40, 52, 66, 85, 120, 142a, 146, 156, 157, 173a, 185, 196, 216a, 218, 240, 204b, 234a; Art Archive/National Maritime Musem: 118; Kate Attwooll: 5c, 75; The Bridgeman Art Library: 5d, 5f, 5g, 16b, 49 (both), 105, 123, 138, 149, 165, 195, 198; 204a, 216b, 217; British Library Board. All rights reserved: /Cotton Claudius D. VI: f.12v: 39; /Royal 13B. VIII: f.22: 41b; /Maps.920.(39): 48; /Maps.c.7.1:9: 51; /Add. 11564, ff.10v-11: 89; /Maps.C.7.c.20: 129; /Maps.K.Top.9.8.k 172; British Museum: 81; Cambridge University Library: 79; Nicholas Crane: 5a, 15, 20, 22, 23a, 24a, 25, 112b, 130, 147, 175 (both), 183, 186, 202; Collections/Alan Spencer: 21; Corbis: 23b, 41a, 77, 100, 101, 112a, 166, 167, 199, 219, 220, 228, 247, 250, 251; Courtauld Institute of Art: 139; Epicscotland.com/Ashley Coombes: 182; Getty Images: 106, 109, 229, 235, 237, 246; /Ellen Rooney: 90; Hampshire Record Office: 213 (both); Impact Photos/Michael Good: 241; Andrew Lawson: 83; Simon Ledingham: 136; Loop Images/David Sellman: 53; /Graham Bell: 16a; Mary Evans Picture Library: 50, 76 (both), 94, 108, 125, 142b, 215, 226, 227; /Grosvenor Prints: 98; National Library of Ireland, Dublin, 700, fol. 48r: 24b; National Library of Scotland: 168, 181; National Motor Museum/ Heritage Images: 230; National Portrait Gallery: 5b, 5e, 5h, 45, 135, 225; National Trust Holiday Cottages: 201; Natural History Museum: 169; PhotolibraryWales.com/Chris Warren: 19; /Kevin Fitzmaurice Brown: 26; /Ruth Hargest: 33b; Richard@earlymaps.com: 87 (both), 96, 145; Royal Geographical Society: 177, 178; Salisbury Cathedral.co.uk/Steve Day (both): 78; stockscotland.com/D. Robertson: 242; /Hugh Webster: 184, 190, 243; Tate, London 2007: 140; Tern: 54b, 57, 59, 187, 179 (both), 233; The Bodleian Library: University of Oxford Ms.Top.Gen.c3: p203: 60; The National Trust: 80; TopFoto.co.uk: 121, 126, 171, 197, 200 (both); Weidenfeld & Nicolson: 111, 141, 150, 153, 158; Warrington Museum & Art Gallery: 173b; courtesy of Pip Wilson: 47.

First published in Great Britain in 2007
by Weidenfeld & Nicolson
10 9 8 7 6 5 4 3 2 1

Text copyright © Nicholas Crane 2007
Design and layout © Weidenfeld & Nicolson 2007

A CIP catalogue record for this book is available
from the British Library.

ISBN: 978-0-297-84456-3

Design director: David Rowley
Designer: James Alexander, Jade Design
Design assistance: Justin Hunt , Tony Chung, Jo Cannon
Maps: Nick Robertson, Wordsalad
Editor: Robin Douglas-Withers

Colour reproduction by DL Interactive UK
Printed and bound in Spain by Cayfosa Quebecor

Weidenfeld & Nicolson
The Orion Publishing Group Ltd
Orion House
5 Upper St Martin's Lane
London WC2H 9EA

An Hachette Livre UK Company

The Orion Publishing Group's policy is to use papers that are
natural, renewable and recyclable products and made from
wood grown in sustainable forests. The logging and manufacturing
processes are expected to conform to the environmental regulations
of the country of origin.

www.terntv.com